INSIDE OF TIME

My Journey from Alaska to Israel

INSIDE OF TIME

My Journey from Alaska to Israel

RUTH GRUBER

CARROLL & GRAF PUBLISHERS
NEW YORK

ALSO BY RUTH GRUBER

Ahead of Time: My Early Years As a Foreign Correspondent
Exodus 1947: The Ship That Launched a Nation
(formerly titled *Destination Palestine*)
Rescue: The Exodus of Ethiopian Jews
Haven: the Dramatic Story of 1,000 World War II Refugees
and How They Came to America
Raquela: A Woman of Israel
They Came to Stay
Felisa Rincón de Gautier: The Mayor of San Juan
Israel on the Seventh Day
Science and the New Nations
Puerto Rico: Island of Promise
Israel Today: Land of Many Nations
Israel without Tears
I Went to the Soviet Arctic
Virginia Woolf: A Study

PHOTOS BY RUTH GRUBER IN
DOCUMENTARIES, BOOKS, AND EXHIBITIONS
Exhibit, Tyler Art Gallery, State University of
New York, Oswego, New York, 2002
Exhibit, Art Gallery, Jewish Federation, Jewish Community
Center, Long Beach, California
Exhibit, Art Gallery, Jewish Federation, Austin, Texas, 2002
Exhibit, University of Judaism Theater, Los Angeles,
California, 2002

The Long Way Home, 70th Annual Academy of
Motion Picture Arts and Sciences Award for
Documentary Feature, 1998
Steven Spielberg's Survivors of the Shoah Visual
History Foundation, in category of
Rescuers and
Liberators, 1998
Photo Essay and Exhibit, New York UJA-Federation, 1998
Photo and Essay Exhibit, The Jewish Community Centers of
Greater Philadelphia, 1998
Photo Essay and Exhibit, Finegood Gallery, West Hills,
California, 1998
Photo Essay and Exhibit, Hirsh Gallery, Los Angeles Museum
of the Holocaust, 1998
Permanent Photo Collection, U.S. Holocaust Memorial
Museum, Washington, D.C.
Jewish Women in America: An Historical Encyclopedia, 1998
Permanent Exhibit: "Bitter Hope: From Holocaust to Haven,"
New York State Museum, Albany
Truman, TV documentary, 1997
Exodus 1947, TV documentary, 1997
Exiles and Emigrés, documentary, 1997
Jewish Historical Society of Maryland, 1997
The Aftermath: Europe, World War II series, Time-Life Books
"The Generations of Israel," A CBS Legacy collection
Exhibit, Academy of Fine Arts, Berlin, 1994–5
Exhibit, Goethe Institutes at Milan and Rome, 1994–5
CBS *Sunday Morning,* 1986

Inside of Time
My Journey from Alaska to Israel

Carroll & Graf Publishers
An Imprint of Avalon Publishing Group Inc.
161 William St., 16th Floor
New York, NY 10038

First Carroll & Graf edition 2003

All maps and photographs are courtesy of the author.

Library of Congress Cataloging-in-Publication Data is available.

ISBN: 0-7867-1083-7

Book design by Paul Paddock
Printed in the United States of America
Distributed by Publishers Group West

To my young grandchildren
Michael and Lucy Evans
Joel and Lila Michaels

CONTENTS

INTRODUCTION

It was on my first trip to Alaska during World War II that I learned to live "inside of time." I might be sitting in a place like Nome. I would send a radio message to Anchorage for a bush pilot to pick me up and fly me to Point Barrow.

The answer would come back, "See you Tuesday—WEAPERS." "WEAPERS" meant weather permitting. Tuesday came. The next Tuesday came. Then the next. But no bush pilot. Usually it was the weather. Or the pilot was sick or on a binge.

Until that fateful voyage, I had been a restless fighter against time. If the elevated train from my shtetl in Williamsburg, Brooklyn to Manhattan was a few minutes late, I screamed at it under my breath like a longshoreman.

Now, instead of sending my blood presssure rocketing, I began to utilize the days and weeks of waiting. Wherever my lap was became my desk. I could fill more pages in my notebooks, send more reports to Harold L. Ickes, secretary of the interior—for whom I was working as field representative and later as special assistant—and interview more people, especially the Eskimos, whose serenity and affirmation of life I so admired.

Time was no longer my enemy. Now it enveloped me, liberated me. Living in a magical circle of space and energy helped fuel my love for words and images, the tools with which I would later fight injustice.

The patience and perseverance I learned stood me in good stead when Ickes, making me a simulated general, sent me to war-torn Europe in 1944 to shepherd one thousand refugees to safe haven in Oswego, New York. When we were blacked out, our engines silenced while Nazi planes flew over us and U-boats hunted us down, some of the wounded soldiers we carried shouted to me, "It's these damn Jews—we survived all the battles, from Casablanca to Anzio, and we're going to die because the Nazis know what we're carrying."

To show the soldiers what we were carrying, I arranged to have our gifted singers and actors perform for them. When the soldiers, their heads bandaged and their arms or legs in casts, watched and listened to some of our beautiful young women, they began to applaud with delight. It seemed to me they were seeing these artists not as objects of derision but as human beings.

Some talked to me of how amazed they were by the vitality and determination to survive of people who had suffered the greatest evil the world had known. The captain's early order to me, "We don't want any fraternization on this ship," blew into the sea. The soldiers kept coming to our part of the ship bringing chocolate and cookies for our children and spending hours learning the life stories of some of the refugees. Anti-Semitism and hostility evaporated.

When the war ended, I traveled as a foreign correspondent through Europe and the Middle East with the Anglo-American Committee on Palestine. In Germany, we visited the terrible Displaced Persons camps taking testimony from the refugees. Some of the DP camps were former death camps and army camps in which these survivors of the Holocaust were now sleeping on the same wooden shelves where thousands had died during the war. I wanted to shake the world by its lapels: "Get rid of these camps. Open the doors of Palestine! After what they've suffered, let these Holocaust survivors go home."

A year later, Helen Rogers Reid, the vice president of the New York *Herald Tribune*, sent me to cover UNSCOP—the United Nations Special Committee on Palestine. It was only the twentieth committee studying the problems of Palestine and the Arab-Jewish conflict.

We were listening to eloquent Jewish and Arab leaders in the YMCA in Jerusalem when I learned that a small American excursion boat named *Exodus 1947,* holding forty-five hundred Holocaust survivors, was being attacked by British destroyers and *Ajax,* the famous British cruiser. I rushed to Haifa and stood at the dock watching the battered ship enter the harbor. Three were dead: Bill Bernstein, the American second mate who had been bludgeoned to death, and two sixteen-year-old orphans.

The British officers made no effort to stop me from shooting pictures of soldiers dragging people off the ship and forcing them onto three ships sitting in the harbor. The commanding officer told me they were bound for Cyprus.

I flew to Cyprus to wait for them. It was a hellhole of sand and wind. No plumbing. No water. No privacy. I tried to capture it all in the articles and photos I kept sending the paper.

Cyprus became Helen Reid's passion. Determined to use her influence with the British to get the Jews out of Cyprus, she used my articles as her weapon, but she failed. The British kept the Jews imprisoned on their island even after Israel was born.

David Ben-Gurion, the architect of the new nation, moved to Kibbutz Sde Boker in the Negev in the last years of his life. "If we do not conquer the desert," he told me, "the desert will conquer us." After his wife, Paula, died, he returned to his modest home in Tel Aviv, where I visited him shortly before his death in 1973. One of the soldiers stationed at the entrance told me, "It's good you've come—so few people come to see him now."

He was lying on the upper floor on a narrow bed, covered with a white quilt. On the floor below him were his sole companions, soldiers who guarded him, cooked for him, and occasionally ventured upstairs to make sure he was all right.

"Pull up a chair," he spoke in a soft voice. I took a tape recorder out of my bag. He noticed it immediately.

"Put that thing away," he demanded.

"B. G.," I protested, "I want to have a record of your voice."

"You don't need a record—it's in your head."

I slipped the tape recorder back in my bag and took out a fresh notebook. A little smile played on his lips. It was the fall of 1973. I had come to write a book on the Yom Kippur War called *Israel on the Seventh Day*. A sadness swept over me realizing that the air in the room talked of death. I knew how badly the country would miss him.

"Master," I asked, "will there ever be peace between the Arabs and the Jews?"

"Yes."

"When?"

"Not in my time," he sat up in his bed. "But in yours and your children's."

"Where will it come from?" I pressed.

"Egypt," he said.

"Egypt?" I was incredulous. "That's where the *fedayeen* (terrorists) come from. Egypt starts every war. They're the ones who throw the grenades into children's homes. How can peace come from Egypt?"

He waved his hand as if brushing the thought away.

"Forget that," he told me. "There is a whole generation of young people rising up who know we can cooperate. They still have diseases we cured fifty years ago. Our doctors and our scientists can help cure them. They have natural resources and raw materials that we need. Yes, there will be peace."

I took his hand, knowing it was the last time I would see him. He died on December 1, 1973.

Readers who may wonder at my recollections of whole scenes and dialogue may feel reassured to know that they come from the 350 notebooks I filled with descriptions and interviews recorded right on the spot in my own idiosyncratic version of short longhand.

They also come from my reports to Secretary of the Interior Harold L. Ickes, which began in Alaska in 1941 for eighteen months, and then continued through my years in Washington as his special assistant until January 1946.

Returning to journalism as a foreign correspondent in early 1946, my articles and photos have given me the eyewitness material I use here in covering the postwar years through the birth of Israel, and on to 1952, when *Inside of Time* ends as Eleanor Roosevelt asked me to show her how Israel was absorbing tens of thousands of new immigrants.

In these difficult days, with heartbreaking stories of suicide terrorists and innocent victims, I find it more important than ever to live and write inside of time. It does not mean living life without urgency and passion, or expecting immediate rewards. We must keep working for peace, fighting injustice, and raising our children and grandchildren to live with decency, dignity, and hope.

—RUTH GRUBER
NEW YORK CITY, OCTOBER 2002

Part 1

ALASKA

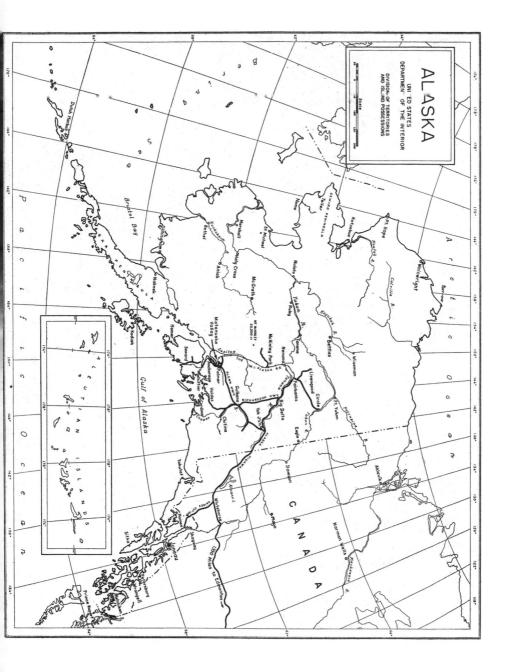

ALASKA

UNITED STATES
DEPARTMENT OF THE INTERIOR
DIVISION OF TERRITORIES
AND ISLAND POSSESSIONS

Scale

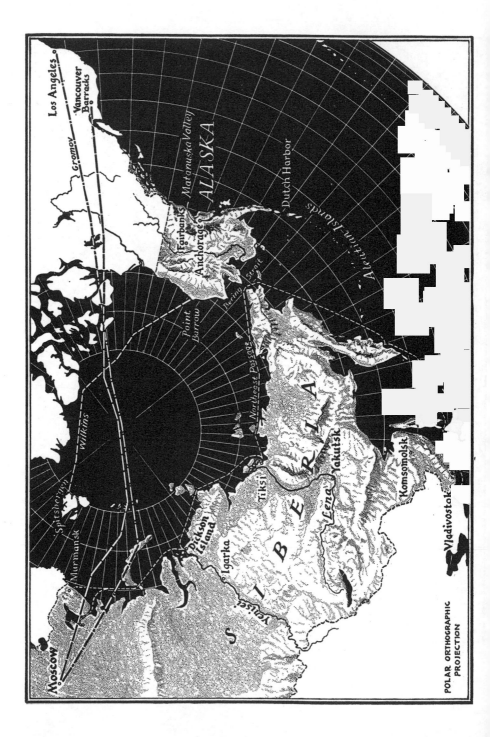

Los Angeles

Vancouver Barracks

Gromov

Wilkins

Matanuska Valley

ALASKA

Dutch Harbor

Fairbanks

Anchorage

Bering Strait

Aleutian Islands

Point Barrow

Northeast Passage

Spitsbergen

Murmansk

S I B E R I A

Dickson Island

Igarka

Tiksi

Lena

Yakutsk

Komsomolsk

Yenisei

Moscow

Vladivostok

POLAR ORTHOGRAPHIC
PROJECTION

Chapter One

MISS GRUBER GOES TO WASHINGTON

On a halcyon spring morning in April 1941, I jumped out of bed in a small Washington hotel room. My mind was churning. At eleven o'clock, I was to interview Harold L. Ickes, the secretary of the interior. In a few days, I was to leave for Alaska to write a series of articles for the New York *Herald Tribune*.

Interviewing Ickes was a *must*. Alaska, still far from being a state, was in his department.

What would he be like, I wondered, as I dressed carefully in a navy blue suit, white blouse, and a blue hat with an upturned brim of white satin. I wore dangling earrings and high heels, hoping they would make me look taller than my five feet two inches and more sophisticated than my twenty-nine years.

Long before eleven, I hailed a cab, drove through Washington's quiet streets and stared at the Greek-style monuments with excitement. "He'ah you are," the cab driver sang out. "Here's Interior." He stopped in front of an elegant building with bronze-sculpted doors. An attractive, dark-skinned elevator operator, immaculately dressed in a summer dress, rode me up to the sixth floor, and pointed me to the secretary's suite.

Inside a waiting room with benches lined against the wall, Ickes's appointment secretary sat like a sentinel guarding the gates. She took my name and motioned me to take a seat. The outer office was filled with men. One after another, she waved them through an inner door. I heard her calling them by their titles: Senator, Ambassador, Governor, Mr. Mayor. No one stayed in Ickes's office more than ten or fifteen minutes.

Exactly at eleven, the appointment secretary, whose name I kept hearing was Ellen Downes, beckoned me. I followed her as she knocked at the door and then left me at the open entrance. I hesitated for a moment. Ickes sat at a desk at the far end, looking up as I began what would have been a two-block walk in Brooklyn. Even as I headed toward him, I noticed that he must have favored the color blue. The heavy drapes that looped around the windows from the ceiling to the floor, the chairs that encircled a conference table, the deep rug in which my high heels sank—all were blue.

In New York I had read whatever I could find about this former newspaper man/lawyer. As secretary of the interior, he had cleaned up a corrupt department. The Teapot Dome scandal about twenty years earlier had been in Interior under President Warren Harding. It was said of Ickes, who was unimpeachably honest, that he would fire anyone caught stealing even a postage stamp. He was saving the environment, conserving its beauty, guarding wildlife, fighting for minorities, especially Indians, building parks, changing the face of America.

He was sixty-seven, born in 1874 on a farm near Altoona in western Pennsylvania His father was an alcoholic womanizer.

His older brother was a bully. But his mother wielded the greatest influence on his life, teaching him to be self-sufficient, courageous, and a skillful organizer. She died when he was just sixteen, but her influence was his legacy.

Now, he came in from his Maryland farm before eight every morning, checking up to see who was not yet at work. The picture I had drawn in my head was of a New Deal Democrat who was politically liberal and socially a tyrant. Instead, I found myself sitting in a leather armchair next to a warm, approachable man who looked like the editor of a country newspaper. His body was small and round, his eyes glinted behind gold-rimmed glasses, his jowls moved when he turned his head. He had a pug nose and a pugnacious jaw.

"I'm glad you came," he said. "Because of your book we tried out many of the things we're doing in Alaska."

A chill of excitement ran down my spine. My book *I Went to the Soviet Arctic* was published on September 1, 1939—the very day Hitler invaded Poland. Two years later and it was influencing our government! I hoisted myself in the chair trying to appear cool. I squeezed my hands so he wouldn't see them trembling.

"My wife, Jane," he spoke the three words like a love song, "my wife, Jane, found it in a bookstore and told me, 'Harold, you had better read this book.'"

I had seen newspaper pictures of his young, red-haired, beautiful wife, Jane, who was pregnant. In 1938, the press had gleefully exploded with the story of the sixty-four-year-old widowed secretary of the interior marrying the twenty-three-year-old member of the Cudahy meatpacking family. He had met her through his son's wife. Somewhere I read that she had told an interviewer, "I would rather spend five years with Harold than forty years with a less exciting man."

"So you're leaving for Alaska for the *Tribune*? That's good," he said, wasting no time. "Alaska's going to be very important once we get into the war."

I nodded. "The war will teach people that Alaska is the shortest route for our planes to ferry guns and butter to Europe. And at the Bering Strait, we're just three and a half miles away from Russia." He sat silent, waiting for me to go on. I continued, "That's why we have to populate it fast. But it's that perennial contradiction when you're opening new land. You try to conserve a frontier land and at the same time fill it with people who might lay it waste."

"You're right," he said, "but time's not on our side. Populating Alaska is a wartime priority."

"That's why the *Herald Tribune* wants this series now."

He swiveled in his chair to face me directly. He was smiling. "Will you be going alone?"

"Yes."

"You're single?" he asked.

"Yes."

"Jane and I went to Alaska. The country is beautiful. I want to create more parks there to keep that beauty untouched. But Alaskans aren't enthusiastic about what we're doing. The spirit isn't right up there. Most of the white people are only interested in making money and taking it out to spend in Seattle and California."

He continued talking about Alaska, obviously enjoying his description of this huge empty land, bigger than Texas, one-fifth the size of the United States, with only thirty thousand whites and thirty thousand native peoples.

Then, silent for a few moments, he searched my face. I glanced surreptitiously at my watch. We had been talking for half an hour.

Now I waited for him to go on.

"Between you and me," he broke the silence, "I'm very unpopular up there. Recently the legislature passed a unanimous resolution asking the president to accept my resignation, or if I didn't resign, to fire me. When the *Chicago Tribune* read that resolution, they sent a reporter up there to dig up dirt. Today they're starting a whole series of articles attacking me."

Though I had just met him, I had begun to feel we had the same goals for Alaska. "What are you doing about it?" I felt outraged for him.

"It doesn't matter. I can stand it. I'm glad you came to see me and I'm glad you want to go to Alaska. Don't go for the *Herald Tribune*. Go for me."

I felt blood rush to my head. I had come expecting to interview him for the *Herald Tribune*. Instead, he was suddenly offering me a job. What would it be like to work for the government? To work for such a man?

I was a child of the Depression. To be offered a full-time position was almost unheard of. Nearly everyone I knew was unemployed. If there were jobs, they went to young men, not to young women. True, I was lucky. I was part of the *Herald Tribune* family, with credentials and a serious byline, "Special Foreign Correspondent." But I was paid by the article and the syndication. This would be different. A real job.

"How long would you expect me to stay?" I asked, though the words "yes, yes, yes" were ringing in my head.

"A year, maybe longer. You would be my field representative, reporting directly to me. Your work would be pretty much what we've been talking about—how to populate the territory, and at the same time conserve its natural resources and its beauty. You'd be making a social and economic study, and sending me reports as you go along."

"Mr. Secretary, I would be honored to work for you."

He pressed one of the row of buttons on his desk. Within moments, a solemn man with a pale face and pale brown hair entered.

"This is Mr. Burlew, First Assistant Secretary," Ickes introduced us. Mr. Ebert Keiser Burlew always signed his name 'E. K.' "Dr. Gruber wants to go to Alaska and we've got to send her."

Mr. Burlew's voice was flat, emotionless. "We're pretty low in funds, you know."

Ickes was undaunted. "How about getting Colonel Ohlson to put her on the payroll of the Alaska Railroad?" He turned to me, a mischievous smile around his lips. "Careful. We're horse traders."

Some fifteen years later, I read in *The Lowering Clouds* (Volume I of *The Secret Diary of Harold L. Ickes*) his account of our first meeting.

> *Dr. Ruth Gruber . . . wants to go to Alaska and do a job there. She is a writer and lecturer and is the youngest Ph.D. in the world. Her book on the Soviet Arctic was very good indeed, although I have not read all of it.*
>
> *Dr. Gruber is a very attractive young woman and is quite good-looking. I could not quite make out whether she is Jewish or not, but she may be.*

Hmmm, I thought. Later, he told me that growing up in western Pennsylvania he hadn't met a Jew until he was sixteen years old. But he must have had some kind of mystique about Jews. The legal department was staffed with brilliant young Jewish men. I once wrote him a letter with a New Year's greeting in which I told him, "You don't have an ounce of anti-Semitism in you." He had written back, "Barney Baruch told me the same thing."

> *Anyhow I confess that I fell for her line and decided that I would like her to go to Alaska. She wants to go at once and will stay a year if necessary. However, she has to be financed.*
> *. . . In the meantime, however, Dr. Gruber got everyone by the ears down here. I suspect that she is an imperious young woman who does not stand on ceremony and wants to have her own way. Anyhow, she got Burlew sour on her and Mrs. Hampton and the people in Territories and Islands as well.*

I chuckled. I knew I had made people angry because I was too impatient. I had wanted to cut all the bureaucratic red tape and get up to Alaska. Others in the department, I later learned, were asking, "Who is this dame from Brooklyn who sashays into the boss' office and he gives her a job we would have given our eyeteeth for?" I went on reading in his diary:

> *However, I think that it is worth the experiment to send her to Alaska . . . it may be that Dr. Gruber has come at just the right time. If she comes back with some of the conclusions that I have formed, she will be in a position to do a great deal of useful publicity. Her point, which I think was well put, is that Alaska cannot be popularized in Alaska but must be popularized here. I think she can do it.*

Chapter Two

FDR AND ELEANOR
HOLD SEPARATE PRESS
CONFERENCES

From Ickes's office I taxied back to my hotel and telephoned Joe Barnes, my editor at the *Herald Tribune*. "Hi, Joe," I tried to contain my excitement. "Guess what? I have a new job. I can't go to Alaska for you. Harold Ickes is sending me."

"Wow! Congratulations, Ruth," he said. "That's a real coup. But I'm disappointed. H. R. will be too. " H. R. was the name everyone called Helen Rogers Reid, the wife of Ogden Reid, the owner of the paper. "We were really looking forward to running the series," Joe said. "But make sure to call me when you get back. We can run it next year."

Next I phoned Brooklyn. Mama answered the phone.

"Put Papa on the extension," I shouted. "I've got something to tell you both."

"I'm on," Papa said.

"Listen, the government is offering me a job."

"Where is it?" Mama demanded.

"In Alaska."

"At least Alaska is in America." Mama took a deep breath. "With you, it could have been China."

I laughed. "One day maybe it'll be China."

For several days I appeared in Mr. Burlew's office only to be told by his secretary that Mr. Burlew had no word on when I was to leave. As a political journalist for more than a decade, I was no stranger to bureaucratic foot-dragging.

Five years earlier, on my second trip to the Soviet Arctic, I had spent weeks in Moscow trying to get a visa to the Yakutia Soviet Socialist Republic. Russia was a bureaucratic nightmare. Government agencies warred against each other until finally Otto Yulievich Schmidt, the czar of the Soviet Arctic, pulled a magic cord and I took off. My experience there should have immunized me against the slow motion of Washington bureaucracy.

To fill the time waiting for orders to leave, I began interviewing some of the bureau chiefs. All were men, generous with their time and advice, and one woman, Ruth Hampton, who was the assistant director of the Division of Territories and Island Possessions. Alaska was part of her province. A few days before meeting her I spent a whole morning with Felix Cohen, a tall, thin, bespectacled lawyer, the son of the famous philosophy professor Morris Raphael Cohen of City College in New York.

Felix told me how he had helped write a bill that would bring five thousand Jewish refugees from Europe and five thousand American settlers from the States to Alaska each year.

"Ickes was determined to help refugees," Cohen explained. "The bill had a two-pronged purpose: to save refugees and to open Alaska."

I was awed by how Ickes and his staff were linking the rescue of Jews with opening Alaska.

"What's happening to the bill?" I asked.

He shook his head. "It never got out of committee. Ickes was livid when it was killed."

"Who killed it?"

"So many. The isolationists and restrictionists in Congress. The labor unions who said every refugee you bring in takes a job away from an American. The anti-Semites. Even a whole group of Alaskans came all the way down here just to fight us."

"Alaskans," I blurted out. "Didn't they see how five thousand refugees and five thousand Americans coming up every year would bring in doctors, teachers, pioneers, homesteaders—?"

I stopped speaking. His face was a mask of pain.

He spoke in a low voice. "The Alaskans said there was no anti-Semitism in the Territory now because there were only a few Jewish families in each town. Bringing five thousand Jews a year would start race riots." Then, in a strained voice, he said, "They all helped to kill the bill."

His words hung in the air as I left his office.

Still no word from Mr. Burlew. Evenings, I prowled the quiet unhurried streets of Washington. Along the Tidal Basin the cherry blossoms were exploding into pink-and-white balls of cotton candy. But my mind was not on the snowscape of cherry blossoms. I was consumed with getting to Alaska before we went to war, but right now the likelihood seemed far away.

Marking time, I visited friends in the Washington bureau of the *Herald Tribune* who invited me to President Franklin Roosevelt's press conference in the White House. We waited in an anteroom outside the president's office. I overheard reporters priming each other: "What's your timetable? When are we going to war?"

The door to the Oval Office opened. My friends broke a trail through the herd of men, pushing me to the front of the president's desk. His desk was littered with ashtrays, miniature horses, small boats, toys, and a long cigarette holder.

Up close Roosevelt was even handsomer than the rotogravure picture my father had hanging on the wall. If only Papa could be here. Papa adored Roosevelt. Papa, who had come here at sixteen from czarist Russia to escape pogroms, considered Roosevelt the greatest president in the greatest country in the world. How thrilled the whole family would be when I told him how close I had stood to the president.

I jotted a quick description of him in my notebook:

> Sits comfortable and relaxed. The useless legs hidden behind the desk. Gray striped suit. Black-and-orange polka-dot tie. The weather-beaten skin is a road map of black telltale marks of sun and wind and sailing. He beams that famous smile with its fascinating crooked teeth directly at you like a klieg light, making your heart stop.

The only ones seated were the president, who was reading papers on his lap, and his press secretary, Steve Early, who sat directly behind him. Four Secret Service men stood in the background. He had been wheeled in before we were allowed to enter. Journalists never mentioned his polio-ridden legs.

While he remained silent, continuing to read, my eyes swept around the crowded room. I recognized Walter Lippmann, the *Herald Tribune*'s most influential columnist, and Elmer Davis, later to become head of the Office of War Information.

"There are no other women here," I whispered to one of my friends. "Why?"

"Roosevelt likes only men journalists at his press conferences. That's why we thought it would be fun to sneak you in, and then get you right up front. Once you're in, we figured they wouldn't throw you out."

I wanted to laugh, but the president, looking up from his papers, was talking of sending aid to Britain. Suddenly, here in the White House the surface calm of Washington vanished. Our minds were focused on the war as Roosevelt described the British standing alone against Hitler. There were hang-ups, the president complained, in rushing war equipment to help them. We knew that FDR wanted to get us into the war to help Britain and defeat Hitler, whose armies had already conquered most of Europe. Now in the spring of 1941, the war in Europe was heating up. Hitler's U-boats were decimating the British fleet. Yugoslavia, trying bravely to hold out, had been overrun in a week and a half. Knowing how vulnerable and unprepared Alaska and the Philippines were, defense areas were being established around them. But Roosevelt couldn't get the country behind him. Using the press conference, he involved us, maneuvering us to carry his message of frustration: The country had to move faster to help our closest ally and friend, the British.

Three months earlier, on December 18, 1940, Hitler had issued war Directive Number 21, "The German Wehrmacht must be prepared. Also, before the ending of the war against England, to crush Soviet Russia in an Active Campaign." Hitler called the operation "Barbarossa," a reference to the leader who had ruled Germany's First Reich in the twelfth century and conquered much of Europe. Barbarians.

"I am not pointing with pride," FDR's eyes narrowed. "I am not satisfied." He flung the word *not* at us like an angry prophet.

"How can you accelerate the work?" a reporter asked.

The president puffed his cheeks out as if he were thinking. Then he pulled his right hand over his head and scratched his left eye. "By using chestnut burrs."

Even Walter Lippmann looked bewildered.

Roosevelt waited. The reporters did not move.

"You boys," he said at last. "You know where they put the chestnut burrs on horses to make them go." He threw his head back and laughed. The men roared with him. I was no farmer, but I could imagine what part of a horse's anatomy was involved. Welcome to the boys' club.

That night, unable to sleep, still raging that the mills of bureaucracy ground so slowly, I jotted notes swiftly. Perhaps, alone in his room at night, the president tossed in his bed as I was tossing now. If he had any misgivings or doubts, he never showed it. In his patrician voice, he said, "There are some smart people in this country—and in this room too." He stopped and smiled as he said it, and you felt he liked you, trusted you, admired you—until he lashed out, "and there are liars, enemies, appeasers, and they are in this room too."

You looked around to see which enemies he meant. He manipulated the reporters like a lion tamer in the circus.

Early the next day I was back standing at Mr. Burlew's secretary's desk. This time, Burlew himself came out of his office. Before I could say a word, he blurted, "We're sending radiograms back and forth to Colonel Ohlson in Anchorage."

I was about to inquire why my orders were moving so slowly, when Mr. Burlew said, "These things take time," and vanished into his office.

What was causing the delay? Was it me? Was I trying to speed up the wheels of government? I knew my faults. I was restless, always fighting against time. What did I need to learn so that seasoned bureaucrats would not be as hostile to me as

Mr. Burlew seemed? Or, I wondered, was there a whiff of misogyny and anti-Semitism?

One morning at ten, I entered the office of Ruth Hampton, the assistant director of the Division of Territories and Island Possessions. She was in her fifties—large, buxom, white-haired, and as icy as the glaciers I was impatient to see. I hoped she could speed up whatever maddening process was holding up my departure.

"The secretary suggested I read your book," Mrs. Hampton told me. "I don't know. I can't get behind the word communist. I hate them so. I can't bear to read anything about them, good or bad. They're no different from those Nazis. I hate them all. To think those poor lovely people in the North you wrote about have to be victimized by those brutes."

Sensing hostility, I thanked her and hurried out of her office. On the street, I hailed a taxi to the National Museum to meet Ales Hrdliçka, the anthropologist who had led a four-year expedition to Alaska in 1899.

Dr. Hrdliçka was a young seventy-two-year-old, short with soft smiling eyes. "So you were in the Soviet Arctic," he beamed. "They're doing a wonderful thing there in the inter-marriage of the races, openly and willingly, not like our whites and Negroes. They're creating a taller, stronger race, and bringing out very good things."

I shut my eyes for a moment. In a half hour I had traveled the arc of Washington's obsession with communism—from right to left, from Hampton to Hrdliçka.

"You are American?" he asked suddenly, squinting at me as if I were an anthropological specimen.

"Yes."

"You are Jewish?"

"Yes."

"Good. But don't go to the Eskimos with those fingernails and red lips. And that hat. . . . They'll be afraid of you. They'll disappear right off the street."

I laughed. "I don't expect to dress this way in Alaska."

He seemed not to hear me, as he continued. "Most of the stuff written about Alaska is trash. This is not against you, but against the rhapsodic stuff women novelists write. They go only where the tourists go." He flung his arms out and raised his eyes to the ceiling as if he were imitating their rhapsody. "But few people ever go where you will go—"

Rapidly I changed the subject. I found his views amusing but I hadn't come to interview him on women novelists. "What future do you think Alaska has?"

"No future at all," he tossed the words at me.

Surely, I thought, he's teasing me. "I think Alaska has a brilliant future—if we can get people to develop it," I said.

He wasn't teasing. "You can lead a horse to water . . . you know the rest. But it's good you're going. If you're the right kind of person, you will enrich your life up there. Your whole life will be different. It won't make you a good person, but it will make you a better person."

His enthusiasm, quixotic as it was, lifted my spirits. I taxied back to the Interior Department to keep my next appointment. It was with Mike Straus, Director of Information for Interior.

Straus paced the floor in front of me, a burly giant whose bronze face looked more like an American Indian's than a smart Jewish newspaperman who had come out of Chicago with Ickes. I liked him instantly.

"You're young to be the next target of a lot of political machinations," he said. "Be prepared. The big fish canners and gold miners up there hate Ickes, and they're going to pick on anyone he sends. Better get yourself ready for it."

I felt no fear.

He continued pacing. "I think we'd better send out an announcement about your appointment. I don't think we should play you up as 'Youth Personified' or 'the Lady Explorer.' We'll keep it on a broad base that you're going up to make a social and economic study—"

"And that's the truth. I want to find new ways to help open the Territory—"

"Okay, okay. But we've got a campaign to work on," he said.

One day, I attended one of Eleanor Roosevelt's all-women press conferences. Her conferences were a gentle poke in the stomach to her husband for his all-male conferences. Little I had read about her prepared me for her presence, or for the mixture of sadness and strength in her face. Her high voice and buck teeth took nothing away from the passion that fueled her words.

The women asked her questions about welfare, childcare, the evils of poverty, and the role of women in politics. She answered with skill and honesty, often admitting, "I really don't know, but I'll try to have the answer next time we meet." Here she was—a journalist among journalists. Even in the way they questioned her, the women journalists showed their admiration and affection. She was never cynical or judgmental, never mean or cruel. She won their trust, and they showed it in the stories they wrote about her.

But her enemies were legion. They hated her power and her influence on the president. No First Lady had ever acted as she did—popping up everywhere, in mines wearing a miner's helmet with searchlights, in factories, in airfields, in army posts, and aboard naval war ships. She was always speaking out with courage, always concerned with human rights. Yet, she was constantly lampooned by reactionary cartoonists and writers, especially Westbrook Pegler, a columnist syndicated by the Hearst newspapers. Later when I was "Peglerized" for working for Ickes, she told me, "You learn how to handle people like him. You ignore them." Now in her press conference, surrounded only by women, I hoped she took comfort from the women and, of course men, too, who came to her defense.

At long last, Mr. Burlew called me to his office. "Colonel Olhson sent the radiogram we've been waiting for. He's ready to put you on his payroll."

"So I can leave immediately?"

"Not so quick. You have to fill out these civil service papers, questionnaires about your educational background, jobs you've held, things you've published, everything—"

That day, doctors in the Public Health Service examined my eyes, my ears, my throat. I was fingerprinted and later learned that J. Edgar Hoover himself assured Ickes that I was clean.

At nine the next morning, I was back in Mr. Burlew's office. It was Good Friday and Passover, April 11, 1941.

"We wired Colonel Ohlson your assignment as of today," Mr. Burlew said. "You can take the oath of office right now."

I raised my hand, swore to uphold the Constitution of the United States and was sworn in as "Field Representative of the Alaska Railroad."

Outside I flagged a cab for Union Station and a train to New York City. I was determined to reach Brooklyn in time for the first Passover seder.

Papa, dressed like a noble Jewish king in a white caftan and a white yarmulke, led us in the prayers and told the story I loved, of Moses leading the Israelites out of Egypt up to the Promised Land. Ickes, I thought, was trying to lead terrified Jews out of Hitler's Europe. But he, like everyone else in Washington, had failed.

I looked at Mama, short and strong, in a freshly starched white blouse, dark skirt, and spotless apron, ladling out the holiday food she had cooked all day. I loved listening to my three tall handsome brothers, Bob, Harry, and Irving, singing the prayers with enthusiasm. I sat close to my sister, Betty. Until she married Sam Sobel, the medical student she had fallen in love with at New York University, we had shared a bedroom and all our secrets.

My parents, like millions of immigrants, had worked to make us educated, honest, and decent human beings in a country where you could be anything you wanted to be. Education was their highest priority, but my mother had to quit school in the eighth grade. She was needed to do the laundry for the newcomers who stayed at her parents' apartment for two dollars a week.

I shut my eyes listening to the prayers. I was home.

But Mama was worried about Alaska. "It's so cold," she shuddered. "God forbid, you could even freeze to death in all that ice and snow."

"It isn't all ice and snow."

She hardly heard. "So when are you going to stop running? You're not so young anymore, you know."

Mothers and daughters, I thought. On good days we embrace like dancers clinging to each other in a Spanish tango, and on bad days we condemn each other in a tug of war. "Why can't you be like the daughters of my friends?" my mother asked rhetorically, knowing I had no answer. "They get married. They have children. They have a nice easy life. But you—you're too busy traipsing around the world."

I realized she wanted me to fulfill her dreams for me. But I couldn't, though I knew I was giving her pain and anxiety. I tried to make her understand. "Look at it this way, Mom.

Maybe I can help people who have no jobs, or who don't know what they want to be. If I handle this job well, maybe I can help them build a new life for themselves."

"So maybe you could build a new life for yourself."

I tried to forestall the tug of war. "Some day, Mama. But not now. I'm leaving in two days."

I could hardly wait.

Chapter Three

A Controversial Bath

The whole family helped me pack a suitcase with winter and summer clothes. I slung my Leica, and my eight-millimeter movie camera over my shoulder, picked up my portable typewriter, and walked around kissing everyone good-bye.

"Don't forget this," Mama handed me a brown grocery bag with a jar of prunes she had soaked overnight in my father's best scotch. "In case you have a headache or get sick while you're traveling." Inebriated prunes were Mama's cure for every disease. It was the gift she gave me before I left on any assignment.

Papa kissed me on the forehead. "Go with God and be careful."

In the comfort of a roomette on the Pullman train, I spent five days reading, planning, reveling in the beauty of America, until the train reached Los Angeles.

I was to spend the night in Los Angeles, and then continue by train up the coast to Seattle, where I would board a ship for

Alaska. In the L.A. station, I walked to a newspaper stand. A San Francisco tabloid called *This World* caught my eye. Was it possible? On the front page was a photo of me with the caption:

DOCTOR GRUBER
WANTED TO TAKE A BATH
ZDRAVSTVUITYE

The article described how Republican Congressman John Taber of New York had interrupted Congress' discussion of the budget for the Interior Department. Holding up a copy of *I Went to the Soviet Arctic,* he barked, "It's time to stop the propaganda of communism. Any of us who vote to pay this woman's salary is not fit to sit in the House of Representatives!"

Representative Jed Johnson, a Democrat from Oklahoma, jumped to the defense, asking for a quotation from the book. "How can we prejudge a woman without even giving her an opportunity to be heard? . . . Even the worst criminal has his day in court."

Obviously no one in Congress had read the book. There was a long silence.

"Until someone reads it," Johnson announced, "I'm not going to condemn her."

Noah Mason of Illinois quickly read the last sentence: "But I know that some day I shall go back and bathe again in the Yenisei at Molokov Island . . . swim in the Arctic Ocean, and come back to a steaming breakfast shouting, *Zdravstvuitye* (which means hello)."

The thought of a government official shouting *Zdravstvuitye* was enough for the House. It quickly voted 64 to 49 to remove me from the Interior Department's payroll.

North Carolina's Alfred Bulwinkle, a Democrat, plaintively murmured, "The only thing she said is she wants to take a bath."

I found a seat in the railroad cafeteria. So this was what Mike Straus had tried to prepare me for.

"It's a rotten lie!" I heard myself say so loudly that people at nearby tables turned to look at me. I was angry and frightened. What did it mean? Was I fired already?

Surely they knew I was no communist. If they had only read the book, I thought, they would have known that I had written for the leading newspaper of the Republican press, the New York *Herald Tribune*. Where had they gotten their ideas? Certainly not from the book. If I had been a communist, the Russians would never have let me go to the Arctic. They knew that a communist would have been prejudiced in their favor, and wouldn't have been believed in the States.

I checked into the Women's Club of Los Angeles. As the morning wore on disturbingly, newspapers began calling for statements on my political views. I thought how ironic it was. I was no political evaluator; my interests were people. The only thing revolutionary in the book, I thought, was its proof that any nation's share of the Arctic needn't any longer be a barren, uninhabitable wasteland. The great overthrow that I recommended was the overthrow of medieval prejudices against the North by people of more southern descent.

I telephoned Ickes. He was jovial. His wife, Jane, had just given birth to a son, Harold Jr.

"How's the communist?" Ickes laughed.

"She only wants to take a bath," I said.

"Communists don't take baths," he joked.

"I know, that's what confuses me."

"It's not you they're after, it's their way to get me," he explained. "Get everyone important you know to write me a letter. I'm going to fight it in the Senate."

Ickes sounded like a boxer dancing in the ring. This was what he loved. Only Ickes, I thought, would have taken on the fight for someone he hardly knew. Most cabinet members would have said, "Sorry kid, can't help you. You're out."

I got to work. I realized what it meant to have friends. Wires and letters poured in from people like Professor George Cressey of Syracuse University; Quincy Howe, editor at Simon & Schuster, the publisher of my book; Mary Beard, historian, and the director of the CBS Lecture Bureau. My brother Harry cancelled his appointments and trudged around New York picking up the written recommendations. Of all the letters and telegrams that came in, the gesture of support that gave me the most confidence and strength was from the Arctic explorer and author, Vihljalmur Stefanson. Stefanson wrote:

> I have known Dr. Gruber for seven or eight years and have frequently heard her discuss political and social questions. Her views are essentially those of a New Dealer—very strongly anti-Fascist, strongly anti-Communist, and certainly not farther Left than those of President Roosevelt in his fireside chats and messages to Congress . . .
>
> I have seldom seen book reviews that were more uniformly favorable, and do not remember that one of those I read suggested that she might be a communist or might have communist leanings. There were several who complimented her on not taking sides—on being objective and pointing out the favorable as well as the unfavorable sides of life in the country she traversed.

A call came from the *Herald Tribune*. It was Helen Rogers Reid. "Ruth, this thing is a political move, and utterly ridiculous." She repeated what Ickes had said. "It's an attack against Ickes and you happen to be a pawn. I'm writing a letter of outrage."

The next day the *Herald Tribune* ran an article that announced:

DR. RUTH GRUBER
PRAISED, OUSTER
DRAWS ATTACK

FRIENDS INDIGNANT AT HOUSE
FOR DROPPING HER FROM
PROPOSED ALASKA SURVEY

Several days later, Ickes entered the Senate chamber armed with a fat briefcase of letters and affidavits. He never opened it.

"I don't believe," he thundered, "that a citizen of the United States—which of course Dr. Gruber is—becomes a communist by visiting Russia." He described the action of the House as "a reflection upon our democratic form of government. None of us can afford to let such fabrications go unchallenged."

Senator Bankhead (Tallulah's uncle) asked, "Do you know what race she is a member of?"

Ickes answered, "I do not know. I never asked her that. I have seen her twice. She looked like an American." He quoted from the *Los Angeles Times*. "She has won the friendship and admiration of explorers and learned folk all over the world."

In the end, it was Ickes's wit that won the senators. They began to laugh as he pointed out that Herbert Hoover and Shirley Temple had both been to Russia, and they were not communists.

He sent me a telegram after the hearings, "You may proceed to Alaska with the understanding that if the language eliminating you from the Interior Appropriation Act is continued it will be necessary to recall you. After my statement before the Committee I do not believe this will occur."

The next morning I boarded a train to Seattle.

Chapter Four

SCHOOLMARMS AND WHORES

T he morning after my arrival in Seattle, I drove down to the docks of the Alaska Steamship Company, ready to sail at nine for Alaska. The ship was to leave an hour late, officials said. At ten, it was to be an hour later. At eleven, it was set to sail at noon. Finally, sometime in the afternoon, amid shrieking of whistles, grinding of cranes, rather sparse flurries of confetti, and people waving from the narrow wooden pier, we departed. The SS *Denali* was finally heading north.

A light mist fell on my face as I stood at the rail watching the ship pull out of the harbor. The ship nosed around the great industrial buildings of Seattle on beyond Vancouver, and pushed leisurely through the thick green timbered islands of the Canadian archipelago. A few hours north of Vancouver, and you were in a northern jungle of islands and fur-clad fjords, hidden bays, and circling inlets. I breathed in the clean washed air and the sweetness of evergreens along the banks. We were on our way to Alaska's Inside Passage.

Soon the deck was alive with construction workers, sour-doughs (the name for early Alaskan settlers), fishermen, and women of different ages, some in elegant coats and high heels, others in sneakers and slacks. I wore slacks, too, and a sweater and low-heeled shoes to walk the decks.

In Seattle, a steamship officer had prepared me, "There are only two kinds of women going on that steamer—schoolmarms and whores," he said. "The purser sizes them up when they come aboard and seats them according to their profession. He never guesses wrong."

It was on that ship sailing to Alaska that I got my first inti-mation of the special brand of Alaskan humor, its virility, its enormous lies, its rich Bunyonesque imagination. The run from Seattle to Ketchikan is misnamed. It ought not to be called "The Inside Passage," but rather "The Munchausen Tour." The officers on the ships, and most of the old-timers, have huge and lusty fun at the expense of all the newcomers. Each year the tall stories grow taller, the bears bigger, the ice worms slimier, and the cold winters colder. At least half the misinformation taught to children by unsuspecting school-teachers who have taken summer cruises to Alaska must be laid at the cabin doors of men like the *Denali*'s Swedish pilot.

A round, middle-aged sailor with his flaming red hair, his pipe, his thick brogue, and his joy in fooling all newcomers, especially schoolteachers, was famous on the run. Almost everyone had an anecdote about him that made you roar. I was with him one afternoon, walking the deck in the silver sun-light, when someone came up to him.

"Pardon me, sir," a young man asked in a Harvard accent, "but can you tell me if the gulls sleep at night?"

"I don't know," he said, "I never slept vit vun."

The young man walked away quickly.

"How do you like Alaska?" I asked to change the subject.

"Fine," he answered.

"What part do you like best?"

"None," he said firmly. "I can't vait till I get turned around and go home again." He was talking like Greta Garbo now. "Like de fellow said," he philosophized, "what's de use of chewin' tobacco if you're agone to spit out de juice? What's de use?"

In the early evening, rain driven by a strong wind began to pound the ship. We were passing north of Alert Bay, near the island on which the Doukhobor sect lived. They had left Russia about seventy-five years earlier in search of a communal utopia and some few years later staged a nudist parade in protest against a Canadian decree forcing them to send their children to government schools. Now the purser assured us very seriously that the mounties constantly poured itching powder on the Doukhobors to keep them from going around naked.

"At five o'clock," the purser said, "they blow a whistle over there and each man picks his woman for the night."

The Swedish pilot didn't think that story was very good. "Oh, them Doukhobors, they lost their pep. Now they got only one wife and one farm apiece."

The construction worker slapped his thigh with laughter and ambled off.

More passengers ventured out on deck. An attractive blond woman in her twenties approached us. I wondered where the purser had seated her.

"Where you going?" the pilot asked her.

"Kodiak."

"Your husband there?"

"Yes."

"He don't love you, or he wouldn't take you to Kodiak."

"He loves me," she protested.

"What do you expect Kodiak will be like?" I asked her.

"Terrible. It'll be something like hell, but I'll get used to it."

Despite the assurance that I would meet only schoolteachers and prostitutes, there were young women on the ship traveling as clerks, stenographers, telephone operators, and brides. Rumors chased around the ship purporting to identify the prostitutes. Prostitution was big business in Alaska. Someone said that many of Alaska's first ladies, wives of mayors, and church leaders in the towns had been dance-hall girls who came up in the gold rush days and then settled down to marry. It was inevitable, in a frontier, that you would get the extremes of society: the empire builders and the drifters. Even on our ship, you could see that there were few people who were regular, middle-class types firmly tied to their roots. Contented people rarely strike out for a new frontier.

My fellow passengers offered me daily advice on how to get by in this new land. "The secret of getting along in Alaska," someone told me as we walked on the deck, "is to hear all you can, and keep your mouth shut." Someone else quoted an Alaskan expert who had warned her, "When you go to a new town or village, everyone you meet will be friendly. Be a friend to everyone and an intimate of no one."

The steamer traveled up the Inside Passage to Seward, stopping at all the towns along the way. In each one, officials, alerted by Ickes's office, came aboard to greet me, show me around, and discuss their problems.

The crew of the Alaska Steamship line, like most people who lived under the midnight sun, had lost all concept of time. When you have twenty-two hours of sunlight each day, you never know when to go to sleep. Some of the officers seemed to think that sleep was altogether primitive, and in the summer, unnecessary. There was plenty of time to sleep in the winter, during the long nights.

Each evening, I would walk on deck, thinking over the events of the day and waiting for the sun to set. I was overwhelmed with the beauty and serenity of the place. After miles of rolling silent majestic hills, after thousands of small green islands freckled with trees, after motionless water and numberless gulls, here was a sun that refused to slide straight down into a pocket, but that kept swinging, round and fiery, like a mirror that a small boy had tilted up to our eyes.

At long last, the sun hid behind a hill, leaving a brilliant lambent halo where it had stood. The sky flushed yellow and saffron. The mountains grew purple and shadowed and a sliver of moon rose modestly, as though it were apologizing for coming into the stage-show put on by the sun.

And while I stood at the rail trying to hold on to all that beauty, a construction worker walked to the rail beside me.

"Hell," he said, "Alaska ain't nuthin' but rain, mist, and a little blow."

As the ship swung in and out of Indian villages, each one fascinating, inviting, and important, I had to decide whether to get off at each stop, stay for several weeks, learn all that I could, and then take the next steamer northward, or to stay with the ship and see the things that the tourists and the "round-trippers" got to see. The second plan seemed better to me. Then, while the waters were all open and transportation good, I could travel as far north as possible and, having defined the problems and chosen the places I wanted most to study, I could return south and make a careful survey.

My first overnight stop was Alaska's hilly capital, Juneau. It rose from the waters of the Inside Passage like a quaint waterfront town in Holland with small pastel houses and wooden steps that led from one level of the city to another. Dark mountains filled the skyline.

I checked into the Baranof Hotel, a new nine-story building named for the Russian governor who had ruled Alaska in the late eighteenth century.

Protocol dictated that I pay my respects to Governor Ernest Gruening. "Gruening was picked for the job by the president," Ickes had told me. "I had no voice in it. He's as unpopular up there as I am. He's bright, he was the editor of *The Nation,* but we disagree on a lot of things. He's like a bull in a china shop."

I phoned the mansion and was told the governor was out of town. Instead, E. L. (Bob) Bartlett, the secretary and acting governor, would be delighted to see me the next morning.

It was ten at night and still strong daylight, so I strolled along the narrow streets with signs that read, 5, 10 AND 25 CENTS STORE, DRUGLESS PHYSICIANS AND CHIROPRACTORS, and my favorite PAY N' TAKIT.

Six blocks from the hotel on South Franklin Street, I walked past rows of saloons and wooden shanties. Girls with brightly rouged faces peered out from behind cretonne curtains. A few waved at me. I waved back. Three Indian girls hung outside a pool room. I figured they were freelancers. A poster in a window proclaimed, ALASKA: LAND OF THE MIDNIGHT SUN. I looked more closely. Someone had changed the caption to read, LAND OF THE MIDNIGHT FUN.

The next morning I called on Bob Bartlett in his office. He was a slim, homespun man with narrow-set eyes and an aura of honesty. On his desk were neatly folded copies of the *Juneau Daily Empire* and several issues of the *The Nation*. I began the interview quickly. "What are your biggest human problems up here?"

"Drinking," he said. "The natives and the sourdoughs drink enough to float a fleet. Drinking's going to kill off the Eskimos and Indians if we don't work out some way to prohibit its sale. Another big problem is gambling."

"It's a curse." I said.

"That it is," he agreed. "Another big problem is taxes. The big mining and fishing companies pay federal taxes but refuse to pay local taxes. This is empty country. There are thirty thousand whites up here all together. The rest, another thirty thousand, are natives. The federal government runs practically everything up here. It's your boss, Secretary Ickes. What do those officials in Washington know about Alaska?"

He waited, obviously pleased I was writing his criticism of the federal government in my notebook.

"Listen, Ruth," he said suddenly. "You can't be in Juneau without seeing the Mendenhall Glacier. How about seeing it now?"

He grabbed his hat. I shut my notebook.

In minutes we were driving up and down the hilly streets. The sky was cloudless and the temperature warmer than in Washington. An outdoor thermometer read eighty-four degrees. The Mendenhall Glacier was sixteen miles out of Juneau on a smooth concrete highway framed with shining trees.

"You don't see many roads like this in Alaska." He said it like a man caressing a woman's skin. "That's another thing we need desperately. Roads. The only way you get in and out of most places is by air or ship. Well, here we are."

I bounded out of the car holding my breath. The Mendendall Glacier, a gigantic ice mountain, was blue-white marble come to life.

"This is one of the bigger ones," Bartlett boasted. "You can't see it all unless you fly over it. Seventeen miles long and about three miles wide. That's bigger than some states."

Fascinated by the behemoth before me, I peppered him with questions. "Are those glaciers like the iceberg that sank the *Titanic*? What's their mystery?"

"There's no mystery," he chuckled. "They've been forming for hundreds of years. Winter snow falls on the mountains and freezes. That's what makes glaciers. They go down maybe a thousand feet. And they flow, but so slow you can't detect it. Glaciers are different than icebergs. An iceberg can sink a ship, but glaciers are safe."

My mind flashed back to P. S. 141 in Brooklyn. The ice mountain was the image that most books about Alaska imprinted on our young brains. They were mysterious and slightly terrifying. The Mendenhall Glacier was indeed mysterious, but also majestic, and not terrifying. I felt as if I were seeing the first day of creation.

Chapter Five

ANCHORAGE BOOMS

Anchorage. Not Fairbanks or Nome, not the familiar names from the gold rush, but Anchorage. I liked the sound. Anchorage, the biggest town along the Alaska Railroad was to be my workplace and my home.

At the station I caught sight of a man in hunter-green leather striding the platform like Paul Bunyan. It was Col. Otto F. Ohlson, the Alaska Railroad chief. He was five foot six, straight as a telephone pole, with steel-gray hair and a dashing white mustache. He had dark weathered skin, a strong nose, and gold-rimmed glasses through which his blue-green eyes commanded the landscape.

"Welcome. Welcome." He greeted me in a jovial voice, enriched by a Scandinavian accent. "You won. Your boss did it. The Senate voted for you to stay."

I whispered to myself, "Thank you, Mr. Ickes, thank you."

"You got a big job ahead, Doctor," Colonel Ohlson said, bundling me into his car. "This is our plan today. First I'll take you to your office in the federal building. You have the penthouse."

"Sounds good. What floor is it?"

"The third."

"Then what?"

"Then I'll take you to the Westward Hotel, and you can check in."

My office was a large airy room with a desk and chair facing the window and a row of new filing cabinets lining the opposite wall. Outside the window I saw Anchorage's main street, Fourth Avenue, stretched out like a checkerboard, with bright wide streets and winding alleys. White mountains rose on both ends of Fourth Avenue, bracketing the town.

We drove to the Westward Hotel, a clean hotel built essentially for salesmen. It had a bar and a fair-sized dining room.

"I'll pick you up tonight at six o'clock," Colonel Ohlson said. "You'll be a guest at the Atwoods. Mr. Atwood is the publisher of the *Anchorage Times*."

I unpacked swiftly and chose a cool summer party dress to wear. Promptly at six, Colonel Ohlson appeared. We drove to a handsome, modern house. We were greeted at the door by Evangeline and Robert Atwood.

She shook my hand, and told me, "We've heard so much about you. I couldn't wait to meet you."

I liked Evangeline almost immediately. She seemed to be in her late thirties and was strikingly handsome. Dressed in a long silk evening gown and stylishly coifed, she could have been a hostess in Los Angeles or New York.

Soon the house began filling up with women in long dresses and men in tailored suits and army uniforms.

The upper crust of Anchorage society was invited to these dinner parties, along with the military brass. Burly Lt. Gen.

Simon Bolivar Buckner Jr. and his slender wife, Adele, daughter of Southern aristocracy, were always the guests of honor.

General Buckner, red-cheeked with ice blue eyes and a leathery face, was the head of the Alaska Defense Command. He had been chosen for the job of preparing Alaska for war because he was known to be tough and mean. He was a Southerner, born in Kentucky to an army family. His military grandfather had assumed the name "Simon Bolivar" in admiration of the South American hero. His father, also named Simon Bolivar, was sixty-three when Junior was born.

He had arrived in Alaska in 1940, a huge empty territory, which he began blanketing with soldiers. Less than a year later, in addition to its original population of 60,000, Alaska now held 22,000 army troops, 2,200 army and air force personnel, and 550 navy officers and sailors. Air bases were built almost overnight in Kodiak and Sitka. A radio station was installed at Dutch Harbor, and a huge army base at Fort Richardson became the central refueling station for planes flying between the United States and the Soviet Union.

Buckner quickly came to love Alaska. The hard frontier life suited him. Each morning, the fifty-six-year-old general bathed in a tub filled with ice-cold water. At one point, his aide used a blow torch to unfreeze the pipe carrying the water for his bath.

Now, at Evangeline's dinner party, General Buckner held center stage, telling stories, laughing as jovially as the rest of us. He was in full uniform, with rows of battle ribbons covering a good part of his chest. After the meal, we adjourned to the salon, where the guests themselves provided the entertainment, telling stories and jokes and singing songs that most of us knew.

General Buckner suddenly turned to me. "Something tells me you can sing," he said. "Why don't you honor us with a song?"

I racked my brain. There was a song that my Aunt Francie had taught all the children at the Sunday afternoon gatherings at our house in Brooklyn. I decided to try it out. I cleared my throat, straightened my skirt, and began to sing:

> She's more to be pitied than censured,
> She's more to be helped than despised,
> She's only a lassie who ventured,
> On life's evil paths ill-advised.
> Do not scorn her with words fierce and bitter,
> Do not laugh at her shame and downfall,
> For a moment you'll stop to consider,
> *That a man was the cause of it all!*

"Good girl!" General Buckner applauded. "Let's hear it again!" He made the song his own. At every dinner party from that night on, he would ask me to sing it, and in his booming voice, would join me in belting out the last line. Eventually the whole dinner party, laughing and applauding, would sing along.

Anchorage, in 1941, was the most hopeful town in Alaska. It had everything it needed to become the biggest city in the territory: farm land in the Matanuska Valley, gold and coal in its mountains, a harbor for ships to sail into, and a railroad linking it to Mount McKinley and Fairbanks.

It was a Wild West town of saloons, storefronts, and sawdust-covered restaurants. Every few feet there was a bar, and off the main street there was a whole row of brothels in wooden shacks. But it was also a growing young city, filled with women's dress shops, drugstores, women's and men's clubs, churches, and overflowing hotels. It had no gentle patina of age. Even the churches had a brand-new, unfinished look, unhallowed by years of births, deaths, and marriages.

My days in Anchorage were filled with interviewing people on every level of society. I prowled through the city, making friends, trying to capture the essence of Alaska in my notebooks and on film. Often, I worked fifteen hours a day taking notes and sending constant reports to Ickes by telegraph and by airmail.

In my reports and letters to him, I had to walk a fine line. I had to balance my enthusiasm for Alaska with its realities. I wanted to show how much potential the territory had, but I didn't want to oversell it. Alaska was a land of many stereotypes that had suffered from its own picturesqueness. Travelers returning from this vast land told not of the schools in every town and village and of the university in Fairbanks, but of the wild no-man's-land of ice, snow, and if you were lucky, gold. I didn't want to perpetuate these stereotypes.

One evening Colonel Ohlson invited me to dinner at his home. He lived in a large wood-framed house with a manicured lawn, a two-car garage, a cook, and a housekeeper. He greeted me on the street and ushered me into his home.

In Washington I had been warned against him. "Keep out of his way," several people had told me. "He's a tough guy to deal with." They were wrong. He was the last word in gallantry and chivalry, and without question the most gracious host in a territory famous for its hospitality. He was straight out of a textbook for European officers, who shook your hand when you entered a room and bowed when you left. He was the Grande Army officer who made you feel like a grande dame.

He gave me a quick tour of the elaborately decorated house. He told me it was all his wife's work. She had died of cancer two years earlier, but I felt her presence throughout their home.

Over dinner, the colonel offered me fatherly advice. "You

have a very serious problem, Doctor," he said. "You might write what a wonderful country this is, and a lot of people would read it and come up here, and what would they find? Nothing. They would blame you. You would be held responsible for years for their failure. They would forget everything good you had done. They would forget that you were sincere. They would only say, 'Oh, she was the one who started that terrible failure. Gruber's Folly.'"

"Colonel," I said. "I can't tell you how grateful I am for your advice.

I need all the advice I can get. I want to know the truth about Alaska, how we can help open it for homesteaders, for GI's, for farmers, for men and women who love frontier country, for teachers and nurses—"

I stopped abruptly, thinking I was talking too much.

"Go on," he said, puffing his cigar.

I hesitated. "You don't want to hear me. I want to hear you. I even brought my notebook."

"Keep on," he blew smoke in the air. "I really want to know what you're thinking."

Encouraged, I went on. "I have this mental map where I can see all kinds of people coming up here: farmers escaping the dustbowl in the midwest; women who want to be adventurous and live independent lives; doctors and nurses who want to help the native people, especially those whose lives are being destroyed by alcoholism and the white man's diseases."

He nodded. "I think you're being too optimistic about the kind of people who will want to come up here. Life isn't easy here, you know. Many who come stay a little while, then turn right around and land back in Seattle or Los Angeles or even New York."

"Colonel, that's what happened in the opening of the West. According to some historians, half the people turned their covered wagons around and went back east. Even if half of those who come up here turn around, those who stay would fall in love with the beauty and richness of this land."

"I still say you're too optimistic. Be careful."

"I'll try. I'm writing your advice in my head."

Back in my hotel room, I reconstructed much of the colonel's advice in my notebook. I understood his warning. One of the waitresses at the Westward Hotel, with whom I had become friendly, confided in me. "People who come in are gossiping about you. They all ask me questions, but I tell them, 'I don't know anything you don't know. It's all in the newspapers.'"

I was the proverbial fish in the goldfish bowl. Anchorage society continued to eye me with a certain curiosity and suspicion. One evening at Evangeline Atwood's house, she said, "Ruth, you're a mystery woman. We're trying to figure out why Ickes sent you. We think maybe he wanted you to find out how you could bring Hebrews up here."

"No," I answered her, "I'm hoping to bring Americans up here." Her use of the word "Hebrew" as if "Jew" were a dirty word reminded me of how some people used "Nigra."

I wished I could have said that I was bringing Jewish refugees fleeing Hitler. With their skills, they could have filled this frontier with engineers, artists, musicians, and writers. But I had no power. Ickes's bill, to bring five thousand refugees and five thousand stateside men and women each year to Alaska, was dead.

Other rumors floating around were that I was Ickes's daughter, or that I was part of the Office of Naval Intelligence. That rumor was eventually knocked down by an army officer, Lt. Joe Hauser, who explained to one rumormonger, "It's impossible—we don't use women operatives in this country; she would have to be the first exception."

One rumor that made me chuckle was that I was a child welfare specialist sent to teach birth control to the natives. But my favorite rumor contended that I was a lady doctor writing a novel on the love life of the Eskimos.

I decided to dispel the rumors. A reporter for *Jessen's Weekly* in Fairbanks covered a speech I gave to a women's club. The article was headlined DR. GRUBER RAPS RUMORS AND GOSSIP BY ALASKA WOMEN, and read:

> Anti rumor and anti gossip clubs were recommended by Dr. Ruth Gruber, government social and economic research writer, to the Homemakers' Club of the University of Alaska Extension Service Tuesday afternoon.
>
> She would have members of an anti rumor club pay a fine of ten cents every time they spread a rumor, the money to go into a treasury for the purchase of War Bonds.*

---

* Misunderstandings of my work in Alaska have persisted for years. Even in 1990, T. H. Watkins wrote in his massive and brilliant biography, *Righteous Pilgrim: The Life and Times of Harold L. Ickes, 1874–1952*, that Ickes had hired me to "snoop around in Alaska and keep him informed." Watkins's explanation was, "Since he did not fully trust the reports he got from Gruening, Ickes had hired his own correspondent." I was grateful to Watkins for all the kind things he wrote about me, but I was never a snoop.

Chapter Six

THE SILVER BULLET

Colonel Ohlson had the distinction of being the third most hated man in Alaska. Numbers one and two were Ickes and Governor Ernest Gruening. Alaskans disliked Ohlson largely because they felt he was overcharging them for carrying freight on the railroad.

"People in the territory want their goods sent free," he explained to me, "but the people of the United States have to pay if the Alaskans don't, and that isn't fair. It's the people's money."

We were on one of his "speeders," a small private train called the *Silver Bullet*. It had two engineers, two sets of double seats, and a long bench in the back. The colonel, sitting in front of me on the train, took the cigar out of his mouth only long enough to point out sights of interest. Traveling on the *Silver Bullet,* stopping at designated sections, I was intrigued by the way he talked to the men or telephoned ahead that we were coming. He looked and sounded like the railroad executive, giving commands to the two engineers. He was one of those rare men who was even bigger than his big job.

Stretching up in the distance, as we neared Talkeetna, was Mount McKinley. The tallest mountain peak in North America, it was a sculpted mass of ice and snow and rock. Once again I became aware of how empty this land was, how easily newcomers and refugees could have lived here, liberated from the fires burning in Europe.

In the early evening we reached Curry, where the railroad managed and owned a light green, modernistic hotel. As we sat around the sumptuous dinner table with other guests, eating steaks one and a half inches thick and costing one dollar and fifty cents, everyone told stories about Alaska.

After dinner, Ohlson and the men played bridge with the young wife of the hotel manager. The colonel's gambling was legendary. He squinted his eyes and concentrated as hard on his cards as he did on his railroad. I was sleepy after the long and not too steady journey, but the colonel refused to let me rest.

"What?" he exclaimed, "You don't play bridge?" he shook his head in amazement. "Bridge is very good for you, Doctor. You just have to forget everything else." He asked me, "You don't play cards, you don't drink. So what do you do for fun?"

I admitted to him that I was a social failure, and went on to bed.

The next day, after a breakfast that a lumberjack would have considered more than adequate, we left at 9 A.M., bound for Mount McKinley. The *Silver Bullet* moved swiftly toward the highest peak in the United States. The colonel, fresh, rested and puffing a new cigar, told me that for him, the section ahead was the most beautiful in the whole country. Great fields and valleys rolled between the mountains. At noon we reached McKinley Park. Pine trees and animals flew by us as I stared up at the snow-capped peaks. It was 6:30 in the evening, with the sun as bright as noon when we reached Fairbanks.

A friend of the colonel's met us at the station and drove us to Fairbanks' best hotel, the Nordale. I unpacked my bag, changed into a cool summer dress to withstand the eighty-degree heat, and then, eager to see the city for myself, went out for a walk.

Fairbanks had a spirit of its own, a town of small, one-storied gabled cottages with a thousand radio poles and antennas stuck everywhere. After walking aimlessly down the broad avenues, some of them paved and others planked, I returned to First Avenue on the banks of the Chena Slough River. This, I imagined, was the way Fairbanks had looked in the first days of its development. A few sparse trees told the old story of pioneers who felt that the first step in building a town was to tear down all the trees. There was an ancient, sagging hotel facing the Slough, a two-storied, faded green relic of the early days. Old-timers, dressed in rough mining clothes, walked by slowly in the hot sun.

Suddenly I came upon the Fairbanks cemetery. The history of the city was in this cemetery. The army of gold seekers had their own unsung fallen heroes, and I noticed a grave that bore the fitting inscription:

> In Memorial to the Unknown Prospector
> Whose Bones Were Found
> Near Mile 441 Alaska Railway

Fairbanks was founded by anonymous prospectors who had struck gold on Pedro Creek in 1902. The graves of men who stayed and died in Alaska were marked by wooden crosses laid flat on the ground. You couldn't stand the wooden crosses up, because the winter frost would heave them out of the ground.

Across the street from the cemetery was a dog pound, and while I walked, the dogs, imprisoned in their pens, kept whining pitifully. The mosquitoes bit the unfortunate canines hard, recognizing fresh blood. I was about to quit the cemetery, driven out, not by the memories of dead men and women, but by the howling of living animals, when I came to a section where prostitutes were buried. The cemetery showed in frank, bold segregation how sharp the line was between the "good" women and the "bad" ones. Even in death, they couldn't associate.

Going back to the city, I walked through "The Row," the warren of brothels on Fourth Avenue. It was a row of wooden cabins and wooden outhouses, connected by a narrow planked street. Slop pails were everywhere. I learned later that the "girls" in this town were so well organized, they wouldn't let any newcomers in. It was one of the few professions in Fairbanks where people died of old age.

Further along the street were small houses that belonged to working men and women. I stopped to talk with Belle, a black laundress with an expressive face, glasses, and bad teeth. Formerly a prostitute, she was now working as the laundress for the army. Her house was a jumbled workshop: All the clothes were washed and dried in one large room and then bundled together in brown paper. Belle's lover, a small Italian man, came into the house. He delivered the laundry that Belle washed and packaged. Both of them had rich, lush laughs, and they laughed at almost everything. Belle walked me to the door of her house as I was leaving.

"This sure is God's country," she said. "I've been to all the big cities, and then I come to this dusty little hole, and I love it. Now, why?"

There is something epically unlovely about pioneer towns; they often have no unity of construction, no integrity, no plan.

Fairbanks was dirty and muddy, a constant conflict between the fine front of the new post office building and the terrible alley of Third Avenue, behind which people threw their food and garbage. Winter is the only time Fairbanks looks clean because a coat of snow blankets the garbage and makes the dilapidated log cabins and mud holes look lovely. But spring and summer exposed the mud and garbage all over again.

Fairbanks, preparing for war, was a preview of what the Arctic world of the future might look like. The broad streets were filling up with airmen from foreign lands: Great Britain, Canada, Australia, and the USSR as well as the United States. The route that these airmen followed took them from Canada, to Fairbanks, then across the Arctic Ocean to Siberia and Moscow. The Soviet flyers, dressed in high leather boots and army tunics dangling over their breeches, walked down Lacey Street saluting American and Canadian and British airmen. They sat at long counters of the Co-operative Drug Store drinking chocolate malteds with American girls who worked for the army engineers or studied at the university. Nearly everyone in Fairbanks was picking up a few Russian words, like *da* and *nyet.* Meanwhile, the Russians burned the midnight oil trying to pronounce *though, enough, bough, bought,* and *schizophrenic.*

Every day, in the hot dry summer and the cold dry winter, the good townspeople of Fairbanks watched their sky grow dark with Russian planes flying westward. Far from the battlefronts of Europe, the Russian pilots were veterans of the war we had not yet entered. Locals were sitting in their movie theaters next to men who had already been decorated for bravery in action. Girls from Minnesota and Brooklyn danced in the friendly Sky Lounge with men from Stalingrad and Sevastopol, who kissed their hand after each dance and bowed deeply. These were Russians who smoked long cigarettes and seemed to have stepped right out of newsreels from the Old World.

In Fairbanks, we stayed in touch with the world through the radio. We listened to speeches by Winston Churchill, Franklin and Eleanor Roosevelt, and other leaders. Hitler's planes were bombing London. We could even hear the bombs exploding across the radio airwaves. I kept in touch with my family through radio operators, who patched me into other shortwave aficionados. They in turn made collect calls to Brooklyn, where I was able to tell Papa that I wished him a happy Father's Day. He later wrote me that hearing my voice made it the happiest Father's Day of his life.

For a whole week in July, the temperature in Fairbanks hovered at eighty-five degrees. The nights were no cooler, because there *were* no nights. I could read a newspaper and type my reports and letters without turning a light on even at 11 P.M. I spent the days in light cotton clothes, interviewing and jotting notes in my notebooks; at nights I furiously typed my reports and letters. Air conditioning was unknown, and with no fan, my room in the Nordale Hotel was so hot I often did my typing in a bathing suit.

On June 21, the longest day of the year, Pan American Airlines invited a few of us to take an airplane flight so that we could see the sun set and rise within a few minutes. It was 12:30 A.M. The sun was setting as our plane climbed twelve hundred feet to get above the clouds. Soon we were in near darkness, with a line of red encircling a cloud. It looked to me like a soft, dark animal with a luminous fringe of red hair. Suddenly the sun shot like a huge ball through a slit in the clouds. It was a brilliant, gorgeous red, such as I had never seen before. The clouds began to reflect the light of that sun; cumulus clouds that had been black and amorphous before were now vivid and fantastic with color, shape, and depth. The earth, which had been dark for a few minutes, was now bright as high noon.

Fairbanks was a different city from the air. The white and brown houses were tinged with gold. The gold that miners scraped from the ground and shipped out to the banking center was a transient gold. The permanent wealth of Alaska, the gold that transcended time and space, was the gold that lit up the hills and the rivers.

The midnight sun did strange things to people. For one thing, sleep seemed a waste of time. There was something in the air, something so electric and vibrant that you actually needed less sleep in Fairbanks than you did in the States. I knew women who came home from parties in evening gowns at two in the morning and felt so alive with the beauty of the sky and the land that they lifted their long skirts, went out to their gardens, and picked the bugs off their potatoes. Some of the miners mined for gold twenty-four hours a day in the summer, planning to sleep all winter, like hibernating bears. You could play tennis and baseball at midnight, and to get the sunlight out of your eyes when you finally wanted to sleep, you slept with a sleeping mask.

My notebooks were rapidly filling up with interviews, especially with working women. Women in Fairbanks were doing everything, from owning and running businesses and shops to serving as judges and community leaders. I even met a woman miner, whose name was Grace Lowe. "She's the boss of her mine at Livengood," a man told me, "and believe me, she's the boss all right. She can run the 'Cat' [the bulldozer] and the truck. She can cook and do most everything. She came up here in the middle twenties and ran a roadhouse with another woman. Then in the early thirties she got her mine and ran it with some helpers. She's made a lot of money and has properties

'Outside,' too. She's a real character—intelligent, easy to look at, and has the respect of a lot of us men in town."

Grace Lowe lived up to her reputation. She was wearing a red sweater and blue denim slacks the day I met her, and she looked like Rosie the Riveter, tough and glamorous at the same time. "It's hard on some women up here," she told me, "but I get along fine. It's just as hard on the sourdoughs. Take this week—it's been eighty degrees each day, and half of them nearly keeled over from heat prostration."

Peggy Gordon, another hard-working woman, owned a successful dress shop in midtown. Sweltering in the heat, I dropped in and chatted with her. Because laundering was so costly (blamed like everything else on the high cost of transportation), it was cheaper for me to buy a new white blouse each week from Peggy than to have the one from the previous week washed and ironed.

Peggy had spent twelve years "Outside"—in the lower forty-eight—bringing up her son, who was now thirty, and her daughter, who had been "Miss Fairbanks." Moving back to Alaska, Peggy became head of the Women's Club in Anchorage. But in Fairbanks, where she now lived, she was too busy running her shop to go to meetings.

"I'm really in love with this town," she told me. "The people here are so warm and democratic. Everybody digs in. It's awfully hard on women though. They have to keep the fire burning all winter. The days are so short, and it gets so cold, and there is so much to do, but there is a real heroic spirit." She nodded, watching me jot her words in my notebook. Then she went on. "The real trouble with Alaska," she said, lowering her voice confidentially, "is that Alaskans think they are so much better than everyone else who comes up here. They think they are just the best people in the world." She conjured up an image of Alaskans standing with one leg on the gravy train and the other leg free to kick everyone else off.

Her husband, Frank, a small man with a shock of white hair and a Scottish brogue, entered the shop. He was a member of the legislature, and for long intervals left Peggy alone while he worked on bills and committees in Juneau. He joined the conversation as if he were making a speech.

"I'd like to see ten or twenty thousand people come up here when they build the Alaska Highway. But the thing I have against your boss Ickes is that he wanted to bring six hundred thousand refugees here."

"No, Frank," I said to the local legislator, "the bill Ickes tried to introduce would only have brought five thousand people from the states and five thousand Jewish refugees a year to Alaska." I shook my head, thinking, *This is the way anti-Semitism takes root. "The Big Lie."*

Where did Frank get the six hundred thousand figure? Oddly, it was the number of people Moses had taken from Egypt to the Promised Land, a mass escape from bondage that led to freedom for a mixed multitude.

A few days later, I climbed aboard the *Nenana,* a paddle wheel steamer owned by the Alaska Railroad, bound for Nome.

Chapter Seven

SAILING DOWN THE YUKON RIVER

On a quiet Sunday in June, sailing down the Yukon, I learned that Hitler had broken his pact with Stalin and had invaded the Soviet Union. The terrifying news splintered the air. Every evening at eight, all of us, passengers and crew, crowded around the radio listening to the *Hollywood Richfield Reporter* describe the Nazi onslaught.

It was strange to be sailing down the Yukon while Europe was burning. This was a peaceful river, that ran for eighteen hundred miles from St. Michael in the Bering Sea to Whitmore in the Yukon Territory. It had been an important artery ever since ancient times; now the shadow of war stretched across it. Walking on the deck or sitting in the mess hall, we talked of the war, how soon we would be fighting side by side with the British, the French, the Russians. Even the most passionate anticommunist Alaskans felt a sudden reversion of feeling toward the Soviet Union. We all were sure that soon our soldiers would be fighting and dying together.

I love water. I love oceans and rivers. I'm happiest living near water. Now, on the Yukon, I kept thinking of the rivers I had known: the Hudson as a child; the St. Lawrence, which I sailed on a circuitous trip to college in Madison, Wisconsin; the romantic Seine; the Rhine, along whose banks in Cologne I walked each day; and the Lena and Yenisei in Siberia, whose spirit I had tried to capture in my notes. And now the Yukon, so serene in sharp contrast to my fears for my relatives as news came of Hitler's march across Poland. I did not know then, but all the aunts and uncles and cousins I had visited in 1936 on my way to Yakutsk in Siberia had already been forced to run to a river, undress, and then were shot. Those who did not fall into the river were pushed into it.

Listening to the radio reports of Hitler's armies storm-trooping across Europe inspired some of the men on our ship to tell me stories of the Russian traders who occupied Alaska before it became part of America. One of the sourdoughs at dinner described how the first Russian trader had lined up Indian and Aleut men to see how many could be killed with one bullet. Seeing my horror, another sourdough described how Russian traders sought out people who had died of smallpox, gathered up the infected clothing of the dead, and packed it into boxes made of copper to protect themselves. They then gave the clothing to the Alaskans along the Yukon River. This was all to save gunpowder. I judged that even if there was some truth in their stories, time had added trimmings to the atrocities.

Still, I felt the impact of the Russian colonization along the river. Rising from the riverbanks was a tiny town called "Russian Mission," with the same log cabins and sod-covered roofs I had seen in Siberia. Children jumped around as a group of us from the riverboat walked by racks of drying salmon and fish. Old women with Slavic faces crouched in front of their homes, chatting away. I asked the postmaster what language they spoke.

"They speak native," he explained, "not Russian or English."

Walking slowly through the village, I had the feeling that we were disturbing it, pulling it out of its timelessness. An aged woman in a fish-stained parka stood in front of a wooden igloo, vigorously chopping wood. She stopped for a moment as we passed, looked at us with curiosity, and then went back to her chore.

On the evening of June 27, our last day on the *Nenana,* we reached Marshall, the end of the line for the riverboats owned by the Alaska Railroad. From here I traveled down river to the Bering Sea on a small motor ship, the *Mildred,* owned by the Northern Commercial Company that locals used to go from village to village.

The *Mildred* had four bunks and about twelve passengers. In honor of the arrival of another female passenger and myself, they covered the bunks with unwashed blankets as sheets. I appreciated the gesture but slept in my clothing.

A young couple who had come down the river on an outboard motorboat immediately took two of the bunkbeds. I slept in the third and never knew in the morning who had slept above me the night before. The bunks, of course, were all in the same compartment, wedged between the pilothouse and the mess hall. Privacy was unknown. So was plumbing. There was a toilet on the the stern deck, a small closet that you backed into.

The boat had sprung a leak and water was flowing into the engine chamber. Each passenger took turns happily pumping water out as if it were a Saturday afternoon sporting event. I enjoyed talking with a lovely young Eskimo mother with a round face, skin the color of maple syrup, jet-black hair, and soulful dark eyes. She wore a blue sweater, a yellow-plaid cotton dress, store shoes with Cuban heels, and a brown beret. She had a four-month-old baby boy who cried constantly and an older little boy who was as beautiful as Gainsborough's "Boy in Blue." All during the trip, she kept rocking the baby in her arms. I told her how much I admired the patient way she consoled her child. In Brooklyn, I often saw mothers so irritated by a crying baby that they would slap them across the face or on the buttocks, yelling, "Stop crying!" Of course, their slaps only made the babies scream louder.

In sharp contrast to the gentle young mother was the talkative Eskimo cook and engineer, Alex Johnson, who looked like a wolf in an old picture book. Every time he opened his mouth, which was practically always, he showed you a yawning cavity of no upper teeth except the two incisors.

"Do you know Dr. Hard-liquor?" he asked me almost immediately.

"Yes, I do," I said, knowing he meant Dr. Ales Hrdliçka.

"Fine man. Fine man. But what for he dig up skulls all the time? What for?"

I tried to explain that Dr. Hrdliçka was an archeologist and was studying the migration routes of man from Siberia through Alaska to the United States.

Alex Johnson shook his head. "Still he dig up graves." He looked thoughtful for a moment, and then slapped me on the back. "Old Hard-liquor a good man. He gave me five bucks," he said with a laugh.

There was an eighty-four-year-old Russian Eskimo who was Alex's equal in humor. They rarely stopped teasing each other.

"I got weak heart," the old man announced one day while we were eating canned peaches. "Nearly kick over the other day."

"Why didn't you?" Alex asked.

"Too much work for you fellow," the old man replied with a sly glint in his eyes. "You got to dig grave, build cross—you too busy."

Alex slapped me on the back, joining in the laughter.

Our captain was a Russian Eskimo, too. He stood each day in a small pilothouse and navigated our small boat.

"How old do you think I am?" he asked me one day.

"Forty-five," I replied.

"Fifty-four," he answered. "I have eight children. My grandfather on my father's side was Russian. Where I live in Hamilton, down the river here, we're all related. Hamilton is one big family. They are all my uncles, aunts, and cousins. Most of these villages on the river are one family. That's why so many of them are dying off."

When I jested about our luxurious cruise ship, the *Mildred,* my fellow passengers told me, "Oh, she's nothing. You should have sailed on the old *Agnes.* She was a gas boat, and everybody on her would breathe in too much gas, start passing out, and be knocked over into the river. They would have to be fished out. The *Agnes* had two bunks and she carried at least sixteen passengers. The passengers would have to sleep standing up like planks."

The *Mildred* should have been honorably retired years earlier, but she still transported sewing machines, washing machines, food, and miscellaneous cargo down the river. She was the mail boat, too, and carried mail to the coast at St. Michael, where it was picked up by another small boat, which took it on to Nome and Kotzebue.

The riverbanks were gradually beginning to look bareheaded as the hills and trees gave way to tundra. I spent a day in Hamilton, a trading post and Eskimo village in the delta of the Yukon. Herbert Lawrence, an Eskimo trader from Black

River, south of Hamilton, led me past the twenty driftwood houses that comprised the village.

We stopped at the home of an old Eskimo man. His furs and skins hung outside his house, drying in the sun. Inside the single room, a fire burned on the earthen floor, and fresh salmon hung from racks on the ceiling while dry salmon lay stacked on shelves. A typical Russian wall hanging with sculpted tin figures of saints hung on the wall.

Herbert and the old man took turns telling me that the 116 natives living in the village attended two churches: the Catholic church, presided over by Father Endal, and the Swedish Lutheran church, which had a native minister. The old man told me that if one church closed down, the natives would all attend the other church. At one time they were all Russian Orthodox. He described a girl who was baptized eleven times. Whenever she moved back to the village they baptized her; she eventually went insane.

We visited an elderly woman named Agnakjluk who fascinated me from the start. She laughed with delight as we entered. I had the feeling she was excited that we had selected her home to visit. She greeted us in a printed percale dress, still sitting on the floor, holding the rag she was using to mop the floor.

There were dimples in her large round face. Her teeth were strong, but filed down from years of chewing fur to make *mukluks* (boots). She lived in two small rooms: The first room had a stove and a wooden crate; the adjoining room had a large wooden board with a mattress. She pointed to the bedroom, where a baby sat on a bundle of rags and furs. "Eskimos love babies," Herb said. "The smaller the child, the more he rules the family." Three other boys came trudging into the house. They pretended not to understand English. Then one seemed to listen more intently than the others. Herb said, "He understands."

"Do you speak English?" I asked the boy.

"Yes," he said hesitantly. I smiled, hoping to encourage him. Herb had told me earlier that most villagers were ashamed to speak English.

The boy told us in fluent English that his parents were dead and the baby's parents were also dead, so his grandmother took them both in. Agnakjluk smiled and nodded her head, knowing we were talking about her.

"Now I'm supporting the family by fishing and trapping," the boy said. "I was in school one winter and then they expelled me because I had to go trapping for fur."

We returned to the *Mildred*. At midnight, I stood on the deck. It was still daylight. A ridge of pink shimmered on the horizon. The tundra was bursting with buttercups and white Alaska cotton. I tried to absorb it all: the brown, quiet, rippling river; the yellow flowers; the absolute stillness. Now and then I heard the call of a bird. Mosquitoes ate at my skin and sat in my hair. All the calamine lotion I layered on my skin was no deterrent. I was unfailingly popular with the mosquitoes. I was sure they flew in from miles around to attack me.

In the boat, other passengers moved silently toward their bunks. Daylight and night descended on the *Mildred*. Tomorrow we would enter the Bering Sea.

Chapter Eight

THE RIME OF THE BROOKLYN MARINER

The next day, an Eskimo trader took me on his outboard motorboat to the village of St. Michael. In the dense fog of the evening, the trader had a hard time navigating. Whenever we lost our way on the narrow channel or the engine stalled, we both rowed until he started the motor again and we found our way. A loon flew close to us, sticking its outrageous neck forward. Two cranes marched majestically on the fertile treeless tundra. As we broke through the water, the smell of oil from dead seals reached our noses.

St. Michael looked as though someone had painted a picture of a European seaport town. The towers, masts, churches, and houses looked two-dimensional from the water, but gradually transformed into a gray and somber ghost town. A graveyard of abandoned riverboats lay rotting on the beach, and long empty warehouses sat tumbling into the sea. The wooden homes looked dilapidated, ready to sink into the moist earth. I felt as though I had been dropped into Coleridge's "Rime of the Ancient Mariner." I kept waiting for ghosts to start dancing around me.

Only the schoolhouse, the church, and a few small homes stood in good repair. Dominating the whole village were the onion-shaped domes of the Russian Orthodox church and several deserted army barracks. St. Michael had been an important settlement in the early days of Russian colonization, and again as an army post during World War I.

As we rowed to the beach, a crowd of children from the village rushed across the rocks to help us. We walked to the schoolhouse across the wooden planks of the sidewalk covering the flowering tundra. The two schoolteachers, Mr. and Mrs. Thomas, were as delighted to welcome me as Agnakjluk had been. They had spent a whole year in this isolated spot and were anxious for news from the "Outside." Mrs. Thomas had been a teacher in Virginia and Mr. Thomas had been an assistant principal.

I spent the night at their house, and we stayed awake in the kitchen, laughing, eating sandwiches, and talking. The teachers poured out a whole year of loneliness, telling me of the constant feud between teachers and traders. "We are trying to educate the children," Mrs. Thomas explained, "but the traders here resent our efforts to help the Eskimos. They call us 'government bums.'" The feud between the traders and the teachers reached a climax when the government helped the Eskimos establish cooperative stores. The traders, losing money and power, were furious.

I suggested the Thomases take a few days off and I would run the school for them. As an activity, I handed out copies of *Life* magazine, which came once a year on a ship bringing food and supplies and asked the students to write a short essay on what they were reading. I was startled to find that every single student wrote about the ads. So much for serious journalism.

One child described a familiar Listerine ad: "This is the story of a girl. She is very sad. She is waiting at the church. The groom has left her. She has bad breath."

I could think of no other writer who could have explained that plot with such economy of words.

One of St. Michael's most famous residents was Sinrock Mary, known as the "Queen of the Reindeer." She owned one of the largest reindeer herds in Alaska. Part Russian and part Eskimo, she had acted as an interpreter for the Russians who had come with the reindeer in the early 1900s. She was a complete mixture of the two cultures, and you knew it the moment you entered her wooden cottage. Where the Eskimos were reticent, Sinrock Mary kissed my hands with effusive thanks for honoring her with my visit. She wore Eskimo mukluks, but had a Russian handkerchief tied around her neck. Her chin had three stripes tattooed on it in Eskimo fashion.

I entered her home through a vestibule where furs and skins hung from the ceiling and continued through the kitchen to her bedroom, which also served as her living room. The house was spotless. The floor was made of wood and painted white. The wooden bed on which she sat and the two straight-backed chairs emphasized the simplicity in which she lived.

We understood each other immediately and spoke a mixture of Russian, English, and a few words of Eskimo that I was beginning to understand. Sinrock Mary told me that she had lots of money and many reindeer, which the village herders were watching for her. But she was very lonely. She had had two husbands and they were both dead. She kept saying in Russian, "*Mne ochen grustno.*" (I feel very sad.) "I miss both my husbands and my adopted son is dead, too."

Like many Eskimos, Sinrock Mary had adopted a flock of children. She gave the children food, clothing, a good home, and love. In return, they helped her: the girls cleaning her house and doing the cooking, the boys hunting, trapping and fishing for food.

A famous story about Sinrock Mary was that she first belonged to the Catholic church, to which she contributed a great deal of money. Then she quit and went to the Greek Orthodox church.

"What made you leave Catholicism?" I asked her.

She laughed, looked thoughtful for a moment, and said, "Catholic Jesus—he all the time broke."

While we were talking, a woman entered. She had flaming red hair, white skin, and blue eyes, and was dressed in an Eskimo parka. On her back, she was carrying a baby, and a dozen other children followed her in.

"My adopted daughter," Sinrock Mary introduced her.

"Are you part Russian, too?" I asked.

"Oh, no!" she exclaimed. "My mother was Eskimo but she died."

"And your father?" I prompted.

"I don't know," she said with a smile. "I was too young."

From Sinrock Mary's house, I went back to the Thomases. At midnight, the three of us walked across the tundra to see the reindeer. I was breathless when we reached the herd of over four thousand deer. Silhouetted against the water and the sky, their horns etched in soft twilight, they moved slowly and silently until something frightened them and they would gracefully leap away. There were dark brown ones, light tan ones, and pure white albinos that would become rare because of the popularity of their hides for clothing. All night the little fawns raced back and forth, playing hide-and-seek with their elders. Three herders sat around a fire drinking coffee, in their white parkas and hoods, looking like nomads in a desert.

In the glow of my midnight walk, I found the crumbling town transformed. St. Michael was the westward gate to Alaska, the marching point of the old Russians, linked to the world only by the river and history itself.

Chapter Nine

NOME

The dirt-paved streets of Nome were raw, damp, windblown, and unpaved. They carried the shattered hopes of twenty-five thousand gold miners. The log cabins shook in the frost of winter and smelled year-round because of the lack of indoor plumbing. To me, Nome was the essence of the Alaska I had learned about in school, and I was eager to explore it.

Like a pilgrim in rubber boots, I trudged each day down the broad muddy main street within sight of the Bering Sea. The shacks and wooden stores housed a food market, an outdoor clothing store, a barber shop, and a tailor. Farther down the street, a movie house boasted: "The Dream Theatre—100 Percent Talking Pictures."

In the gold rush days, Nome was the most famous camp in Alaska. Now it was growing increasingly smaller, deserted by the gold hunters who had built it up. In 1897, gold was discovered on the Klondike in Canada. Men lost their lives crossing the dangerous mountain passes leading to the gold fields.

Then, in the last year of the nineteenth century, gold was discovered outside of Nome.

Back in the United States, people hungry to get rich quick dreamed of taking a brief trip to Nome, picking up the nuggets, and returning home to build palaces and to regale their friends with their exploits.

By June 1900, over ten thousand people were on their way to Nome. In July, it was reported in the States that smallpox had broken out in Alaska and that an epidemic of typhoid was expected. By August, hundreds of letters from disappointed prospectors began to trickle home. The stampede slowed down. People felt betrayed. The long, wide, golden beach they dreamed of panning for riches was really a narrow strip three quarters of a mile long. A thousand men earned less than ten dollars a day working the beach. The "great, peaceful city of Nome" advertised back home was actually a camp of two mud streets that boasted neither sewers nor sidewalks.

There were not enough tents, so not only men but women and children were sleeping on the beaches. Most of the gold was in the saloons, and the best prospecting was done by ladies of easy virtue. With every ship, a thousand new hopeful men and women arrived, and with every ship hundreds of disappointed gold seekers went home.

The ruin of Nome when I saw it in 1941 was the ruin of a town that had accepted its fate. The failure of Nome was in large part responsible for the prejudices that emerged in the States against Alaska. I realized now, as I walked each day along Front Street and heard the wild waves of the Bering Sea beat against the shores, that Nome was a state of mind, a state that would have to be changed if we ever wanted to open Alaska for development.

I wrote to Ickes, "One should never visit Nome. One should

remember it only from the gold rush days. It is hard on its white settlers and disastrous for its natives. Nome is a great well of drunkenness, juvenile delinquency, and disease."

General Buckner and some of his aides flew into Nome to celebrate July Fourth. The general was to be the keynote speaker. He may have had larger audiences in his life, but never a more unique and enthusiastic one.

Nome was proud of itself on the Fourth of July. It was dressed up for the Day of Independence. Across the gray wooden city hall—which was also the fire department, police station, and library—hung a huge red, white, and blue banner. A dais had been erected in front and was draped in red, white, and blue bunting paper. Everyone knew that we were on the brink of war, and patriotism was running high. For weeks, posters had proclaimed the celebration: JULY! JULY! BIGGER! BETTER! COME ONE! COME ALL!

On the morning of the Fourth, the celebration began in true military style. A little after 9 A.M., three army bombers maneuvered over the city, so big and so fast that for a terrified moment I thought they were going to sideswipe every pole and telephone line. The noise over Nome was that of a mighty armada. By ten o'clock, a huge parade was in progress, and Front Street was lined with cars, all covered in streamers and crepe paper. Elderly Eskimo women, swathed to their chins in furs and calico, stood in silence. Young Eskimo mothers, with slacks, high-heeled shoes and short homemade reindeer jackets, rocked their babies. High school boys sat on decorated bicycles and scores of children giggled explosively. After the parade, performers lined up on the wooden platform and sang, "Alaska, My Alaska." The Nome citizens sang along.

Finally Buckner got up to speak. The general looked stern

and military, as befitted the occasion. His face was ruddy and handsome; he sucked his stomach in and his white hair glistened in the cool gray morning.

"Fellow Americans," the general began, looking into the horizon far beyond the faces before him. "We think too little of our obligation as citizens. In this period of prosperity, we have grown fat and lazy. People think not what they can do for the government, but what they can get out of the government. If we are not efficient for ourselves, we will be efficient for some other country." Years later, President John F. Kennedy would echo this same sentiment.

The whole audience listened respectfully and when he finished, applauded loudly. Automobiles parked on the cross street honked their horns. Eskimo children broke into smiles.

In every city and town and farming village in America, mayors were making speeches. I felt that none was more truly American than this one, that no celebration captured the frontier spirit more sharply than in Nome; no speech was given before an audience that understood the words less and the meaning more.

In the evening, everyone moved into the high school, where a dance was held. Dancing was important in Eskimo folklore. It usually followed great events like a hunt or a long trek on the ice. Each movement had a meaning, creating a story. Many missionaries misunderstood the dancing, thought it was pagan, and tried to forbid it. But the Eskimos paid no attention.

Ten young men sat in a row beating on seal-gut drums. While men dancers danced, rhythmically flailing their arms, women sat on a table with their left legs stretched out and their right legs bent over the left. They began to sway. Men leaped ecstatically as the music grew louder and wilder. Even the drummers began to sing with the whole audience shouting in accompaniment. A baby girl with a blue hair ribbon and tiny mukluks started crawling toward the drummers. The dancing women smiled lovingly. One of the men stopped drumming and put her on his lap. Then he began to drum again.

By midnight, the festivities were over. The general flew back to his post at Anchorage, and the three bombers flew away, dipping their wings in farewell. The people of the town went back to their shacks and tents and houses. Nome fell asleep.

The Nome Eskimos were a tragic example of the effect that Western society had on native people. Problems of disease, poverty, alcoholism, and prostitution plagued Eskimo communities. They had no resources within their culture to cope with the problems we brought them.

Tuberculosis was taking a deadly toll. One of the nurses took me to the home of a boy who was dying of tuberculosis of the larynx. He lay naked on a reindeer skin on the floor. He could hardly talk, but he kept repeating to us over and over, "It's my tonsils." Two women and babies, all dressed, slept on the floor as well. The nurse and I decided to come back the next day so that she could give him a bath and I could get a picture of him and his family to send to Ickes. I wanted the secretary to see the need for a tuberculosis hospital at Nome. When we returned the next day, the boy was dead.

Another day, I walked among the wooden shacks and tents of the Diomede and King Islanders who were camping on the outskirts of the city for the summer. Nome was a resort for the native people of these villages. In the summer, they pitched tents there and spent days picking berries on the tundra or drying a day's catch of fish and cleaning reindeer skins.

I sat on the floor in one of the tents and talked with its owner, a woman named Inez Big Jim. Inez was interested in having the stateside nurses give classes to the Eskimo women in midwifery and first aid.

In another tent, a bedridden Eskimo woman swapped travel stories with me. She was lying on a hard bed surrounded by books. On hearing I was from Washington and New York, she said, "I love to travel. When I read about a place, I don't know it like when I see it. Once in the States, in Chicago I met a girl from Egypt. I was from a cold place and she was from a warm place. We got along fine."

Nome led to King Island, an unspoiled Eskimo village I was eager to explore.

Chapter Ten

LEARNING TO LIVE
INSIDE OF TIME

You should take pictures of Eskimos dying of TB,"
Dr. Victor E. Levine told me. "Whole families lie
on one bed—the mother dies, then the children die
one by one."

I met Dr. Levine, a short, middle-aged man, on the boat
bound for King Island. He was making a study of the King
Island Eskimos, who lived about ninety miles outside Nome.
Dr. Levine horrified me with his stories of the lack of medical
care for Eskimos. He told me that the average life span for an
Eskimo was twenty-four years. He railed against government
policy that placed teachers in many villages but actively resisted
sending doctors and nurses.

When he saw how disturbed I was by his accounts, he added,
"The situation is only made worse by the lack of knowledge
surrounding TB. Dogs don't have TB, so people drink dog
urine thinking it will cure them. Mothers cough and touch
babies' mouths, thinking they can rid themselves of the disease
by passing it to their children."

Despite his tragic stories, Dr. Levine kept me and the other passengers on the boat to King Island laughing with happier tales of Eskimos he had known.

"I was traveling on a ship called the *Northland,*" he told us. "We stopped in a village where an unmarried Eskimo girl was pregnant. Her family was very distraught. I asked her if she knew who the father was. She nodded eagerly. 'Well, who is it?' I asked her. She pointed to the harbor where my ship, with over a hundred sailors on it, was anchored. 'The *Northland,*' she explained."

My guarded laughter encouraged Dr. Levine to continue. "In one village there was a red-haired Eskimo baby. This was very unusual, so I asked the young mother if the father had red hair. She looked thoughtful. 'I don't know. He didn't take his hat off.'"

King Island, no more than a quarter-mile long, was a beautiful array of rocks and foliage rising out of the blue Bering Sea. The houses were built on high platforms into the face of cliffs. Many of the walls and roofs were covered with walrus skin.

Friendly King Islanders invited me into their homes. To enter, I climbed over a sawed-off door into a foyer, then passed through an arch to the living room. We sat on the floor, where they helped me fill my notebooks with their rich folklore stories of hunting and sealing. This community was healthy. Tuberculosis and alcoholism had not invaded them. I was relieved to spend time in a community not ravaged by white men's diseases.

Each afternoon, flocks of birds flew over King Island. They were of bright colors and a variety of sizes, a far cry from the pigeons in Brooklyn. The midnight sun was so bright that I could describe the birds in my notebook by the light that came through my window.

The Catholic church was the spiritual and social center of life on the island. Its priest, Father Bellarmine LaFortune, was a little French Canadian who had learned to speak the native tongue. His services were held partly in Latin and partly in local vernacular. On Sunday, he gave a short sermon in English, and afterward the congregation sang hymns in Eskimo.

Each night, the village turned out to watch movies. There, in the basement of a clubhouse on the water's edge, people who lived in a more picturesque place than anything a Hollywood writer could concoct came to see films of New York and Paris, of steamboats and skyscrapers, of historical dramas of the Deep South and Wild West cowboys.

Whole families came to see the movies that arrived by ship with the food and medicine once a year. Mothers shifted babies from their backs and nursed them through the picture. The children were amazingly quiet. They cried only when a picture grew too terrifying, especially when someone was shot. One night, we were watching a film called *BooLoo,* about the Sakai tribe in the Malaysian jungle. The King Islanders were delighted with all the jungle animals, but they shrieked with horror as a boa chewed up a man and swallowed him.

The movies brought the war into this peaceful Arctic island. There were newsreels showing Hitler's armies marching across Europe. The Eskimos knew that Hitler was evil. Whenever he appeared on the screen, the men jumped up, mockingly raising their hands in ridicule of the Nazi salute.

After the nightly movies, we sat on top of the clubhouse with the midnight sun playing on the Bering Sea making that bluest of all waters reflect a silver color. One night a young Eskimo mother named Ursula sat beside me with her baby daughter, Louise. Ursula spoke fluent English and we soon became constant companions.

"Some people in the United States," I told her, "still think Eskimos kiss by rubbing noses together."

Ursula roared with delight. "We kiss American way," she explained, "like movies." She looked down at her baby and added, "We kiss 'Eskimo' way, too." She smiled and rubbed her baby's nose against hers.

Ursula began to teach me Eskimo. Each day my vocabulary increased. It was a musical language. Little Louise was the one who taught me my most important Eskimo phrase, "*Na-ghua-ghiek-pin,*" or "I love you."

Meals on King Island were huge tributes to the canning industry. One day I was having lunch with Nurse Stanton, my roommate, and Dr. Levine. We went into the large storage room of the schoolhouse, where we stayed and looked at the fascinating array of colorful cans, discussing whether we would have peaches, pears, sausages, coffee, condensed milk, or other preserved foods.

At the table, Dr. Levine and Nurse Stanton immediately began discussing the health problems of the Eskimos. They agreed that every village ought to have a nurse, and several ought to have a doctor. But the two disagreed violently on how the Eskimos were being educated.

Dr. Levine, who rarely raised his voice, spoke sharply to Nurse Stanton. "You want to educate them to be white men— we should be educating them *and* allowing them to keep their culture."

After I had been on the island for several weeks, I felt that it was time for me to move on. I sent word to an airline company in Anchorage asking for a bush pilot to pick me up and fly me to Nome. The answer came back, "Pick you up tomorrow WEAPERS," which meant "Weather Permitting." The next day came, but no pilot. Days passed and still no pilot. Excuses came: "Fog. Storm. Broken engine. Pilot sick. See you next week WEAPERS."

It was on King Island that I truly learned to live inside of time, instead of fighting it. I sat wrtiing for ten days, practically marooned, and did not complain. Usually illiterate in anything technical, I learned to fix my typewriter and my cameras on my own. I learned I could not control time, but I could live and work inside of it.

Finally a bush pilot appeared. My friends came to the landing field, smiling and waving good-bye. From the plane window, I watched King Island disappear, grateful for all it had taught me.

Chapter Eleven

THE MAD CRUISE OF THE
ATALANTA

After a brief stay back in Nome, I left on the Coast Guard cutter *Atalanta* for Nunivak and on to the Pribilof Islands. The ship was named for a mythical Greek heroine who was nursed and raised by a bear. It was a small 165-foot patrol vessel with a flock of teenagers learning to be Coast Guard sailors, along with eight nonmilitary people on board, including myself. The captain was Lieutenant W. C. Hogan, a stout man who looked older than his thirty-six years. He had gray eyes, a flabby shaven face, pouting red lips, and a weak chin. His white hands, soft as a woman's, trembled constantly. Hogan was rumored to be the most hated man in the Coast Guard. He had a peculiar hobby: creating tiny little models of railroad cars out of copper bearings. He strung them all together with a cord, and exactly at eight each evening, he emerged from his cabin and marched up and down the deck pulling his long procession of tiny railroad cars. He was totally unaware that a small band of his young trainees marched behind him, while the rest of us clasped our hands over our mouths so he couldn't hear us giggling. Most of us quickly came to the conclusion that he was out of his mind, a judgment bolstered by his frequent refusal to come out of his cabin during the twenty or more hours of daylight.

One night, making a swift appearance, Hogan told me that the cutter's mission was to comb the Bering Sea in search of illegal Japanese floating canneries. "We are the Bering Sea Patrol Force—in fact, the whole force—and we represent the seagoing power of the United States in these waters." He spoke proudly. "We are the only armed vessel north of Dutch Harbor."

The first few hours of our cruise were calm and peaceful. We ate lunch and laughingly discussed our personal theories about seasickness and how to prevent it. I was a great believer that never missing a meal would prevent illness.

It was two hours later that the *Atalanta* began to show her true colors. From the beach, she was a trim-looking ship: streamlined, secure, and battleship gray. But on deck, she was a washtub. She rocked at the the lightest swell and rolled with the slightest breeze. She was safe and seaworthy, but she moved in the water like a drowning cat. The boat rolled up on her port side and stayed that way contentedly for four long seconds, while we passengers skidded to the starboard side. Then, she lurched suddenly and swung to her starboard side. Again, like a cat, she seemed shy of water and determined to keep out of it as much as she could. Climbing one wave, she shook herself madly and then, as if she were heaving a sigh, dove under another one.

We took to lying on our bunks and staying there. I had the feeling I was going over Niagara Falls in a barrel, but the barrel wouldn't turn over. Nights were not so bad; I slept on an army cot in the officers' mess hall. I woke once every hour or so, when the ship changed its mind in the middle of a wild swing.

The days were long and hard. Some of the teenage sailors, most of whom were so new to the Coast Guard that they had not yet been trained, slept in the hold down below on hammocks. They were often so seasick that they came up for air and stretched out on the desks of yeomen, clinging tightly to the wood. I joined them, stretching out on the last available surface, a typewriter table. Lying there next to a young sailor, I looked closely at his agonized face and thought, "Some day I will be walking on Forty-Second Street and I will see this young man and say "I know you! You were with me on the mad voyage of the *Atalanta*!"

I hadn't yet gotten actively sick. This was fortunate, because the sailors hogged the rails, and I would have had to fight for a spot.

We dropped four of our passengers at Nunivak Island, one of the most untouched islands in Alaska. After briefly going ashore to visit the island and give my stomach a chance to settle, I reboarded the *Atalanta*. The good ship cruised and cruised and cruised. My sickness began in earnest. The *Atalanta* was sailing in figure eights, water rushing over the deck with each loop. The captain refused to explain why the ship was maneuvering so erratically instead of heading straight for the Pribilof Islands, my destination.

I used to be a good sailor. In fact, I had been in far worse waters than these. I don't think I would have been half as seasick if we were not traveling in circles. It was the aimlessness that exhausted me. The sheer purposelessness of the ship's course made me grow sicker each day. I was living on three slices of bread a day. Now and then I dared to eat a canned peach, and I grew thinner all the time. If Mama could have seen me, she would have screamed, *"Ess, mein kind!* Eat, my child, if you eat you won't get so sick." But my stomach warned me not to listen. My mother had never been on the *Atalanta.*

More days passed; I gave up counting. Eventually I started sleeping through the days. When I was lucky, I got to lie on the couch in the wardroom. My fellow passengers and I took turns sharing it. We were limited to a third of a bowl of water a day for cleaning. Nobody could bathe, and we all smelled. The sailors joked, "We all hate being clean, but we take a bath every three weeks to keep in practice."

That summer of 1941 was only months away before Pearl Harbor would change Alaskan life forever. The fishing vessels in the Bering Sea were filled with prewar tension. After I had been on the ship for several days, I was stretched out on a yeoman's desk when I heard someone shout, "There's one! There's a Japanese fishing boat!"

In a second, the days of sickness were forgotten. I ran to my bunk, grabbed my Leica and movie camera, rushed to the deck, and began shooting. In a rare daylight appearance, the captain stood beside me and proceeded to stare silently through large black binoculars. We both looked out at the great maroon-colored freighter with at least six hundred Japanese men and women crowding onto the decks to look at us.

"When are we going to board that ship?" I asked Captain Hogan, remembering we were an armed vessel.

"We're not," he answered, still holding his binoculars. "We just want to show them that we know they're here illegally."

A young sailor turned to me and whispered confidentially, "If that ship takes one shot at us, we're sunk!"

The Japanese cannery ship, undaunted, kept fishing in our waters. I was frustrated as we sailed away, and I soon became seasick again.

Chapter Twelve
THE PRIBILOF ISLANDS

After seven days on the Bering Sea, we reached St. Paul, the largest of the Pribilof Islands.

"Hurrah!" Our shouts of relief rolled across the deck, loud enough, I thought, to startle the fish in the water, the fur seals on the beach, and even the birds flying over us.

Captain Hogan made a sudden appearance. "All officers and visitors who want to go ashore can leave now," he announced.

Why only officers? Why can't those seasick sailors get off the ship too? I decided to confront the captain, but he had already vanished into his cabin.

The crew lowered our lifeboat down the side of the *Atalanta,* and within minutes, holding tight to the rope, all of us happy campers climbed down the Jacob's Ladder and jumped onto the dock.

We tied up at a concrete loading wharf, and had started walking up a red clay road when we heard a noise that sounded like a Gregorian chant. It was the noise of the seal harems. We were on the largest seal rookery in the world.

An official-looking man in a truck drove up and approached me. "I have orders to take you to the government office, " he said.

I said good-bye to my shipmates and waved to the sailors still standing sadly at the rail of the *Atalanta*. In the office, I met Edward Johnston, the superintendent in charge of the Pribilof Islands. He was a small, friendly man, a scientist who collected beetles in his spare time. He told me later that he had a collection of twenty thousand moths. I wasted little time in the office. I wanted to see the seals as soon as possible.

Soon I was hiking with Johnston down the bright lava road toward the rookery. The air was cool and damp, the ground treeless and rocky. We saw a number of dead "Road Seals," called that because they had been driven out of the hauling grounds and had died of exhaustion on the way.

As we neared the rookery the sound of the seals kept growing louder and more insistent. The rocks and boulders of the beach were alive with sleek, graceful, bellowing, fighting, fussing, shaggy, battle-scarred seals. The sights and sounds reminded me of Coney Island on a Sunday afternoon. Huge bulls, four to six feet tall, looking savage and brutal, towered over the smaller animals. Johnston told me they weighed about five hundred pounds. Their fur was deep brown with long yellow-white hair on the back of their neck, forming a mane or "wig." Surrounding them in their harems were the cows, weighing a mere seventy or eighty pounds. Pups played together in nurseries between the rocks. The baby seals kept bleating like lambs. They were as amorphous as a blot of ink, continuously in motion.

The Pribilof Islands were among the few places in the world where the seals came out of water to mate and bear their young. They arrived in the spring, and by October they left. Where they came from, and where they went, remained a mystery.

We had lunch in the dining room of the government house, meeting all the government officials and the representatives of the Fouke Fur Company who had come, at government expense, I was told, to assist in the sealing. They came from St. Louis, Missouri, to make sure the seals were being handled exactly as their company desired. The Fouke Fur Company had the exclusive contract with the federal government for the seals' skins.

After lunch, Johnston shared his incongruous hobby with us—a collection of mounted and preserved beetles. Then the inevitable question arose—where would I stay? The question of my housing was an ongoing amusement.

Ben East, a government worker, suggested I might stay with the resident doctor and his wife, who were visiting from Washington. He helped me into his car and drove to the doctor's house. He knocked at their door and shouted merrily, "Here's Dr. Gruber."

Dr. Sam Berenberg, a young, slim physician, shouted, "Not of the famous bath incident?"

"The very same," Ben laughed.

Dr. Berenberg and his wife, Fredericka Martin, welcomed me like a long lost relative and immediately offered me a shower. I accepted gratefully. I was all soaped up and singing loudly to myself when, suddenly, the water stopped. There was no repairing the shower, so I toweled off.

Mrs. Berenberg was a large, handsome woman dressed in bright green slacks and a matching shirt, which brought out the reddish color of her hair. She was to have a baby in a month, but she joined us on our excursions around the island, doing whatever it took to keep up with the group. Without being paid for it, she was helping her husband run the hospital, using the experience she had gained as a trained hospital organizer. The two of them had determined to make the most of their stay on the island. They were studying the Aleut language, which few people ever learned, and reading everything they could get their hands on about the people, the islands, and the fur seals.

They took me on a tour of the village, four rows of concrete houses in which 270 Aleut men and women lived surrounded by chickens and children. We visited the hospital, a clean concrete building with wards in which Aleut patients lay reading books and listening to the radio.

While the Eskimos used the church as the center of community life, the Aleuts of the fur seal islands used the canteen. In one corner, men were playing pool; in another, a little girl practiced "Swan Lake" on the piano. An upper floor held the recreation hall, where dances were held, basketball was played, and movies were shown. I learned that the movie theather was segregated. During the pictures, white people sat in the balcony while the Aleuts sat below. I had found Jim Crowism in other parts of Alaska, but this was the first place where I found it sponsored by government employees.

Notices of future events were posted on the bulletin board in the hallway leading to the village store. It was on this board that I first saw how the Aleut sealers were paid on the Pribilofs. Instead of wages, they received bonuses for each seal they killed, sixty cents a skin on St. Paul Island and seventy-five cents a skin on St. George Island. I would later discover that the government sold the skins in auctions back in the States for up to forty-five dollars apiece.

In addition to the bonuses, the men received a yearly allowance based upon classes. The first class of workers received approximately five hundred dollars; the second, four hundred dollars; and so on. The lowest class was for boys, who received about twenty dollars. Their work consisted of watching the seals.

A list of the men in each class hung on the bulletin board in the hallway. Below the list was a typed notice:

> As it now stands, the above is the proper sealing division for 1941. There will be changes made if any trouble is made.
>
> Nekifer Kachutin was reduced to third class for being drunk and disorderly and Iosef Molovidor has been put on one year trial and will be reduced two classes should he make any more liquor.

This notice continued at great length, giving harsh warnings to anyone suspected of drunkenness or illicit distilling of spirits and brewing. It gave me a clearer picture of life on the island. Here, Agent L. C. McMillan controlled the most intimate details of the native people's lives. Here, the Aleuts were forced to accept prohibition and punishment for drunkenness. The agent in charge (McMillan) chose the houses in which the Aleuts lived. The native people were forced to endure a class system that had been inherited and left practically unchanged from czarist days.

When Russia had owned Alaska, Russian hunters had come across Siberia through the Bering Sea to the Pribilofs, enslaved the Aleut men, and forced them to kill seals, then brought the beautiful pelts home to be sold in Russia and across Europe. When we bought Alaska from the Russians in 1867, we picked up where the Russians had left off, treating the Aleuts as government slaves.

The situation enraged me. I wanted to know why, in a democracy, people were treated like government property. I understood that while these terrible practices were ostensibly under the U.S. Fish and Wildlife Services, in actuality they took place under the auspices of the Fouke Fur Company. Nowhere in America had I seen a wider gap between what democracy said it stood for and what it was doing in the Pribilofs where the Aleuts were living in disease-ridden, sewage-filled work areas.

Mr. Johnston invited the Berenbergs and me to come to the early morning seal slaughtering. I had been working furiously all day, and unable to sleep, so I accepted. Exactly at 2 A.M., Johnston drove up to the Berenbergs, and swiftly the three of us piled into his car and left for the coast.

Before the hunt, we ate an enormous breakfast in a low-ceilinged mess hall. All of us, the government men, the Fouke Fur Company people, the Aleut workers, the Berenbergs, and I, ate pancakes and drank hot coffee. Someone gave me rubber boots and a yellow oilskin raincoat. I pulled the coat tightly around me as we walked toward the sea.

The heaving cries of the fur seals swelled toward me like a giant symphony with minor notes warning of coming danger. The killing was brutal and quick, elemental and noisy, full of terrible sounds and the smell of decay. In the gleam of a beautiful, misty morning, with the tundra flowers perfuming the air, death began to wind like a snake over the flat land toward the water where the seals lay. The gleam of the seals' sleek bodies hit my eyes, and the sight and sound of men beating seal skulls turned my stomach.

Some of the men seemed to enjoy racing from seal to seal, slamming heads with large silver pans or sticks. Soon huge flies began to feast on the dead carcasses.

In the early morning light, men ran around the rim of boulders, yelling loudly to be heard over the unbearable grunting and wheezing of seals, whose screaming, sliding bodies were flapping awkwardly down the road, trying to escape the fate of those surrounding them. This eerie death field was all for a thousand ladies fur coats.

Ten Aleut clubbers, young boys and older men, kept the seals in a tight herd while others encircled them, barring their escape. The old bulls seemed resigned to their fates. They stuck their heads up proudly, almost begging to be clubbed with the long hickory sticks that looked like overgrown baseball bats. A few cows had come along on the death march. The Aleuts pushed the cows out of the killing herd, away from the bulls being clubbed.

I sat a few feet away, unable to believe what I was seeing. I felt hot tears rolling down my face in spite of myself. I tried to remain the brave, professional government official, but I was overcome with horror at the spectacle before me. My government companions, seeing my horror, assured me that clubbing was the humane method of killing the seals. "Their skulls are almost paper thin," Johnston explained. "One blow kills them instantly or knocks them unconscious."

As soon as the clubbing was over, the men pulled the clobbered seals a short distance to the skinning grounds. Here, the animals were laid out in rows of ten. The "bleeders" came in. These workers began stabbing their knives into the hearts of those seals who were still breathing. This had to be done quickly enough to prevent any half dead seal from reviving enough to nip the men.

Now the tally and measurement men came along. They were white employees hired by the Fouke Fur Company; all the other workers, by congressional law, were Aleuts. The company men measured the length of each seal and numbered it carefully.

The "splitters" entered, working methodically, skinning the carcasses. They were swift operators—it took Mr. Johnston longer to explain each step to me than it took the men to perform them. The "skinners," holding sharp knives as though they were an extension of their own hands, ripped up the entire length of the belly, around the flippers, and around the neck.

They were followed by the "pulling gang," four men who began the swift stripping. One man jabbed a long fork with two steel points through the neck of the seal into the ground; the other three men clasped metal tongs that looked something like ice tongs on the neck. With ropes attached to the tongs, the men peeled the skins off with a single wrench the way a child yanks a Band-Aid off tender skin, with one quick movement. Aleut boys then picked up the pelts, still hot and bloody, and placed them fur side up in a long line to cool.

Mr. Johnston told me that 1,182 seals were taken that morning at the fifteen Pribilof rookeries.

We were then led to the blubbering plant, where men, handkerchiefs tied around their heads, stood behind slanted beams and worked rapidly and strenuously, shaving blubber from the pelts. At their feet, rivers of pink and yellow fat ran in circles, collecting in square trays. This fat would be used to make soap for the army.

The government also sold the oil from the seals. Seal oil, a superior grade of oil, sold for the same price as the much valued whale oil. More revenue came in from the ground-up carcasses, which were sold to companies manufacturing dog food, fish food, and fertilizer.

Back at the Berenbergs' house, I read a short piece published by the Fouke Fur Company mentioning in one slick sentence how humane they were in killing the seals. So much, I thought, for truth in advertising.

The injustices I saw on the Pribilofs enraged me. But in the end, I realized discrimination and especially segregation, were the order of the day. The military was segregated until President Harry S. Truman desegregated it after the war ended. The South was segregated. Washington, D.C. was the segregated capital of the United States. The Interior Department. was one of the first cabinet departments to desegregate its own cafeteria so blacks and whites could eat lunch at the same tables. Knowing all this, I still felt that the exploitation of the Aleuts and the clubbing of the fur seals was unjust and immoral.

Sixty years later, while rereading my notebooks from the period, I telephoned Tom Loughlin in Seattle. He is the leader of the government of Alaska's ecosystem program in the Marine Mammal Laboratory.

"Have they stopped clubbing the fur seals?" I asked him.

"They ended the 'commercial harvest' of the fur seals in 1984," he explained. "The government was connected with the Fouke Fur Company to the end."

"How many fur seals are left?" I asked, fearing his answer.

"There are nine hundred thousand now," he told me, "but at the peak, when you were there, there were three million."

Chapter Thirteen

ON MY WAY TO THE TOP
OF THE WORLD

It takes a long time to get to the top of the world.

The Eskimo village of Point Hope was on the way. North of the Arctic Circle, it was a picture-book study of wooden houses and mud igloos, all guarded by huge sun-bleached whalebone jaws that ominously jutted out of the earth.

Since there was no available lodging in Point Hope, I lived in the jail. Ida Susuk Lane, a delightful Eskimo woman, was my cook and helper. Like many Alaskans, Ida had a mixed heritage—she was part Portuguese and African and part Eskimo. She had dark straight hair, a strong, athletic body, and a wide gap-toothed smile.

Ida was adventurous and fun-loving. One warm day, she took me swimming in the Arctic Ocean. The water was only a few degrees colder than the Atlantic or Pacific in late August. After a brief invigorating swim, we climbed onto the beach. Ida tucked her white slip into her white bloomers, raised her arms, and danced happily over the sand.

A few days later, Ida took me to the Wednesday night open testimonial at the Friends Church. First, fifty Eskimos sang songs in English. Then Eskimos and missionaries all rose and told how much Jesus meant to them. We sat next to a woman named Molly Berryman. Molly was the wife of an English trader named Tom. She was a huge woman, weighing at least 280 pounds. Late in the meeting, she stood up, her dark brown face smiling, and gave her testimonial in a deep alto voice.

"I was a high-class lady in my day." she began. I knew this meant that she had been a prostitute. "When I got Jesus," she continued, "I decided to pay back all the two dollars that men had paid me. I made a list, but if Tom had paid it, he would have gone broke. He did make good on a lot of my sins, but he's practically broke anyway."

After a week, I decided it was time to go on to Point Barrow, the northernmost village in Alaska. I radioed the airline office in Anchorage and asked them to send a plane.

At 10:30 on a warm bright Saturday morning, a tiny black Stinson 105 that looked as big as a baby carriage dropped down on the beach. Point Hope had a good dirt airfield, but Herb Hager, the pilot, opted for a flashy entrance and landed on the beach. The whole village ran down to shore. The boys and some of the men picked the plane up and pulled it toward the landing field near my jail.

I couldn't figure out if Herb was trying to frighten me. "The Arctic," he said, as if he were preparing me for disaster, "is the hardest flying country in the world, even in the summer. Most of the time there's no place to land, and if you manage to land there's not a soul in sight. You have to be damned good to fly here."

By this time, I had learned that if you planned to take even a short flight in the Arctic, you ought to take emergency rations for at least thirty days. Ida and I had prepared a box of emergency rations. Herb looked at the box and said, "What kind of pilot do you think I am to be traveling without rations?" Not wanting to offend him, I handed my box, overflowing with sandwiches and fruit, back to Ida. Surreptitiously, I hid a Hershey's chocolate bar in my bag.

Herb then noticed the winterized sleeping bag that an army colonel had let me borrow. "What kind of a pilot do you think I am," he demanded, "that I'd be traveling without a sleeping bag? I've got one in the plane." Reluctantly, I left my borrowed sleeping bag with Ida as well.

We took off as the whole village waved farewell. It was excellent flying weather. A small thermometer in the plane read eighty degrees Fahrenheit. I was wearing light slacks and a blouse, and I felt toasted. The Arctic Ocean was calm beneath us. We flew over a school of white beluga whales spitting up foam in the aquamarine water. The mountains loomed ahead like the hides of giant elephants. I leaned back with satisfaction, happy that a smooth flight lay ahead of me.

Herb was definitely not an ideal traveling companion. About thirty-five years old, he was a disheveled, dust-ridden daredevil in need of a shave. Tall, with rimless glasses over his gray green eyes, he had light brown hair and a matching stubble riding across his lips and chin. The tiny plane— "The Flying Bassinet" he called it—was so minuscule that I was forced to sit close to him. I tried to keep a comfortable distance, but there was no room to move.

"Do you happen to have a map?" he asked me after we had been flying about half an hour.

"A map?" I repeated in surprise. "You mean you don't have a map?"

He smiled innocently. "Nope."

I felt a knob of fear rising in my chest. "You know this route so well you don't need a map?" I asked.

"I've never flown it before," he answered matter-of-factly.

Silently, I clenched my fists to give me courage.

For a while I pretended to sleep, but he wanted to talk about his life. I learned that he was born in Tacoma. At thirty, he had bummed his way on freight cars from the West Coast to New York. He had a checkered career as a tobacco salesman, stenographer, welfare caseworker, and finally as a pilot flying his tiny black plane from St. Louis to Alaska.

"Things have been going downhill ever since St. Louis," he told me, "It doesn't get worse than flying in Alaska."

A fog rose suddenly, surrounding us in near darkness. Herb was flying by the seat of his pants, without any instruments.

"There's more soup," he said, referring to the threatening clouds.

"It looks like clam chowder." I tried to put on a brave face.

The plane began to shake violently. Herb shouted expletives, scrambling to steady the small craft. Through the fog, I saw sharp rocks jutting toward our plane. Herb yelled, "You watch these cliffs and see that we don't hit them." I swallowed hard, wondering if I was on my last adventure. "Hold on," he hollered. "We're coming down."

We flew low, then taxied onto a snow-covered path leading toward a small beach. The day that had begun with hot temperatures was now below twenty. To his credit, Herb managed to land inches before we would have crashed into a mountain of driftwood. Snow was falling and I could hear the wind howling around us.

"What happened?" I asked him, half in shock.

"I'm not sure," he replied.

I looked out the narrow window. We were in the midst of a

snow scape that stretched to the horizon. The world here was devoid of human, animal, or even plant life.

I found it hard to talk to him civilly; I wanted to scream at him. My voice was hoarse when I asked him, "Will you radio for help?"

"I forgot to tell you," he said. "The radio went out a long time ago."

"What do we do next?" I tried to speak in a calm voice. There was no point in yelling at him.

"Spend the night and hope somebody will find us." he answered.

I wasn't ready to resign myself to an uncertain frozen night with the charming Herb Hager. Desperately, I said, "We can't be too far from Point Barrow. Shouldn't we just start walking?"

"I can't," he told me. "I'm wearing bedroom slippers."

Despite his assurances that he had packed food, I found nothing on the plane. Sullenly, I took out my Hershey bar, and began to eat, furious at myself for leaving Ida's good food behind.

"Can I have some?" he asked eagerly.

Resentfully, I broke off a chunk of my dinner.

It was a long night. My greatest concern was that the school teachers waiting for me in Point Barrow would send an SOS that I was lost. What if the newspapers carried the story? My poor parents. I could see my mother wringing her hands, crying that her crazy daughter had finally gotten herself killed up there in the wilderness.

A fierce storm unleashed itself. Blinding snow beat against the side of the plane. I settled back. There was no radio. We couldn't walk and we certainly couldn't fly.

"What about the sleeping bag?" I asked him.

"Oh sure, sure," he said, and reached into the mysteries of

the plane again and came up with the kind of thin, unpadded bag you might use on a hot afternoon in Central Park. We opened it and spread it around us. In a few minutes Herb was snoring. I couldn't sleep.

Early in the morning I climbed out of the plane. The temperature had risen to thirty degrees. I began to feel giddy. We were still alive. That was all that counted. I began to sing, "Home, home on the range . . ." in my best bathtub voice, and danced around the beach.

About two hundred feet from the plane, I came upon a monument. I walked toward it and discovered it was a memorial dedicated to Wiley Post and Will Rogers, who had crashed in a fog right on this lagoon. The memorial read, "Ended life's flight here—August 25, 1935." Here we were, I jotted in my notebook, exactly six years later on August 31, 1941. It was eerie.

We decided to try flying again. We unloaded everything that could be carried, left it on the beach, and poured our five gallons of emergency gas in the left wing of the plane. I throttled the crank while Herb spun the props. The plane came alive and Herb was able to take off as neatly as he had landed the night before.

"The Lord sure has his arms around us," he sang out.

I was relieved, but in no mood to sing with Herb Hager.

Soon we were flying over Point Barrow, a welcome sight. It consisted of two clusters of yellow, red, and blue houses separated by a lush lagoon. We searched for a landing field, but couldn't find one. We circled lower and lower. Eskimos in bright-colored parkas came running below us. Herb set the plane down on a beach, which later turned out to be the actual landing field. It seemed the Lord did have his arms around us. And to my relief, I learned that no one had thought to radio my parents that I was missing.

Life in Barrow revolved around whaling and walrus hunting. After I had been in Barrow a few days, I joined a group of Eskimos in a small white whaleboat with an outboard motor. We were on the lookout for walrus.

"The walrus sleep on ice," one of the crew told me. "If it's not icy, we won't see any."

While we searched, I asked the oldest hunter on the boat, "Did you ever meet the American Arctic explorer Vilhjalmur Stefansson?"

It was "Stef" who had paved the way for me to enter the Soviet Arctic, and by extension, Alaska. I knew he had been in Point Barrow on one of his expeditions.

The old man's eyes sparkled in recognition. "I knew him. He good man. He smile all time, and talk Eskimo." In a few words, he had captured the essence of Stef's success—by smiling he showed he was their friend. By speaking their language, he showed he respected their culture.

Suddenly we sighted a walrus sticking its head out of the water. Its smooth long body flew through the air. The men jumped up watching the walrus' movements intently. First the creature dove in the water, then came up with its tail bobbing. The animal looked like a black semicircle in the chilly water.

The creature bobbed down again, and my shipmates lost sight of it for a while. Suddenly it came up about a hundred feet ahead of us. A shot rang out. The bullet ricocheted through the ice layers, but we lost sight of the walrus for good.

Soon the men spotted another one sitting on a large ice floe. We whispered; we stopped the boat's motor, and the men put on white parkas for camouflage. They began to paddle softly. I began shooting my eight-millimeter movie camera. Just as we neared the walrus, it woke and dove into the sea. Two of the hunters raised their guns and shot.

"He's hit!" voices shouted. The ice and sea were bloody, but the walrus swam away. Now the chase began. We started our outboard motor, searching for the elusive creature. Breaking the silence, Abraham Kippy, the leader of the hunters, shouted, "Shoot!"

Shots filled the air again.

"Don't hit him in the head," Abraham ordered, "or he'll sink immediately."

The walrus rose out of the water. We rushed toward him. The captain of the vessel and Abraham prepared their harpoons. When we were within a few feet, Abraham flung his spear with masterly precision. Then he tightened his rope and drew the walrus in.

I was so excited recording the action in my movie camera that I continued shooting long after the film ran out. I realized how different this hunt was from the clubbing of the fur seals on the Pribilofs. These animals were the Eskimos food, their clothing, and even the covering for their wooden huts. Harpooning walruses and whales was their life and their culture. This was not a mass slaughter for the profit of a company thousands of miles away. These hunters were feeding their families and themselves. The air around them was filled with joy.

We made our way to an ice floe and anchored. Two men tied up the massive creature, pulled him toward us, and began the ritual of cutting him up into small pieces of blubber, which they handed to each of us. I took a few bites to be respectful and managed to keep it down.

The hunters explained the ritual to me. The hide of the walrus would go to their leader, Abraham. A portion of the meat would be divided equally among the hunters. The rest would be frozen to sustain them through the long nights of the Arctic winter.

Chapter Fourteen
PREPARING FOR WAR

The days were still long with daylight when I left Point Barrow bound for Dutch Harbor. I was amazed by the clutter of ships filling the naval base. Dutch Harbor was a port preparing for war. I climbed down the rope ladder into a lifeboat, sailed around the harbor, and was helped out by a slim youngish-looking officer in sparkling white naval uniform. He introduced himself as the commander of the naval air force.

"We got a message from Secretary Ickes to treat you properly. I'm turning my house over to you with my staff. I've moved over to the bachelor officer quarters."

I protested. "I don't want to displace you. I know there's no hotel here, but maybe I can find a room in a schoolhouse, or even the jail. I've done that already."

"Wouldn't dream of it," he said, gathering up my gear. "Hop in," he said as he ushered me into his car. We entered his house, a brand-new white cottage with a white porch, a sunny living room, and a dining room big enough for a good-sized party.

In exchange for my lodgings, my host's only request was that I give a dinner party every evening for the commanding officers of the navy, the army, and the air force.

"Now remember," he warned me, "we don't do any drinking until 5 P.M."

I was about to explain that I wasn't really much of a drinker when I noticed his watch. Every number on the watch's face was "5."

The evening meals were banquets prepared by two young Filipino men who became my cooks. We had sumptuous meals: carrots carved into dancing figures, roast beef so rare you could almost taste the blood before you put it in your mouth, delicious pies, and all the liquor you wanted. I was a cheap drunk—a few sips of wine and I would get dizzy and begin to sneeze—so I only pretended to drink.

After dinner, there were dances at the officers' club. Native Aleuts and enlisted men were not allowed to enter. Often, I was the only woman. Sometimes nurses who had officer rank joined us. Because of the scarcity of females, officers were constantly breaking in to dance with the nurses and with me. A dance in a place like Dutch Harbor made you feel like a cross between the Duchess of Windsor and Hedy Lamarr. I wore out more evening clothes in a year and a half in Alaska than in my whole life in New York. I sent a letter to my mother asking her to send me two evening gowns that were hanging in my closet at home. When the dresses arrived, I wrote home, "I expect to wear them as soon as I knock off the five or six pounds I put on with all the food the navy serves me."

A serious problem caused by the swift and hectic militarization of Alaska was the low morale among the young soldiers. It was an issue that deeply concerned me. Most of the servicemen were in their teens, away from home for the first time. In one of my reports to Ickes, I wrote that some of the soldiers were so lonely and homesick in the isolation of Alaska that many tried to kill themselves. Several had succeeded. I described how evenings hung heavily on these lonely young men.

"New saloons open almost over night," I wrote him. "The red light district spreads and flourishes while men and women search desperately for time killers. The boys look upon the territory as a prison, a place of exile. Their general attitude is, 'If the Germans get Alaska, they deserve it.'"

Young soldiers often knocked on my door. "I just wanted to hear you laugh," they said. I would invite them to sit on the terrace and let them talk. Always, they talked of their mothers, their wives, their girlfriends, and how desperately they missed them. At twenty nine, I was too young to be a mother figure, but old enough to be an older sister listening to their fears.

The officers often asked me to lecture to their men on Alaska. "In my own small way," I wrote to Ickes, "I tried to help build morale. I wanted them to see Alaska as I saw it—its incomparable beauty, its pioneer spirit, its promise for the future."

I once told a group of soldiers in the clubhouse, "Alaska is no paradise on earth. Neither is it hell frozen over. Someday you may want to come back and settle here. Alaska needs young people like you—strong, energetic, dreaming of a new life."

From Dutch Harbor, I flew to Kodiak Island, where again I lived in a jail, though this was an unusual one. The warden was given a dollar a day for each convict's room and board. Every morning, he opened the prison gates and the men walked out eagerly to catch some fish. In the evening, they brought their catch back, cooked it themselves, and saved the warden from spending his dollar allotment on their food. It was the happiest jail I ever visited, and one of the best fed.

When I flew back to Anchorage a few weeks later, I found the young soldiers to be as homesick and depressed as the ones in Dutch Harbor. To cheer them up, I played Ping-Pong with them nearly every Saturday night in the *kashim,* the army clubhouse in Elmendorf Field outside of Anchorage. They were so grateful they always let me win. I became the Ping-Pong champion of Alaska.

"Dear Pop," I wrote my father, "you try to do something good, and nobody cares. You do something silly, like playing Ping-Pong and the papers write you up as a local champ."

One of the soldiers who became a friend was Eddie Altshuler from Kansas City. Straight out of college and unable to get a job, he had volunteered for the air force. He told me how he had spent his first night in the military en route to Anchorage, miserable and lonely in the hold of a "dilapidated old ship."

"I wouldn't even sleep in the hold of that ship," he said. "I spent every night on the deck. We reached Anchorage and were immediately quartered on the base in Elmendorf, another miserable spot."

Fast-talking and extroverted, Eddie was placed in the public relations department, where he tried to help lift the morale of the soldiers. Every morning, he spoke on the radio program he created. Nearly every evening he arranged the entertainment in the *kashim* he helped build. Whenever I was free, he would invite me to join a group of soldiers sitting in a circle in the *kashim*. There, I answered their questions as best I could and listened to them talk of their fears and their pain.

Trying to help them helped me find myself. It became the course my life would take after the war, trying to help DPs (Displaced Persons) find a home. These lonely young soldiers were displaced from their farms, their jobs, their schools, and most traumatically, their homes. I tried to teach them the lessons Alaska had taught me—to live inside of time, and that wherever they were, like Eddie Altschuler, they could help themselves by helping each other.

The officers, too, were lonely. Their wives and girlfriends had been evacuated. Unlike the young soldiers, who regarded me as a big sister, the officers' overtures at friendship were less honorable. I soon learned how to keep them at arm's length. One such officer, Major Marvin R. Marston, joined me one day at lunch in the Westward Hotel and made me an offer.

"If you agree to sleep with me, I'll give you a quarter of an acre of land on the waterfront," he said. "Real estate in Alaska is skyrocketing. In a few years, you would be a millionaire."

Controlling my laughter, I answered, "Major, as a government official, I'm not allowed to accept any gifts."

One day, I was set to fly out from Anchorage with one of the best bush pilots, when my phone rang. It was the Army Signal Corps. "We have a message for you from Secretary Ickes. We have to decode it."

The bush pilot knocked on my door. "Ready?"

"I'm waiting for a message from the Signal Corps."

"Sorry," he said, "I've got other passengers rarin' to go," and dashed out.

The next day, the *Anchorage Times* carried a story that the bush pilot had flown through a storm into a mountain and crashed, killing all on board. I couldn't work that day. I cabled Ickes telling him the story and ended, "You saved my life."

Letters from Mama kept me connected with the family. Mama, who could be ascerbic and controlling, showed a sweetness in her letters that she had successfully hidden for years. She worried constantly that I was working too hard.

"Ruth," she wrote, "you say you are working 15 hours a day. In one sentence you write you are feeling grand, and in another sentence you write for vitamin pills. I think you must be in a run down condition. Oh, how I wish you were home already, so I can see you and try to fatten you up a bit."

Mama complained that my letters were too short, although they were usually longer than hers. She chided me, "All week I watched for the mail man, and today I finally got a letter. When I got the envelope, I thought I had a very big letter, but it was a little tiny letter in a big envelope. But as you write you are very busy, I'll have to be satisfied."

After I finished a large report for Ickes, I wrote my mother a fat letter with joy and relief: "Dear Mom, I feel so good tonight I could burst. I put the final words on the report to Mr. Ickes—about 50,000 of them—pasted in the black-and-white photos I had taken, had it bound like a book, and sent it off air-mail. I feel as if I had given birth to a child."

Mama responded typically, "You write 50,000 words for Mr. Ickes, and maybe you will have a few more to write for me."

One of my jobs in Anchorage was to visit and report on the Matanuska Valley, a project developed by the government in 1935, in the depth of the Depression. It was to take farmers out of the Dust Bowl, bring them to Alaska, and prove that you can raise vegetables up here. With a government driver, I drove out to the valley on a sunny autumn day. It was forty-eight miles from the city—forty-eight miles of trees, streams, rivers, bridges, and breathtaking mountains. The road was a two-lane gravel highway that traveled smoothly and reminded me of upstate New York. The birches were gold. Red mountains rose all around me, and at twilight the mountains faded and became pink and purple.

After a two-hour drive, I was beginning to believe I was "Outside" in fertile farmland with the beautiful brown farm houses, red barns, chicken houses, and acres of cleared land. Cow pastures sat in the shadow of Mount McKinley.

We drove on to Palmer in the heart of the valley. It was a neatly carved town with trim white houses lining new streets with all the essentials of a thriving community—a recreation hall, a post office, schools, and a small hospital. Approximately 750 people lived scattered throughout the valley.

I was not surprised when opponents of experimental government projects wrote critical articles claiming that the Matanuska experiment had failed. These stories were untrue. The farmers were cultivating the valley into an agricultural dream of lush fields and healthy cattle. The valley's farmers had already earned more than a million dollars. The army and navy bought up all the food the farmers could grow.

I stayed in the home of the Wilsons, one of the farming families. Mrs. Wilson shared her story eagerly one evening at dinner: "Being here is really our first honeymoon. The Depression had hit us hard. We were sick with worry over how to meet our bills. We never caught up. Now, for the first time in our lives, we don't have to worry. I can go into any store and say, 'I can buy that.' I can buy anything my family needs and anything I want." She stopped for a moment. "But more important than having money, we have won our self-respect again. Alaska has given us back our dignity."

Mrs. Wilson was hard-working, sincere, highly efficient, and full of fun. Everyone pitched in. Her husband, Ivan, worked at Fort Richardson as a carpenter. Her sixteen-year-old son, Jim, did many of the household chores including milking Katy the cow, feeding their calves, and chopping wood. Her father-in-law, old Granddad Wilson, also lived with the family. Granddad was seventy-five, bearded, and an ardent woman-hater.

The women pioneers of Matanuska fascinated me. While many of the men left the farms to work on the army base, the women became full-time farmers and did all the cooking, cleaning, laundering, and the raising of the children. The woman living next door to my hosts showed me proudly how, with her little tractor, she had planted sixty acres by herself.

I spent each day talking to everyone I could, trying to get a range of perspectives on life in the Valley. Cy Johnson, a government field man, took me driving throughout the colony. He was twenty-one, quiet, earnest, and friendly. We drove in his bright red pickup truck through the north section of Palmer. The soil was fertile, wind-blown earth that had traveled from the Matanuska River and settled here.

Stopping at random farms, I talked to both the satisfied settlers and the dissatisfied ones, people who were paying their debts to the government and those who were reneging. After a while, there was a certain pattern. The satisfied people said, "We came here because we thought we'd be better off than we were before. We were on relief and couldn't find jobs. Here we found jobs on farms, sawmills, roadwork, mines, and air bases."

Those who were unhappy in the valley explained that the government had misled them. One farmer complained, "Before leaving the States, I was told that the government would lend each family thirty-three hundred dollars. Instead, the government gave me a seven-thousand-dollar farm, which I had to take. I now owe more money then ever before."

Driving back to Anchorage in Cy's red truck, I realized that Alaska needed both well-meaning government intervention and independent pioneering people working together to shape the new identity of the territory. But it also showed the inevitability of conflict between powerful forces, each with its own agenda. Alaska was big enough to hold them all, and in a few short months, the war would harness their energy and unite them. The naysayers agreed with the enthusiasts—the Matanuska Valley experiment was a success.

Chapter Fifteen

DECEMBER 7, 1941

The Japanese bombs that were dropped maliciously on Pearl Harbor on December 7, 1941, reverberated across Alaska. Four days later, Hitler delivered a hysterical speech denouncing his two chief enemies—President Roosevelt and the Jews.

"With the entire satanic insidiousness of the Jews," he shouted with venom, like a villain in a Verdi opera, "the president and the Jews are set on war and the destruction of Germany." He then declared war on the United States.

On December 11, 1941, knowing how worried my family must be, I wrote to assure them that I was all right:

> Dear Mom and Pop,
> We've been hearing all kinds of rumors up here that the Japanese say Alaska has been bombed and captured. So I'm rushing this note to tell you not to believe any rumors. We're

perfectly safe; don't worry about me and don't believe what the papers say. Even the Associated Press in New York wired up here asking for pictures showing the panic, children running home from school in an air raid, houses burning.

I've never seen anything as inspiring as the way the civilians rushed to the Civilian Defense Headquarters and offered to serve. One man came in with his gun and ammunition and said, "I was going out to the States, but I canceled my reservation. I was gonna have my teeth fixed, but I guess I can shoot the Japs with these teeth."

The face of Alaska changed. The Pacific was now America's front line: Hawaii, the Philippines, and especially the Aleutian Islands, lying like a sword aimed at Tokyo, were obvious targets for Japanese kamikaze pilots. They were the suicide terrorists of World War II, ready to kill themselves and others on their deadly missions.

General Buckner and the military were working around the clock to prepare Dutch Harbor and the Aleutians for the kamikaze onslaught. My mind spun back to images of the Japanese floating cannery I had tried to board during the mad voyage of the *Atalanta*. How many more floating canneries had the Japanese sent prowling these waters? How many were actually spy ships, seeking out the most vulnerable islands to bomb or invade?

My first conversation with Ickes in his office flashed through my head. We had talked of Alaska as the shortest distance between America and Asia. There were a few others who tried to rouse the country, only to have their voices lost in an apathetic void. One was the popular Alaskan delegate to Congress, Anthony (Tony) Dimond, who, back in 1934, had cried out on the floor of Congress, "Defend the United States by defending Alaska." Congress had turned a deaf ear.

A year later, Brig. Gen. William (Billy) Mitchell stood up, like a biblical prophet, before the House Military Affairs Committee. "Japan is our dangerous enemy in the Pacific. They won't attack Panama. They will come right here to Alaska. Alaska is the most central place in the world for aircraft."

Billy Mitchell never saw his warning heeded. He died soon after his rousing speech. Congress had turned a deaf ear on him, too.

Foreseeing the danger before a kamikaze attack, I sent a confidential cable to Ickes recommending that the Aleuts be moved out of the Aleutian and the Pribilof Islands. Ickes cabled back, "We'll do it."

Thank you, Mr. Secretary, I whispered to myself. I remembered Colonel Ohlson warning me to be careful, that some of my recommendations might be called "Gruber's Folly." So be it, I decided. The urgency was to get the people out of harm's way.

Soon, a thousand Aleuts were rushed by the military aboard Coast Guard cutters. They came from Kiska and Attu at the farthest reaches of the Aleutian Islands, from Unalaska, Dutch Harbor, and the Pribilofs. Our concerns were justified. The Japanese bombed Dutch Harbor on June 3, 1942, and captured Kiska and Attu.

Meanwhile, I kept sending almost weekly reports and letters to Ickes. The reports were always stamped CONFIDENTIAL. They were scrambled by the Army Signal Corps in Alaska and decoded in Washington. My letters went airmail. Ickes was furious when he learned that my letters to him had been opened by the army censor. He forced the army to issue an order saying all mail to him was not to be opened.

But the army order, of course, did not extend to my letters to the family and to others. They were all opened and stamped CENSORED. But nothing, as far as I knew, was ever blacked out. I made sure that not one word I wrote would give our enemies any information or confidence.

The letters I received filled my rare hours of free time with comfort. There were even occasional moments of loneliness when I yearned to be back in New York, sitting around the table with Mama and Papa and the rest of the family. I was especially pleased when a letter, dated January 30, 1942, arrived from Helen Rogers Reid, then vice president of the New York *Herald Tribune*.

"Dear Miss Gruber," she wrote. "I have felt the deepest thankfulness for the long ago fracas over your book because otherwise, I would never have had the joy of reading it, of knowing your writing, and last but most important the pleasure of receiving your Christmas message. It was wonderfully good of you to think of me in the midst of your new experience—how you did it I cannot imagine but I am deeply touched."

She concluded, "Your words about Alaska are very moving and they have made me long more than ever to visit our northern territory."

Her letter took months to reach me, and then sat in Anchorage for the three months I spent traveling in Dutch Harbor, the Aleutians, and Kodiak Island. I was finally able to reply on May 31, writing, "This has been a full year of exploration not only into the frontier of America, but into the frontier of my own heart and mind. Each of us has his own Alaska, to which he goes to find voice again, to find thought and vision. I've found them here. My only hope now is that when I go back to the States shortly I can do as much for Alaska as Alaska has done for me."

Her reply came immediately by airmail: "It was a joy to hear from you. When you come back to this part of the world I trust you will let me know. I want so much to see you."

Our letters were the beginning of a friendship that lasted until her death in New York City on July 27, 1970.

Wherever I traveled in Alaska, the experiences enhanced my ability to live inside of time. I was imbued with the energy of the Alaskans, and especially that of the soldiers, who kept asking me to meet with them, lecture to them, and help them understand the importance of this territory they were defending. "If I survive the war," the soldiers began to confide in me more and more frequently, "I want to come back here. How do I go about homesteading?" I was happy to answer their questions.

I was beginning to think of winding down, of starting homeward, when Dorothy Gruening, wife of the governor, wrote and asked me to stay with her in the governor's mansion the next time I came to Juneau. "Ernest," she said of her husband, "is away so much of the time, that I'd appreciate your company."

Dorothy, the First Lady of Alaska and the descendant of the founder of the Unitarian Church, was tall, slender, handsome, and so straightforward and hungry for talk that soon we were friends, calling each other by our first names. She carried herself with such dignity that I never heard a single word of criticism about her anywhere in Alaska.

That was not true of her husband. He came from a distinguished German Jewish family, had become a doctor only because his father wanted it, hated the profession, turned to journalism, and became the editor of *The Nation*. He then turned to politics and was appointed by President Roosevelt to the post of governor of Alaska. Disliked as governor, his image changed when Alaska became a state in 1959, and he was over-whelmingly elected its first senator.

I was helping Dorothy host a dinner party at the mansion when the governor congratulated me, "Your suggestion to Ickes that the Aleuts be moved out of the Aleutians and the Pribilofs was taken up by the army, and the Aleuts are now in Funter Bay, not far from Juneau."

The next day I was in Funter Bay, a huge campsite, watching Aleut men putting up wooden shelters to house their families. Father Baranof, a tall, bearded Russian Orthodox priest, who had served in the Pribilofs, greeted me. He described nostagi-cally how the "quiet peaceful world" he loved had come to an abrupt end when the Coast Guard evacuated him and his wife and the Pribilof Islanders.

Speaking English with a thick Russian accent, he said,

> It was the time for killing seals. On Pribilofs we always have great services on Sunday before killing season, which always begins on Monday. Now it was Sunday, fourteen or fifteen day of June. It was a rare sunny day. Then came two cutters into the harbor, and men got off boats. There was a lot of noise. My wife kept asking everyone around us what was going on.
>
> A young boy answered, "Don't you know anything? The whole island is being evacuated."
>
> I saw a soldier. I asked him also what is going on. He said, "Japanese have taken Attu and Kiska." He said we had to leave right away.
>
> We packed up everything we could carry— we didn't know what the Japanese would do to

our homes if they came. The Aleut people had been on Pribilof Island one hundred and fifty years. They had so many things they didn't want to leave—furniture, washing machines, radios. So they packed up everything. Many people wanted to take their washing machines.

Everyone was so sad to leave. My wife, me, and all of us, we all cried. We didn't know how long we would be gone—how many of us would die and never see our homes again, never see that lovely soil.

In Funter Bay, I had my first experience with refugees. I learned what it means to be a refugee: homeless, displaced, disoriented, and on the run. He knows trauma and loss. His memory of home turns even the simplest cottage in which he once lived into a villa.

The Aleuts were told by the army that at the end of the war, they would be taken home. But how could they believe it? They had lost not only their homes and livelihoods, but even their culture became fragmented. They were living among Indians now called Native Americans, whose language and culture were alien to them.

Some of the Pribilof Island men were sent home during the clubbing season to continue supplying the Fouke Fur Company with seal skins. Neither war nor bombs nor enemy invasion could keep the company from overseeing Aleut men clubbing seals for women's fur coats.

I felt guilty. I was responsible for turning the islanders into refugees. There were a few people who did call the evacuation "Gruber's Folly." I had no idea that the evacuation and life in the camp would be so painful for them, depressing them, turning some of them into alcoholics. But at war's end, they were brought back safely to their homes. The experience, difficult as it was for me to see their hardships, helped prepare me for a life dedicated to rescue and survival.

While the war changed the lives of the Aleuts, it also changed the lives of many of Alaska's women. Wives and children of military men were rounded up to be sent "Outside" to safety in the States.

Very few women wanted to go. They stormed the offices of the navy lieutenants and army captains, pleading, scolding, and demanding to stay. Some tried to get defense jobs. Yet they were all forced to leave. Alaska's women were learning not only the ruthless uprooting of war, but the clutching fear that they might never see their homes, their husbands, and their friends again.

I decided to travel on a train with some of the women leaving the Territory to see how they were handling the evacuation. The taxi cab driver who drove me to the train station captured the general gloom: "Gee, it's gonna be like nothin' human with them women gone. It was bad enough before they came, with ten men to each gal. But now we're really gonna feel it. All we'll see again in this country is men, and their terrible mugs are gonna look worse to us than ever. I guess I'll get out of this business. It won't be nothin' here with all them women gone."

Throughout the Territory—in Kodiak, in Yakutat, in Dutch Harbor, in Anchorage, and Fairbanks—wherever men were bidding good-bye to their wives, there was a finality, an unspoken anguish. As I stood on the platform, I saw countless officers with tears in their eyes. Near me, a young private wept openly with his lips pressed into his wife's hair before she boarded the train.

Of all the women I saw, only one completely broke down.

She was young and was soon to have her first child. Her husband sat with his arms around her waiting in the coach for the train to start. She wept desolately, while he sat staring straight ahead. When it was time to go, he stood up and climbed off the train. She suddenly cried out brokenly, "Oh, God, why do I have to go now?"

A spirit of camaraderie developed among the women riding the train. A general's wife had made dozens of sandwiches, which she handed out. Other women rushed to comfort those who were still visibly upset, and helped each other manage the infants and small children running through all the cars.

After the women left, Alaska settled back to contemplate its loneliness. Something vital had been drained out of it.

The economic effect was felt immediately. Businesses began to fold. One dress shop owner told me, "There is no use in staying. The only business that still makes money is liquor. I should have started a honky-tonk instead of a dress shop."

Alaska was like a man whose wife had gone to the country for the summer. The house was empty. You could hear the echo of children's voices, but only the echo.

After eighteen months in Alaska, I flew back to Washington and made an appointment to see Ickes the following day.

I entered his office, planning to thank him for the rare opportunities he had given me and to say good-bye.

"Oh, no, you're not leaving," he told me, "You're staying on as my special assistant."

My new life was about to begin.

Part 2

WASHINGTON IN WARTIME

Chapter Sixteen

THE WAR BECAME A MEMBER
OF THE WEDDING

The train from Union Station in Washington, D.C., pulled into Penn Station in New York. I raced out to see the whole family waving at me exuberantly. I went down the line hugging and kissing everyone. Mama and Papa first, then in order of birth: Bob, who was working for Upjohn Pharmaceutical Company; Harry, a physician at Brooklyn's Kings County Hospital; Betty, a chemistry instructor at New York University; her husband, Sam Sobel, a medical intern dressed in his white hospital uniform, and their little son, Michael. Finally, I hugged my brother Irving, a dentist. After eighteen months away, the excitement of coming home and the warmth of my family's love embraced me like a feather quilt in winter.

I had imagined they would all look older, but I was wrong. Each of my brothers still looked tall and handsome, although maybe a little heavier than I remembered. Mama and Papa looked especially well. My father's younger brother, Sam, a successful businessman, had recently committed suicide. I expected Papa to look old and rather crushed, but he did not. He kept smiling at me as though he were saying to himself, "She's really home."

We drove across the Williamsburg Bridge to Harmon Street. The autumn trees were golden and crimson. Harmon Street, and our gray stone house, never looked so welcoming and beautiful.

Mama immediately fed us. We sat around the kitchen/dining-room table until three in the morning, talking and laughing. One by one, my three brothers and my sister disappeared to go to bed. Only my mother and father stayed, telling me the family gossip. Papa sat, with enormous dignity, in the background, while Mama and I shared stories. He smiled even more when I told him that Ickes wanted me to stay on as his special assistant.

"What does that mean?" Papa asked.

"It means nearly everything connected with Alaska that needs to be answered comes across my desk. He can also give me any assignment he wants to."

A few days later, I returned to Washington. My first few nights at the Lee Sheraton Hotel came to the lordly sum of four dollars and fifty cents a night. It would have been a comfortable home, except that the desk clerk told me I could have it for one week only. He said they had to keep the room for government officials who were suddenly called to Washington.

Working on a hot Saturday morning, Ellen Downes, Mr. Ickes's appointment secretary, led me to my office, Room 3043, a large, sunlit two-room suite with one room for my secretary and one for me. I unpacked my books and notebooks, wrote a few letters, then set out in Washington's September heat to find an apartment.

I rang doorbells, talked to landladies, and smelled the foul, unwashed odor of old rooming houses until I was ready to faint. After hours of fruitless searching along "F" and "G" streets, someone suggested I try the Defense Capital Housing Bureau in the U.S. Building of Information. I had worn my new tweed suit with a red blouse to look businesslike. After an hour in the heat, I took off the jacket; my red shirt was ready to be wrung dry.

Inside the steaming office, I showed my ID card from the Alaska Railroad to a clerk sitting behind a huge circular counter. Her eyes sparkled.

"What do you do with the Alaska Railroad, if I may ask?" she said.

I told her I had been making a study of how to open Alaska for homesteaders.

"How interesting," she answered. "I knew a woman who went there. She says when she thinks of Alaska, she sees only flowers. When I think about it, I see only snow."

I laughed wearily.

She pulled out two long thin drawers lined with cards listing available lodgings.

"Single room with private bath," she read.

I breathed a deep sigh, "Perfect! Where is it located?"

"Wait, I'm not finished." She added, "It says, 'Man Wanted.'"

"Man Wanted," I repeated, outraged. She flipped open a dozen more cards, each one carrying the same refrain. "Man Wanted." I was depressed and discouraged.

"Ah," she sounded triumphant. "Here's one that sounds good. No 'Man Wanted.' It's only about forty-five minutes by bus from the Interior Department."

I was about to say, "I'll look at it," when she smiled. "No, wait a minute. I have one closer to Interior. It's a studio in a new building and air-conditioned."

I dashed over to the "I" Street studio. It was freshly painted, cheerful, and bright even at dusk. I kicked off my shoes and danced around the room. It was exactly what I had been looking for. I signed the lease and within days, furnished it in white, with a sofa bed, art deco chests, and a Swedish-modern dining table that doubled as my desk.

The next months were hectic. Working as special assistant to a cabinet member meant that, in effect, I would be the head of my own department, responsible only to the secretary. My days were packed with a fascinating array of assignments. One of my first jobs was to edit the film on Alaska I had made for Secretary Ickes traveling all over the Territory. While I was shooting it, the Coast Guard had asked me to give them a copy for use in their training regimen. Ickes approved immediately.

Learning the ways of Washington, I soon discovered that most officials rarely write their own speeches or answer their own letters. I drafted the speeches Ickes was asked to give on Alaska, trying to emulate his style of honesty, idealism, and wit. All mail relating to homesteading was sent to me to draft answers for his signature.

One day, Ben Thoron, director of the Division of Territories and Island Possessions, and John Evans, head of the Alaska section of the division, came to see me. Both had just returned from a trip to Alaska, brimming with ideas. "We're really going to change things," Thoron said. "We're going to put Alaska on the map. We've got real ideas."

They discussed their ideas with me, including the need for more women to move to Alaska. "Now we want your help," Evans interjected. "Take the letter-writing situation. The division for years has answered all these inquiries about Alaska by saying, 'We really don't know anything more about Alaska than you do.' We're going to end that negativism. We're going to make it really positive."

Thoron continued, "We'd like you to write some of those letters and really tell them things, so they'll be interested in homesteading in Alaska." He handed me a packet of letters. I was surprised they did not know I was already answering all the letters that came to Ickes concerning Alaska. "Could you have your secretary type the answers?" he asked.

I was bemused and said nothing more.

Back in my office, I immediately began answering the mail, telling the letter writers that we were glad to answer their inquiries about Alaska. I told them a bit of what Alaska was like, that it was not really a land of ice and snow. I also wrote the women about how much Alaska needed them. My tone was encouraging about the prospects of homesteading.

"Unheard of," said Miss Haney, my secretary. "I nearly fell out of my chair when you dictated that first letter. We never wrote such letters before. Heavens, I thought. It sounds like something human."

I brought the drafts to Mr. Thoron. "No, no, no," he told me, in polite horror. "You'll start a lonely hearts migration to Alaska."

"Great God!" said Mr. Evans, in slightly less polite horror. "We once sent such a letter, and there was such a deluge of mail from women looking for men, we were swamped. We wouldn't want such a thing to happen again."

I was appalled by their condescension: Did they imagine that the only reason women would want to move to Alaska was to find a man? Or were Thoron and Evans anticipating a new surge of female gold diggers, a gold rush in the forties?

They began the work of "de-feminizing" my letters. They deleted a paragraph here, another there, until the letters sounded almost, though not quite, like the letters the bureaucrats had been sending for the last thirty years.

Now I was furious. I wondered if they were trying to undermine the work I was doing for Ickes. I knew there were people in the department who resented that as special assistant to the secretary, I reported directly to Ickes, and not to them.

One day, Miss Haney entered my office breathlessly. "Mrs. Roosevelt's secretary is on the phone."

I took the call. Eleanor Roosevelt said, "I have a whole batch of letters from soldiers in Alaska who want to homestead after their service. Would you be willing to draft replies for my signature? There are many questions for which I imagine you would have the answers. I want so much to help them." Her high-pitched voice was etched with empathy for the soldiers.

"It will be my pleasure, Mrs. Roosevelt."

The stack of letters addressed both to her and to the secretary were so voluminous and so detailed in their questions that I suggested to Ickes that I write a whole book, which we could then mail to every would-be settler in Alaska.

Ickes, who never wasted time or words, said, "Do it."

The book opened with a foreword by Secretary Ickes describing the wild misconceptions about Alaska. One thing is certain, he wrote,

> The war has rekindled the fire of curiosity about our last big land frontier. Much of this curiosity has been stimulated by letters home and tales told by servicemen who have fought in the Aleutians or been stationed in Alaska. The result is that thousands of letters have been coming to the Department of the Interior, asking about conditions and opportunities in the Territory.

This booklet is designed to clear away the misconceptions, to debunk the ballyhoo, and to answer some of the questions. It attempts to give a true picture of Alaska, its opportunities and its limitations. Life on the frontier is not easy, and those who go there must be ready to trade hard work for the right to build on wide horizons.

In sixty-three pages, with black-and-white easy-to-follow maps and attractive drawings, the book covered everything from Alaska's history, which began in Russia during the reign of Peter the Great, to 1867, when the United States purchased Alaska from Russia for 7.2 million dollars, on to the present.

It told the would-be settlers where and how to homestead, farm, fish, hunt, invest, and even have fun. It was a culmination of much of what I had learned and experienced in Alaska.

Soon after I finished the book and began sending it with covering letters to the people who wrote to Eleanor Roosevelt and to Ickes, Mrs. Helen Rogers Reid, publisher of the New York *Herald Tribune* telephoned. "I would like you to come to see me when you are next in New York. There's something I would like to discuss with you."

"I'm coming up next week," I told her.

"Good," she spoke in a soft but firm voice. "Call me when you get in."

What could she want to discuss with me? I had spoken with Helen Reid on the telephone several times, but we had never met. She was said to be the most powerful Republican woman in the country, and was helping her husband, Ogden Reid, run the most prestigious Republican newspaper in America. They also owned the *Paris Herald Tribune*, the English-language newspaper read all over Europe.

A few days later in New York, I sat in her office facing her on the sixth floor of the *Herald Tribune* building on West 43rd Street. Even in her desk chair, she carried her tiny five-foot-one frame ramrod straight. She had porcelain skin, delicately carved features, and wide blue-green eyes that dominated her face. She was impeccably put together in a black suit with a white lamé ascot and a white satin blouse. A black beret trimmed with white satin was nestled over her brown curly hair. Somewhere I had read that Frederick, a well-known milliner, designed the berets she wore to go with her suits and dresses.

"I asked you to come," she said, "because I would like you to speak for our New York *Herald Tribune* Forum in November."

I held my breath. The Forum, held each year at the Waldorf Astoria Hotel, was the most significant lecture platform in the country.

"I'll have to get permission from the department," I said.

"Of course. Just call me when you get back to Washington."

She stood up, took my arm, and walked me down the stairs to see George Cornish, who had been my editor when I covered the Soviet Arctic for the *Herald Tribune* in 1935 and '36.

George greeted me warmly. "We'd like to interview you on the work you did in Alaska."

"George," I shook my head, "so much of the information I gathered is confidential. I'll have to ask Secretary Ickes if I can talk or write articles yet."

Helen Reid smiled. "I hope his answer is yes."

Back at the department, I called Walt Onslow, the acting director of publicity. Ickes was away and Mike Straus, the director, was on loan to the War Production Board.

Onslow was adamant. "You'd better say 'no' to both the Forum and the interview. You were on an official mission. I suggest you tell the *Herald Tribune* you'd appreciate it if they carried nothing at this time."

"I'll call Mrs. Reid and George Cornish right away."

I was relieved. My filing cabinets were filled with reports and correspondence. I wanted to reread and index the hundreds of notebooks I had filled in Alaska. I needed time to absorb it all.

Onslow went on. "Every now and then I have to go to bat for you. We get a lot of funny inquiries. The funniest was an exclusive tip some reporter said he had received that Ruth Gruber had been put in jail in Kodiak as an undesirable person."

I couldn't control my laughter. "Kodiak Island wasn't the only jail I slept in. In some villages and towns, jails were the only place they could house me. They had no hotels, and the schoolhouses, where I usually slept, had no space."

My life in Washington was exciting, and I was happy. I was a workaholic and I loved it. At the same time, I made a number of friends, all of whom were doing important work in the government. Washington, like Hollywood, was a one-industry town.

We spent evenings together, either in restaurants or in our own apartments. Soon I was having almost weekly dinners with Emil Corwin and his wife, Frieda. Emil was working on getting food to hungry people around the world through the Department of Agriculture. He was the brother of Norman Corwin, who wrote, directed, and produced some of the most brilliant radio programs on the air. Whenever Norman's productions were announced, Frieda would call me to come for dinner. We sat, not uttering a word, listening to Norman's voice and words on the radio.

Two other friends with whom I dined frequently were Saul Padover and his wife, Irina. Saul was another of Ickes's special assistants, and Irina was beautiful, vibrant, and Russian-born. At dinner at their home, Saul, a skilled writer, historian, and conversationalist, would often say things I found hard to forget. One evening, in a discussion of war economics, he said to a group of us around the table, "The two most permanent industries in the world are cosmetics and entertainment. Anything that has to do with human vanity and human boredom will survive."

Irina was an elegant presence who lit up a room when she entered. She owned a few expensive outfits, which she hung up to air as soon as she took them off. Immaculate and regal, she could have stepped out of a Tolstoy novel. Her tables were set as if she expected a czar and czarina for dinner. The glasses sparkled. The dishes shone. The food, always Russian-style, was served as if her guests were nobility.

Two other good friends were the brilliant lawyer Felix Cohen and his wife, Lucy. Felix was one of the lead solicitors in Interior, to whom I could always go when I needed to establish the legality of something I was trying to do. Felix's father, Morris Raphael Cohen, the popular philosophy professor at City College of New York, had come to live with his son in Washington. Professor Cohen had had a stroke that left him legally blind. I looked forward each week to reading to him from books and articles he chose.

Lucy was small, dark, and pregnant. She was the quintessential Jewish wife, mother, and daughter-in-law. Effusive and bubbly, she was constantly running back and forth from the kitchen to the dining room, making sure we were all well fed.

Every now and then an eligible bachelor invited me out. I accepted, but never wanted the relationship to become serious. I was too busy. Weekends I often took the train to New York, where other boyfriends invited me to plays and the opera. One doctor even tried to enlist my mother's help in convincing me to marry him. I did not find it hard to resist.

On one of my weekends in New York, I telephoned Marie Mattingly (Missy) Meloney, who had founded the *Herald Tri-*

bune Forum and turned it over to Helen Rogers Reid when Missy became editor of *This Week,* the Sunday supplement of the *Tribune.*

Missy's nurse put her on the phone. "I'm bedridden," Missy said, "but I'm working anyway. When can you come to see me? I'm living at the Waldorf Astoria." I told her I would come the next Saturday at three.

Riding on the BMT subway and crossing the Williamsburg Bridge from Brooklyn to Manhattan, my mind flashed back to advice she had given me a few years earlier when I told her I was writing my book on the Soviet Arctic. "Always do the best you have in you. Remember the men around you may know a lot about life. But you do, too. Always do the best you have in you," she repeated. "Never settle for anything less."

I smiled to myself, remembering that it was a man, Sir Isaac Newton, who had said, "If I have seen farther than other men, it is because I stood on the shoulders of giants." Missy Meloney, Helen Rogers Reid, and Dorothy Thompson—one of the dazzling columnists on the *Herald Tribune*—were among the women journalists upon whose shoulders many of us younger journalists were now standing. They were the kind of women who nurtured and inspired us. Even Winston Churchill, who had no passion for strong women publishers and journalists, once remarked, "If Helen Reid and Dorothy Thompson could do such a job in running a paper, perhaps all papers should be run by women."

Exactly at three, I arrived at the Waldorf. Missy's nurse stared at me in dismay. "She doesn't expect you until tomorrow. But wait here in the living room. I'll see if she can see you today."

I nodded with some concern. "I leave tomorrow morning for Washington."

Fifteen minutes later, the nurse told me to go into the bedroom. There was Missy, propped up in bed. Her deep brown eyes, eager and bright, stared at me. The rest of her face seemed pinched. She wore a pink flannel nightgown out of which her marble-white hands and pink nails gently protruded.

"You mustn't think of me in bed this way," she said. "Tomorrow, if you had come, you would have found me dressed."

I promised her I would try not to think of her this way.

"Bring me those newspapers," Missy said. She pointed to several copies of *This Week*. I picked up one of them. "This is the kind of thing I would like you to think about writing for us," she said, turning to page 2 of the magazine. "'It's the sort of thing that helps people to live better. I think that's the kind of thing you could write. Page 2 was my idea. When I first broached the idea, men at the office snickered. I said, 'Well, *This Week* is my responsibility. If it fails, I fail. I'm going to try it.' So, despite the skeptics, we tried it. It comes out on Sunday; by Thursday we get hundreds of letters from people all over the country."

I was impressed and nodded quietly.

"*This Week* has a circulation of seven million," she said. "It's one of those fantastic successes, and was inexplicable to some of the men who ran the *Tribune*."

I was even more impressed.

"I would love you to write for us," she continued. "It isn't what we pay that should convince you, which incidentally is four dollars for a thousand words."

Despite her apology, it was probably one of the highest-paying magazines in the country.

"What should convince you," she went on, "is the satisfaction you'll get when letters pour in and continue to come even months after an article appears."

I told her I would discuss it with Mr. Ickes. The prospect of writing for someone as creative as Missy was not easy to reject. But I knew that I couldn't possibly find time to write a weekly column and work full time for the government. I would keep my word to her and discuss it with Ickes, but I could almost hear him say, "Better turn it down. You've got enough to do right here."

This Week and the New York *Herald Tribune* Forum, which she created and then turned over to Helen Rogers Reid, were not the only successes that would guarantee Missy's role in history. Her activities were global as she traveled the world in search of good stories and good causes to fight for. She helped organize the American Child Health Association. When she learned that her friend Marie Curie, who had discovered radium, had no more radium for her research, Missy corralled her women friends and raised one hundred thousand dollars, enough to supply Madam Curie with a gram of radium, equipment for her laboratory, and income for the rest of her life. She had access to many of the world's leaders, interviewed Mussolini four times, and when Adolf Hitler failed to turn up for an interview he had promised her and then sent a Nazi emissary to ask for another appointment, she told the representative that she was no longer interested in interviewing him. She may have been the only journalist in modern times to refuse an interview with the Great Dictator.

At eighteen, she was a full-fledged reporter, and later as a magazine editor she introduced the idea of combining nonfiction articles with fiction. Married, with a son who became a novelist, she balanced her life as wife, mother, journalist, editor, and lecturer, and did it all with grace

Looking at her now, fragile and feminine, I asked her, "How did you get the nickname 'Missy?'"

"It came from my Negro nanny in Bardstown, Kentucky, where I was born."

I reached into my briefcase. "I've brought you something from Alaska."

I presented her with a pair of miniature fur moccasins embroidered with colorful beads. She was delighted. She told me she had collected miniatures for a long time. "Why is it," she asked philosophically, "that so many people collect miniatures?"

"Perhaps because there's so much perfection in them," I suggested. "I brought you these as a tribute because all these years I have sat at your feet."

"Oh, not my feet," she protested. "I'm the most humble person living."

"Humble, yes," I said, "but great."

"It's your birthday," she said suddenly.

"How did you know?" I asked, amazed.

She smiled mysteriously. I figured Helen Reid had called her and told her I was coming home to spend my birthday with the family.

"I wish I had some token to give you," she told me.

"Your remembering my birthday is token enough," I said. I left her feeling uplifted, and went home.

The Sunday train returning south to Washington was packed with soldiers, sailors, and airmen. The imminence of war was everywhere. From the peaceful small town I had left in 1941, Washington was now bursting with young men and women in uniforms. Nearly every street had a girl in the arms of a soldier, kissing or weeping. I often thought of the lines from Ecclesiastes that we sing each year during Yom Kippur, the Day of Atonement.

> To every thing there is a season, and a time to
> every purpose under the heaven:
> A time to be born and a time to die; a time to

plant, and a time to pluck up that which is
planted;
A time to kill, and a time to heal; a time to break
down, and a time to build up;
A time to weep, and a time to laugh; a time to
mourn, and a time to dance;
A time to cast away stones, and a time to gather
stones together; a time to embrace, and a
time to refrain from embracing;
A time to get, and a time to lose; a time to keep,
and a time to cast away;
A time to rend, and a time to sew, a time to keep
silence, and a time to speak;
A time to love, and a time to hate; a time of war,
and a time of peace.

I wondered how many of these soldiers holding their wives
or girlfriends in their arms would soon be going off to the
battlefields.

My dentist brother, Irving, like so many men I saw in the
street, was already in uniform. He called one morning to tell
me he had fallen in love with a young woman named Fannie
Davis.

"Congratulations," I shouted into the phone. "Tell me
more."

"It's a hard time for me," he said. "I'm so eager to go over
and serve, but the thought of leaving her now is tearing me
apart." His voice cracked. "Will you be able to come to the
wedding? We're getting married January sixteenth."

"Would I come? Just try to stop me."

The wedding, held in New York, was simple. Fannie looked
radiant in a beige silk tailored suit. Irving was majestic in his
captain's uniform. It was a bittersweet ceremony. Mama and

Fannie's mother, Dorothy, wept through most of it. The rest of us kept smiling and sniffling. Young men in uniform kept squeezing the hands of the young women sitting tightly next to them. *Who shall live and who shall die?* The war was a member of the wedding.

Irving wrote me from Camp Breckinridge, Kentucky, a few weeks later. "So far, my fortunes have been very good. I've been assigned to a camp post, and I am doing dentistry. All I'm doing are fillings. But Fannie is with me, so I am happy."

After several months, Irving left with his army unit on a camouflaged troopship to join General George S. Patton's army in Europe. Sensing how anxious Fannie was, I invited her to spend a week with me in Washington. The city fascinated her. Each morning, while I worked, she trudged off to every museum and government building on her list. Then promptly at five she turned up at my office, regaling me with all the wonders she had discovered.

I could see why my brother had fallen in love with her. Irving, six feet tall and handsome, was quiet, gentle, serious. He spoke sparingly and was always ready to help anyone in need. Fannie, five feet one, petite, and attractive, was cheerful and outgoing, and she was a talker, though never boring. At a dinner party in my apartment, I watched her charm my friends, The world, I thought, can be divided into doers and talkers. Maybe that was why when Irving, a doer, met Fannie, a talker, in the hospital where both were working, he had fallen head over heels in love.

Early in 1943, Ickes called me into his office. "I need you to go up to the Canadian Northwest Territories to report on the Canol Project and the Alcan Highway."

These were newly coined words in the lexicon of oil. Canol

brought Canada and oil together; Alcan was an abbreviation linking Alaska and Canada, already linked by geography.

I listened closely as Ickes outlined what he wanted me to report on. Among all his other duties, Ickes was oil coordinator for the federal government. It seemed that each time President Roosevelt had a tough nut to crack, he dropped it in Ickes's lap. Six days a week, I watched oilmen come into the building to meet with the secretary or dine with us in the top-brass dining room. The Saudi Arabians, with ink-black hair and ink-black beards, swept in wearing long white robes with white or checkered *keffiyas;* confusing style and culture, they donned modern oxfords so shiny you could almost see your face in them. They sat at the white linen-covered tables with their American counterparts, who wore fancy decorated leather boots, gray felt Texas hats, and spoke in Texas drawls. The little I knew about Canol and Alcan I had learned eating with them. Why would Ickes choose me for such a critical job in wartime?

Ickes was talking with his chin in his hand. "Nobody," he said, "has given me a report on how the army is getting along with the oil project or with the building of the Alcan Highway. You know Alaska, you know the Arctic." He was answering the question I had not asked him.

He looked at me quizzically. "Can you be ready in twenty-four hours?"

"What will I do with the extra twenty?" I replied.

He called his operator, "Get me General James A. O'Connor in Edmonton.

"General," I heard him say, "I want to send my special assistant along the highway."

The general must have answered, "Send him right along, Mr. Secretary," because Ickes then responded, "It's not a him, it's a her."

Apparently the general's objection was the usual one—"We don't have the proper plumbing for women."

Ickes's answer was a boisterous laugh. "You don't know the plumbing this gal has lived with. She was in Siberia, where the outhouses were built for Cossacks. You needed a ladder to get up on them."

For a fleeting moment, remembering outhouses not only in Siberia but also in the jails in Kodiak and Sitka and Point Hope, I thought the book I ought to write someday should be called *Jails and Outhouses I Have Known*.

The general had no further complaints. Ickes told him firmly, "She'll be leaving tomorrow, flying to Edmonton."

After he hung up the phone, he turned to me with a mischievous grin. "Watch out for that general."

Chapter Seventeen

THE ARMY LAYS THE CANOL PIPELINE TO FUEL THE ALCAN HIGHWAY AND STRIKE AT JAPAN

G eneral James O'Connor, a burly army officer, greeted me as I stepped off the plane in Edmonton, Alberta.

"The politicians up here are so excited about your coming that they asked me if you will speak in the Parliament."

"Of course," I answered. "When do they want me?"

"Tomorrow."

The next day the general picked me up in my hotel and escorted me, in his chauffeured army car, to the provincial Parliament building. An official-looking Canadian guard led me to the podium.

If I ever have children, I thought, this is one scene I'd like to tell them about: standing up in a Parliament building, talking to men twice my age and, I was sure, far wiser than me. If there were any women in the chamber, I didn't see them. For a fleeting moment, I asked myself, "What do I tell them?" I had no notes. I never use notes in speaking. I want to look at the audience, see their eyes, watch their bodies. Are they bored? Are they passionate about the things that consume me? Then I can decide what stories I can share with them. Stories? Yes. All of life is a story. Ideas, too, of course. But ideas told in stories.

I felt a calmness. I would talk to these legislators who made the laws by which Canadians live, the way I had talked to the soldiers in Alaska. The stories came rushing through my head, stories of the Alaska that I now felt so much a part of me. Apparently, it worked. When I finished, the men stood and applauded.

General O'Connor was beaming as he escorted me back to my hotel lobby. "To think I tried to keep you from coming."

"And I haven't seen a single outhouse."

He laughed so loudly, people turned around to stare at him.

"We'll find you one," he promised.

A few days later, flying in an army plane, the general was showing me the route of the Canol pipeline. Tucked under the Arctic Circle at Norman Field, it began exactly where oil had been discovered by the geologist Theodore A. Link in 1919. It was a tiny black dot on my map.

The general, exuberant about the pipeline, put my map on his lap and drew a line from that tiny Norman Field dot as if he were trying to lay down the pipeline himself. His pen moved southwest to White Horse in British Columbia, where the oil was to be refined. With precision, his line crossed the border into Alaska and ended in Skagway.

"From here," the general assured me, "we'll funnel the oil into the planes, the ships, the tanks, and the trucks to win the war."

For three weeks, I spent hours interviewing army engineers, architects, and senior officers of the three American construction companies, Bechtel, Price, and Callahan, who had combined their forces and won the contract to build the pipeline.

After sending off a long report to Ickes, I told the general I was ready to see the Alcan Highway. But I wanted to see it from the air before I took to the road.

"I'll get you the best Royal Canadian Air Force [RCAF] pilots up here," he said.

Within a few hours I was wrapped in a warm army jacket, flying with two fatherly looking pilots. I was their only passenger. They took turns telling me where we were in this wild and majestic wilderness. The day was clear, the sky blue. A few clouds hung over us.

Then suddenly the sky darkened. Snow and wind shook the aircraft. A white blanket of nothingness covered the world—no birds, no animals, no human footsteps; only the mysterious and strangely beautiful nothingness. It was a spiritual experience such as I had never known. This is the way, I thought, the biblical nothingness must have looked, before the Lord created the heaven and the earth. I opened the small Bible I carried in my bag and read from the first book of Moses:

> And the earth was without form, and void; and darkness was upon the face of the deep. And the Spirit of God moved upon the face of the waters . . .

The senior pilot's voice, calm and steady, broke into the silence. "We're lost."

Was it his calmness or the Spirit of the Lord that embraced me? I felt no fear.

The pilot went on. "I'm dropping down to try to get below these clouds and see if I can find a river or a road. Then we can follow it and land somewhere. There's no good map yet of this part of the Canadian Northwest Territories."

How different these two RCAF pilots are, I thought, from

Herb Hager, the bush pilot flying to Point Barrow. He was negligent and arrogant; his route was fully mapped, yet he'd brought no maps with him. These two RCAF pilots, with no maps, no instruments, no control tower to guide us, were descending blindly but with such skill that I leaned back, confident they would break through this ominous wall of black clouds.

Some twenty miles later we broke through. "There's a road," the pilot sang out to me. "Now we'll find our way."

I saw a thin pencil line on the face of the earth. *"And God divided the light from the darkness."*

At the airport, I hugged the two pilots. My eyes welled with tears. "I don't have words to thank you."

"That's all right," the copilot smiled. "We're sorry we didn't get to show you much of the highway from the air."

The next day I set out in an army jeep to drive along the first completed section of the Alcan (later called the Alaska Highway). My driver, Tom, a short, friendly black soldier, helped me climb in.

Knowing I would be running to extremes of weather, I had packed cold and warm-weather Arctic clothing, which I promised to test for the quartermaster general in the army. The day was warm, so I slipped into a cool white blouse and khaki pants, and filled my army knapsack with fresh notebooks, my Leica, Rolleiflex, movie camera, and a DDT bomb. I fastened my favorite big, red straw hat on my head.

The hat turned out to be the most useful piece of equipment I had, so useful that I recommended strongly to the quartermaster general that all GIs and WACs (Women's Army Corps) driving on the Alcan Highway be issued a big straw hat—not necessarily a red one.

Part of the beauty of the highway was the way the Arctic sun cast its light, like a warm embrace, on the road. Driving from

Canada to Alaska, you headed north and west. The setting sun blinded you like an acetylene torch. It was the beauty but also the first curse of the highway. Sunglasses were almost useless, and only the large brim of my hat shaded my eyes enough so I could keep watching the magnificence of the world we were driving through.

The second curse was dust. The Alcan Highway was gravel, not concrete. As we drove along, our jeep beat up a miniature typhoon and hurricane. Every time we hit a rock, dust flew up, blinded us, and then settled into our throats, our eyes, our ears, and our noses.

The third curse was mosquitoes. Soon I was attacked on every uncovered part of my body by a flying armada of Arctic mosquitoes. Within minutes a rash of red welts blossomed all over me, even under my clothes. I remembered reading how in Siberia, Russian prison guards hauled their prisoners into the forest, knowing their victims would die of mosquito bites.

Tom, trying to help me, kept one hand on the wheel and the other waving the mosquitoes away.

"It's no use," I thanked him. "Even at home, insects fly from thirty miles away to bite me."

He laughed. "They tell the story in Alaska about an air corps guy who filled his plane up with five gallons of gasoline before he discovered he was filling up a mosquito instead of a bomber."

One of the war signs springing up all over America flitted across my vision. It asked plaintively, "Is this trip necessary?"

General O'Connor had been right when he told Secretary Ickes there was no plumbing for women. But there was no plumbing for men either. As far as I could see, it was a road without outhouses. If there were any, they were the best kept secret of the highway.

Despite the inconveniences, I reveled in the beauty of the trees, the rocks, the lakes along the road as I traveled the fifteen-hundred-mile highway being built from Edmonton to Fairbanks. In my mind I saw this highway linking Alaska through Canada south to all the Americas. Built in wartime, its purpose was to carry food, munitions, and medicines across the top of the world to speed up winning the war. But after the war I hoped it would become the highway to peace.

"Where's home for you?" I asked Tom.

"Louisiana. We're mostly all from the South. We're a black unit building the Alcan. Funny, huh?"

I did not think it funny, watching black soldiers on the road, with sweat pouring down their faces, as they broke rocks and stones, and cleared timber.

That evening in the hotel dining room, an army officer who had been involved with the highway told me, "Somebody ought to be court-martialed for the way those Negros are treated. They suffer from rank negligence and stupidity. In December they were wearing the same clothing they had worn in building an airfield in Florida."

The black soldiers did not strike or rebel. Loyal Americans, they turned the Alcan Highway into an international success linking Canada, the United States, and someday, they hoped, all the Americas.

After bidding farewell to the general, I flew to Fairbanks, where I met many of the American and Russian pilots who were flying the route across the Bering Strait to Siberia and on to the war front in Europe. The liaison between the American and Soviet pilots, which began with such high hopes, had begun to break down. The Russians complained to me that they were not getting what they wanted. The Americans complained that the Russians were cheaters—that they wanted not

Top: I took over the schools in the Eskimo villages at times when the teachers needed a few days off. I gave the children *Life* magazine to read. They all wrote stories based on the ads, never on the articles. **Above:** My boss, Secretary of the Interior Harold L. Ickes, presented a government payment to a woman named Etta Jones. He was a political battler *par excellence;* I was always grateful to have him in my corner as mentor and advocate. **Left:** During a winter in Alaska I received this amusing holiday card from an old sourdough in Seattle.

All photographs are provided courtesy of the author.

WESTERN DEFENSE COMMAND AND FOURTH ARMY
Office of Assistant Chief of Staff, Civil Affairs Division
ALASKA TRAVEL CONTROL

PERMIT TO ENTER THE TERRITORY OF ALASKA
SUBJECT TO SUSPENSION WITHOUT NOTICE

Name   Dr. Ruth Gruber

Occupation   Field Representative

Employed by   Alaska Railroad

Permit Issued   2/10/43   Expires   2/10/44   No.   P-408

By authority of Commanding General
Western Defense Command & Fourth Army
War time Civil Control Administration
Alaska Travel Control Division.

ATC FORM 2 REV. 12-16-42   Officer in Charge

Top (left): In Point Hope, Ida Susik Lane and I have just emerged from a dip in the Arctic Ocean. Ida cooked meals for me and brought them to the jail where I was residing. With no hotels in the small villages, my most reliable accommodations in Alaska were often in jails. **Top (right):** I quickly acclimated to the Alaska winters, and this fur parka was a big help. **Above:** I had to display my government ID card frequently, especially with tighter security after WW II began. **Opposite page (top to bottom):** Mother and child laughing in Hooper Bay. • The village of Unalaska, across the bay from Dutch Harbor. • Women in Hooper Bay were fond of gathering berries in the tall grass outside the village.

Top: Stunning landscape near the Matanuska Glacier, at mileage post 104 of the Glenn Highway. **Above, right, and opposite:** I found the children in Alaska irresistible, and wanted to photograph them all the time.

Right: A fifteen car train rolls cautiously down the slopes between Whitehorse in Canada, and the Skagway rail junction in Alaska. **Below:** Acres of heavy steel pipe dot the route of the Canol oil pipeline from Norman Wells to Whitehorse in the Yukon. These 23-foot lengths laid end to end could make a 30-mile stretch of the pipeline. **Bottom:** Soldiers from an African-American engineering company find road-building a tough, muddy slog. In one of my reports to Secretary Ickes, I described the inequitable treatment of black troops in Alaska.

Left, from top: An open truck carrying newspaper reporters through the Carcajou River Canyon was dwarfed by three-hundred foot high rock walls. • During the war, young railroad men performed jobs usually taken by much older workers. These fellows were only 23 and 24 years old. • Women from Canada and the United States added a bright spot to daily life at Canol Camp. Here, five women are taking turns using the shower. **Above:** Photographers from *America* magazine came to my apartment in Washington, D.C., where I had hung a shaman's mask on the wall, and placed a totem pole on a chest of drawers covered with a map of Alaska.

Top: Two U.S. servicemen and the police chief of Kodiak, Alaska on the streets of their fair town. **Above:** An old fisherman and his dogs pack it in for the night. **Left:** A native hunter scans the horizon for walrus.

only our airplanes, but guns and ammunition. There were even suspicions, never confirmed, that the Russians were turning American planes over to the Japanese. The townspeople had their own complaints. "As soon as the Russians arrive," they told me, "they buy out everything in sight. In one day our shelves are empty. Cigarettes and liquor, they're the first to go."

After more reports and cables to Ickes, I sent him a message saying I was preparing to fly home.

He cabled back. "Would like you to stay on and go to Juneau to cover the state legislature."

In Juneau, Dorothy Gruening, the wife of the governor, invited me to live at the governor's mansion. It gave me a good opportunity, whenever the governor was in town, to listen to his ideas for the future of the Territory. His keen intellect and genuine passion for Alaska filled our evenings with good conversation.

In the halls of the legislature, I spent endless days listening to the lawmakers debate various bills. The representatives passed several laws of significance. They raised the teachers' salaries, brought delinquent children under greater control, decided to face their tuberculosis problem, and set up tuberculosis wards in the hospitals.

But the legislators had little vision for the future. They sabotaged and defeated every bill that would have given the native peoples greater economic and social democracy. They condemned all unemployment compensation as "parasite bills." They flared up at the mere mention of income tax and refused to increase even the tax on liquor. Hovering over the whole city, like the still unmelted brown and dirty snow, was the blood feud between Governor Gruening and the nine-member majority in the House. The question the nine asked themselves was not "Is this bill good for Alaska?" but "Does the governor want this bill?" If Gruening was in favor of something, the nine were against it.

Unlike my days so often filled with frustration sitting in the legislative building, the evenings were scintillating, with Governor Gruening holding forth on his dreams of statehood for Alaska. It was the one issue on which most Alaskans agreed with him. His own background fascinated me. He was born in New York City to a German Jewish family. His father wanted him to become a doctor and sent him to Harvard Medical School.

"The day I graduated from Harvard Medical School," he told me, "I made up my mind. I had given my father what he wanted—I had an M.D.—but I was never going to practice medicine. I went into journalism and then government. It was certainly the right decision for me."

"In a sense, I had a similar experience," I told him. "After I got my Ph.D. in Germany, I tried to become a college teacher. But no college wanted me. I was a woman—the wrong sex. If there were jobs, they went to young men. So I went into journalism and loved it. Being a journalist and an author have given me opportunities I might never have had in academia."

Gruening teased me, "You've had a pretty exciting career. When are you going to write your autobiography?"

"The world isn't waiting for my autobiography," I said.

Governor Gruening reassured me. Sounding like my father, he said, "Ruth, I predict you're going to find ways to help people. You never know what turn your life will take."

A few months later I met him in Washington, and he said, "Remember my prophecy to you? Look what happened to all your hard work covering Canol." I knew what he meant: In January 1944, the Truman Investigating Committee in the Senate had denounced the whole project as an "inexcusable" boondoggle.

I had learned when I returned to Washington that Ickes had also opposed the pipeline, though he had not mentioned it when he sent me to report on it. It was true to his unique management style. He wanted a report from me that would not be influenced by his bias. Oil from the Norman Wells, he believed, was too meager in volume on which to spend millions of dollars. He was vindicated when the project, originally budgeted at 24 million dollars, escalated to 273 million dollars by 1945 and had still not been completed. The end of the war made the controversial Canol project irrelevant, and Congress finally forced the army to abandon it.

Chapter Eighteen

HELEN ROGERS REID AND THE *HERALD TRIBUNE* FORUM

In late May 1943, I returned to Washington from Alaska and had the good fortune to find an apartment half a block from my office. With nearly everyone in the department greeting me like a long lost traveler, I settled in happily and got back to work. Everything was going marvelously, and I even received official permission from Ickes to travel frequently to New York on weekends, which gave Mama and Papa great delight.

In Washington, Ickes told me he had been rereading some of my reports.

"Obviously you hate bureaucracy," he laughed. "You have the longest scissors in Washington; you are forever cutting through red tape."

My joy in being back in Washington was saddened when I read that Missy Meloney had died on June 23, 1943. Her obituary, accompanied by a picture of her as a beautiful young woman with determined lips and deep-set luminous eyes, ran on the front page of the *Herald Tribune*. Since I did not know any of her relatives, I sent a note of condolence to Helen Rogers Reid. I could imagine how much Missy's death must have rocked Helen Reid. The two had been such great friends. I was deeply moved by Mrs. Reid's answer.

"It was wonderfully good of you to write me about Mrs. Meloney," she wrote. "I wish that Mrs. Meloney could have read your letter, so full of understanding sympathy. Her influence on people who came in touch with her was extraordinary, and it meant a great deal to me to know that you had appreciated the quality of her mind and spirit."

A few months later, I received a call from Mrs. Reid.

"I would like you to speak at the Forum," I heard her say.

My stomach tightened. True to her word, a year after I had turned down her first request, she was again asking me to speak.

"I want you to talk about the work you did in Alaska. How we're opening it up. How it's our new crossroads at the top of the world."

I took a deep breath. "I'll have to discuss it with Secretary Ickes."

"Be sure to call me as soon as you speak to him. If you have any problems, let me know."

I called Ellen Downes, Ickes's appointment secretary, and asked for a meeting with the boss.

"Is it urgent?" she asked. "He has a very crowded day."

"It's urgent." I replied

Fifteen minutes later I hurried across Secretary Ickes's blue-carpeted office. He looked up from his desk, which, like mine, was littered with papers. He pressed a button. His private secretary appeared, gathering up the letters he had signed and the reports he had read and initialed. *Government,* I thought, watching her holding the mass of paper to her chest as she moved soundlessly through a side door to her office, *is built not on concrete and steel, but on paper.*

"Sit down," he pointed to the chair at his right. "I hear it's urgent."

"Mrs. Reid wants me to speak on Alaska at the *Herald Tribune* Forum. I told her I'd have to check with you. She wants an answer right away."

His eyes, from behind his gold-rimmed glasses, squinted with pleasure.

"That's the perfect place for the country to learn about what we're trying to do up there. Give her my regards. I'm glad she selected you."

This time I had to write my speech following guidelines that Mrs. Reid gave me for the time allotted. I counted eleven drafts over several weeks as I attempted to sum up what Alaska meant to me. After the final draft, I clocked the speech and discovered it was far too long. I was upset. I could think of no way to cut it, and the deadline hung over me. I sent the speech to Mrs. Reid with a note explaining the problem. One of her assistants, Jessie Knoess, sent me a comforting telegram:

"Mrs. Reid asked me to tell you that she has been able to give you more time and it will be unnecessary to cut the speech."

I left for Brooklyn the week before the Forum. Shopping on Fulton Street, I found a form-fitting black velvet suit, with a rippling lace collar and rhinestone buttons. Even Mama, risking the "evil eye" descending upon me if she complimented me, admitted in a whisper, "You look pretty good in that."

On the evening of Tuesday, November 16, my brother Harry drove me to the Waldorf Astoria on New York's east side. I was to speak in the second session, which was to begin at 7:45 P.M.

I sat on the stage looking out at some two thousand people, representing an array of American and foreign diplomats, scholars, historians, writers, reporters, lecturers, photographers, scientists, and members of various women's organizations. My heart began to beat so loudly I was sure some of the people in the front row could hear it, as I listened to Helen Reid introduce me.

> Our next speaker is an adventure in herself. She has the keen inquiring mind, the vivid aliveness and zest for exploration among the far-flung people and places of the earth that make the perfect reporter.

I had heard how carefully she worked on each introduction, for the speakers at the Forum. They were pure Helen Rogers Reid. She studied the background of each speaker, gathering material that would most interest her audience.

> Her education stems from three universities—A.B. from New York University at the end of three years, an M.A. from Wisconsin in another year, and a Ph.D. with a magna cum laude from the University of Cologne after only one year. At the age of twenty she became the youngest Doctor of Philosophy on record.

I knew how much Helen Reid valued education for women. She herself was a graduate of Barnard College in New York. At a time when only a few women, rich or poor, went to college, Helen, whose father died when she was three, worked her way through Barnard. A woman's college, it had educated some of the most remarkable women of her generation; among them Helen, who ran the *Herald Tribune,* Iphigene Sulzberger of the *New York Times,* and Agnes Meyer, the mother of Katharine Graham, publisher of the *Washington Post.*

I clasped my hands tightly, listening as she continued:

> On returning home she was given a traveling fellowship to study the situation of women under fascism, communism, and European Democracy. With the assignment she scooped the newspaper world by getting inside the Soviet Arctic and writing a remarkable book entitled *I Went to the Soviet Arctic.*

My cheeks grew red when I listened to her use a journalist's dream word, "scooped."

> In 1941 Secretary Ickes sent Ruth Gruber to Alaska to make a social and economic study of developments. For over nineteen months she covered that vast territory by plane, train, truck, boat, and dogsled with more thoroughness than has ever been done by any single person. She lived in schools, hospitals, and even a jail among the Eskimos of the Arctic coast, talking to people in every walk of life, gathering a wealth of material about this undeveloped part of our country. During a trip to the Aleutians as the only woman in an army convoy, she lived on the base at Dutch Harbor. She ate with the soldiers and sailors and came to know all their hopes and fears. Until now army censorship has prevented her from telling the story of this great new crossroads of the world. Tonight the veil has been slightly lifted. We are thankful that we can bring you her first report on civilian life in our Arctic outpost and her picture of its future.

> I am especially proud of introducing to you
> an important government representative and a
> reporter extraordinary, Dr. Ruth Gruber.

Shaken by her words, I somehow managed to keep my knees from wobbling and walked slowly to the microphone. I took a deep breath.

"I am happy to be here tonight," I began. For the next twenty minutes, I described what I had learned in Alaska. I concluded, with my hopes for the Territory: "Historians tell us that in the opening of the west, about 50 percent of the people turned back. In the opening of the north, we would have to expect at least the same proportion. But if 50 percent of the tens of thousands who have heard of Alaska, who have seen it under fire, and who think they want to live here, turn homeward, that will still leave thousands to build homes, to utilize the wealth and give their children the right to live with decency and dignity, without hunger and without fear."[*]

As I finished speaking, people began applauding. I went to take my seat, and Mrs. Reid made me stand up and take a second bow. When I was finally sitting down, I read the Forum program, amazed at what this tiny woman had accomplished. In the middle of the war, she was able to get President Roosevelt, Eleanor Roosevelt, Winston Churchill, and Charles de Gaulle to participate in her forum. At just fifty-six, she was one of the most powerful women in the country. How had a poor girl from Appleton, Wisconsin, achieved such influence? In the coming years, as our friendship deepened, I would continue to try to understand her. Why did she reach out to so many young women? Why did Helen hire more women than any other newspaper publisher in the country?

*See appendix for full *Herald Tribune* Forum speech.

Following the third and final session of the Forum, she gave a reception at the hotel. The chief editorial writer of the *Herald Tribune,* Geoffrey Parsons, said to me, "When you go back to Washington, will you tell Secretary Ickes that even if we do heckle him now and then, and even if he does send us nasty notes, we have the highest respect and admiration for him. We think he's the best man in the cabinet."

Elsa Maxwell—the inveterate party giver who was also an enthusiastic guest—greeted me effusively.

"I'm dying to meet your boss," she told me. "Could you arrange an appointment?"

"I'll try," I said. When I mentioned this to Ickes, he said he would be happy to meet her.

Elsa arrived at Ickes's office on November 30, 1943. We met, by accident, on the elevator going down. Elsa was wrapped in mink, from her head to her ankles. She was short and stout in her minks, and looked like a barrel of butter.

"My dear," she said in a throaty voice, "I'm so happy to see you. I've just come from seeing Mr. Ickes."

I nodded and was about to ask how the conversation went, when Elsa interjected. "That man," she pointed up toward Ickes's office, her eyes looking starry, "that's a wonderful man. We must keep him in power. Such courage, such honesty, such vision. That's the greatest man in government."

Again I nodded.

"My dear, I'm writing my autobiography. It's coming out in the spring. It's already sold one hundred thousand copies. The Book-of-the-Month Club is taking it. I'm writing up the most outstanding women in the country, and you are one of them."

I chuckled, knowing this was one of Elsa's techniques. Everyone she met was the greatest person in the world. Flattery dripped from her lips like a waterfall.

"Women have a great job to do, and we don't do it." Elsa shook her fist dramatically. "This will be a terrible world. Will you come visit me on Saturday?"

"Of course."

I went to see Elsa at Evalyn Walsh McLean's house in Washington's elite Georgetown neighborhood the following Saturday. The house was a crowded jumble of sofas and artwork. Mrs. McLean was an heiress whose Irish immigrant father had struck it rich during the gold rush. Against her family's wishes, she had married Edward Beale McLean, heir to the *Washington Post* fortune. Some years earlier, she had purchased the Hope Diamond and wore it around her neck every day as a good luck charm, though many said the diamond was cursed. Mrs. McLean certainly seemed cursed: Her son had died in a car accident, her daughter committed suicide at the age of twenty-five, and in 1941, her husband was declared insane and institutionalized. Despite all her tragedies, however, she was a woman of power in Washington. And like other women of power, McLean was inexplicably fascinated with Elsa Maxwell, the self-described "short, fat, ugly piano player from Keokuk, Iowa."

A petite maid led me through a long room to a side corridor and into a bedroom where Elsa was lying in a canopied bed with a pink silk comforter. She was wearing a polka-dotted robe, which she kept unbuttoning and rebuttoning.

"My dear," she said taking my hand, "forgive me for being in bed. You don't mind my entertaining you this way? I am so tired." Her hands fluttered to her forehead. "I am doing so much work for the government—selling war bonds, making speeches, traveling around the country. It is good of you to come."

I sat down.

"I just loved meeting Mr. Ickes," she told me. "I have always admired him. How these people here in Washington hate him.

Take Mrs. Patterson. Last night I was at her house, and she said to me, 'Elsa, how would you like to edit a great newspaper?' I mean, my dear, she was offering me the editorship of her newspaper. I could do a wonderful job with it. The first thing I would do is hire you."

Eleanor "Cissy" Patterson was the owner and publisher of the *Washington Times-Herald*. I doubted Elsa's story was true, but I had quickly learned not to upset Elsa's fantasies.

"I would make it one of the most liberal papers in the country. Like that kind Mrs. Reid has made the *Herald Tribune*. My dear, she's a wonderful woman, Mrs. Reid. She's the greatest American in the country. Single-handedly she has made the *Herald Tribune* Forum the great center of intellects in the country.

"'But' I said to Mrs. Patterson, 'I won't edit your paper because you would always obstruct everything I wanted to do. I'll tell you when I'll edit your paper—when you die.'"

Now, I was quite sure those were not the words she had used with Mrs. Patterson, but she knew that her fantasies made for entertaining conversation. Perhaps this was the secret of Elsa Maxwell: she told good stories.

"Mrs. Patterson is one of the worst women in the country," Elsa continued. "I mean she's one of my dearest friends, though why she publishes me I will never know. After all, there are only two women columnists in this country, Dorothy Thompson and myself. Dorothy has frightened her audience away by hammering at them. That's not the way to do it. You've got to get under their skins in a good way. That's what I'm doing when I give the readers all this silly stuff. So when I need to get in a good fight every now and then, I can."

She continued buttoning and unbuttoning herself. While she talked, I kept wondering what made Elsa tick. I thought I was close to understanding her now. Her gossip was three-dimensional. She knew everybody. That was her occupation—to know people and to be able to gossip about them intimately. She was a kept woman, kept by other women. She could count her life out, I was sure, in guest rooms. She even defined herself as "the guest of the world." With several dresses and a few long evening gowns, she traveled across the U.S. and abroad, with intermittent stops in the suites the Waldorf gave her for her parties.

She was the Dubarry of the sewing circles, the Boswell of the right side of the tracks.

"So I refused Mrs. Patterson's offer," she said as she raised her small heavy body in the bed. "She could have made a millionaire out of me. But I don't want money. I can only wear one dress at a time. I told her, 'You're going to die and no one is going to miss you. You're going to die the most hated woman in the country.' But I cannot change her."

She stopped to take a quick breath, then proceeded to embellish this improbable tale of Cissy Patterson . "I told Cissy about Helen Reid and she was furious. She began to talk about Helen's husband, Ogden Reid. I said, 'That's none of my affair. It's not for me to speak of Mr. Reid's intelligence or brilliance. I'm speaking of Helen Reid, the greatest woman in America, the greatest patriot we have.'"

After trashing her dear friend Mrs. Patterson, I was relieved to hear Elsa praise Helen Reid. She was still talking when the door opened. A tall Frenchman walked in, kissed Elsa's hand, and said, "Good morning, my dear, you're looking charming today. Did you have a good rest?"

"Oh, lovely, Henri, thank you so much," Elsa said with a simper. "Henri, I want you to meet one of the greatest women in America. Single-handedly, she is building the north."

I suppressed my giggle.

She introduced me to Henri Bernstein, a French playwright. He had a theatrical face, with white hair and broad gestures. He looked younger than his sixty-five years.

It occurred to me that lying in bed was a well-planned venue suited to help Elsa hold the center of the room. The bedroom was Elsa's theater. People had to group themselves around the bed. But with a professional scene stealer like Bernstein, even Elsa had a difficult time holding her own. Bernstein launched into a discussion of what we should do with Germany after the war. "We've got to lower their standard of living," he proclaimed, "deindustrialize them, do to them what they wanted to do to France."

I did not think much of his plan. We had a vehement argument. He struck me as being emotionally combustible. He was a loyal Frenchman and an ardent de Gaullist. Helen Reid had recently printed nine articles of his that exposed high government officials in France as being Nazi sympathizers.

Elsa picked up the conversation again. "We've got to do something about this country. We've got to do it right away. This is a party-crazy country. The only things that people are interested in are parties."

This was a strange observation from Elsa, the professional party giver.

"But my dear, I'm like you." she said, again turning to me. "I have great faith in the people. They are going to demand good things and we have got to give it to them. Henri, this is a great woman. She is the Jules Verne of the North. She is Mr. Ickes's right-hand man. And Henri, I discovered her in a room. Have you ever heard how I met her?"

Of course he had not.

"Henri, it was at a party at Mrs. Reid's, that wonderful

American." She fluttered her hands and fussed with her robe. "Edward Tomlinson was there. He was a complete fascist, and he had that wide radio audience. He was saying terrible things about de Gaulle. Then he stood up with his champagne glass and said, 'I dare you all to drink with me to General Giraud.'

"Mrs. Reid jumped up and said, 'Of course, we will drink to anyone who will help liberate France.' And then Helen said, "Let us drink to France's number one hero, the great patriot who will lead us to victory, de Gaulle.' Tomlinson almost gagged, but he drank. And then, Henri, I hear Ruth's voice. I turned to Helen and said, 'Who is that girl in the corner? She speaks with such poetry.' And Helen told me who she was."

"Elsa," I asked her, when there was a break in her conversation, "what is the secret of your success?"

She sat up in bed. "Too many people in too small a room. Then you're sure you're in the hottest party in town."

On Friday of that week, I met with Ickes. "What did you think of Elsa Maxwell?" he asked me. Not waiting for my answer, he added, "I never met a woman who talked so much about herself. She certainly isn't much to look at, is she?"

Chapter Nineteen
THE ROAD TO HAVEN

In July 1941, Ion Antonescu, Romania's fascist dictator, began murdering his Jews.

Within a few weeks, his army hauled nearly two hundred thousand Jews out of their homes, shoved them into airless and sealed cattle cars, and then dumped them into concentration camps in Transnistria in northern Romania.

Children were pulled from their mother's arms and squeezed together into squalid orphanages with no caretakers or teachers. Husbands were separated from their wives. In a few months, more than half of the two hundred thousand were dead from starvation, disease, and gunshots. I learned later from survivors that many were hanged on meat hooks like cattle in a slaughterhouse, with signs under their bodies reading "kosher meat."

The Jews were sure the world had forgotten them. They were wrong.

In Switzerland, Jewish leaders knew about the Romanians

in peril. They knew that if they could raise money, they could then bribe the Romanian guards and save the Jews still alive in Transnistria.

The money was to come not from any government and not from U.S. taxpayers' money. It was to be Jewish money, raised from Jewish organizations, especially the American Joint Jewish Distribution Committee, known as the JDC, or the Joint.

But in wartime, in order to send money out of the United States, two government agencies had to sign a simple release—the Treasury Department under Henry Morgenthau Jr. and the State Department under Secretary Cordell Hull. Morgenthau signed immediately. The State Department delayed, delayed, and delayed, as more Jews were dying in the Transnistria camps.

Morgenthau was furious. He sent one of his lawyers, Josiah E. DuBois Jr., to the State Department to find out what was causing the delay. Joe, whom I knew as a bright young lawyer living outside Philadelphia, hurried over to the State Department and asked his friend Donald Hiss, head of Foreign Funds Control, to help him.

The two government officials leafed through cables until Donald discovered a secret message from our minister Leland Harrison in Bern, Switzerland who described the Nazi plan for *Vernichtung,* Annihilation. He quoted startling information from Gerhart Riegner, who was working for the World Jewish Congress.

The two men were shocked reading about the Nazi atrocities in Romania and Poland. But they were even more shocked when they came upon a cable signed by Undersecretary of State Sumner Welles, ordering Harrison not to send any more such cables. The State Department wanted to hear no more of Hitler's atrocities against Jews.

Joe had little slips of paper in his pocket on which he copied the cable of murder and the shocking cable of suppression. He took these little slips of paper with this monumental news to his boss, Secretary Morgenthau, who read them at once.

"I'm physically ill," Morgenthau said. "Write me a report."

Joe spent the next weeks writing a report entitled "Report to the Secretary on the Acquiescence of This Government in the Murder of the Jews." He told how Breckinridge Long, the Assistant Secretary of State in charge of the Visa Division—in effect, in charge of life and death since refugees couldn't enter America without a visa—sent messages to our consulates across Europe and Asia, ordering them, "Delay, delay, delay when Jews come in asking for visas, even if they already have numbers and fit inside the quotas."

Morgenthau brought the report to his friend Franklin Roosevelt on a Sunday morning in January 1944. "Franklin, if these cables become known," Morgenthau explained, "the whole world will know how anti-Semitic our State Department is, and the scandal will extend to the White House."

Six days later, the president created a brand new government agency called the "War Refugee Board," and took the whole job of saving what was left of the Jews of Europe away from Breckinridge Long. Roosevelt tried to get countries like Egypt and governments in North Africa to open refugee camps, to no avail. The director of the WRB, John Paley, suggested the president open a haven in America. The army selected Fort Ontario, a historic army outpost in Oswego, a small river town lying between Syracuse and Rochester, New York, facing Lake Ontario.

Roosevelt turned the whole project over to Secretary Ickes. I rushed to see him.

"Mr. Secretary," I said, "these refugees are going to be terrified—traumatized. Someone needs to fly over and hold their hand."

Ickes looked energized. "You're right," he said. "I'm going to send you."

I held my breath. Now maybe I could do something, anything. Jews were being massacred for the crime of being Jews. Later he told me, "I know this whole thing, saving refugees, means a lot to you, as it does to me. You're going to be my eyes and ears. I'm depending on you."

"Mr. Secretary," I said, "This is the most important assignment of my life."

In my apartment, I called my family. "Mama, I'm leaving in a few days for Europe," I told them. Mama became slightly hysterical. Papa asked quietly, "Will you at least come home so that we can kiss you good-bye?"

"I can't, Pop," I said. "I'm getting briefings and shots for every disease under the sun."

"Well, I'm coming to see you," Mama announced.

She arrived in Washington on a Friday afternoon and immediately demanded to know the truth: Did I really have to go to Europe now? "It's not enough I can't sleep worrying about Irving," she said, "now I won't sleep worrying about you."

To console her, I took her to see the secretary. It was Saturday, July 15, 1944. I was to leave that morning.

Underawed by power, my mother confronted Ickes. "Mr. Secretary, you're sending my daughter to Europe in the middle of the war. How do I know she'll come home safe?"

"Don't worry, mother," he assured her. "She'll come home safe. We're making her a general."

His words consoled her.

He then ordered his chauffeur to drive me to National Airport and then take her to Union Station. At the airport, she kissed me good-bye, and said, "God go with you."

I knew she loved me, though she could never say it.

• • •

U.S. Army planes flew me across the Atlantic to North Africa and finally Naples, where the refugees were waiting aboard the army troopt ransport *Henry Gibbins*. Before boarding the ship, they had signed a promise that they would return to the countries they had come from as soon as the war ended. Instead of the 1,000 that Roosevelt had invited, there were 982 refugees. At the last moment, eighteen people had dropped out and it was too late to find and interrogate eighteen others. Somehow the figure 1,000 has a mystical quality, and so it has remained 1,000 for most of us involved. While we were bringing these 1,000 to America, Adolph Eichmann was in Hungary selecting 550,000 Jews for death in Auschwitz.

In the Bay of Naples, a convoy of twenty-nine ships was assembling; sixteen of them were warships, the others carried cargo and wounded soldiers home. Besides the refugees, our ship carried one thousand bandaged and crippled soldiers from the bloody battles of Anzio and Cassino.

Word came from Roosevelt: "If you are attacked, you must protect the ship of refugees." We were also ordered to protect two ships sailing on each side of us, like bumpers on a car, to guard us from submarines. They were carrying Nazi and Fascist prisoners of war. While in all of World War II, we took in these one thousand refugees plus individuals like Thomas Mann, Lion Feuchtwanger, and Marc Chagall, we also brought in 425,000 Nazi and Fascist POWs.

I have long believed that even if we are born Jewish, Catholic, Protestant, Muslim, or Buddhist, there is a moment in our lives when we truly *become* Jews, Catholics, Protestants, Muslims, or Buddhists—a volitional moment. The moment came for me aboard the *Henry Gibbins*. I spent days and nights walking the deck, taking the refugees' life histories, knowing that as soon as I returned to Washington, I would have to report to Ickes, and through him to Roosevelt. Often I had to stop writing because tears were wiping out the words in my notebook. I realized that everyone aboard the ship was alive through a miracle. But then I realized that every Jew in the world is alive through a miracle.

Standing alone on the blacked-out deck, the wind blowing through my hair, I was trembling with the discovery that from this moment on my life would be forever bound with rescue and survival. I would use words and images, my typewriter and my cameras as my tools. I had to live the story to write it, and not only live it—if it was a story of injustice, I had to fight it.

On the ship, with time pressing against me to collect as many life stories as possible, I continued to live inside of time, trying to help the refugees assuage their fears, and trying to help the wounded soldiers overcome their prejudices against Jews by having our gifted performers and beautiful young women sing for them.

On August 3, 1944, after the thirteen-day crossing we sailed past the Statue of Liberty. The people waved frantically. Some wept. Others held their children up to see this monument to liberty.

"This is the happiest day of my life," an old man said as he took my arm and we leaned against the rail.

"Mine too," I said.

Rabbi Mosco Tzechoval, a thirty-seven-year-old black-bearded refugee from Romania, asked me if he could say a prayer. We made a small space for him on the iron deck. He bent down on the deck and kissed it. Then slowly, he stood up, closed his eyes and recited the Hebrew Prayer of Survival, the Shehecheyanu, thanking the Almighty for having allowed us to survive to this day. We all said it with him, because we, too, had survived.

The rabbi continued. "We must never believe the things the Nazis say about us—that we brought evil upon the earth. We did not. We brought the blessings of the Torah, and truth. The countries that have tried to destroy us have brought evil upon themselves." He looked up at the people and at the Statue of Liberty. "As we enter America, we must speak with one voice, with one heart. We must not live with hatred. We must live with love."

Chapter Twenty
OSWEGO

That evening I took the refugees by train to Oswego. For some, the train was terrifying, evoking memories of standing huddled against one another in cattle cars.

The train pulled into a siding that led directly to the camp. Ahead of us was a fence and barbed wire. Some of the refugees turned on me. They shouted, "We escaped from concentration camps. Now you take us to another camp! How can you do this to us?" I tried to explain that all army camps have fences and barbed wire. I failed to console them.

We entered the camp. The people were given the numbers of the barracks they were to live in, and then lined up to get two towels and a bar of soap. The army, still in charge, gave each refugee an identification card. Hanging on a cord around their necks, the ID read: CASUAL BAGGAGE. It became a sardonic joke among the refugees.

Joe Smart, the director of the camp, led me to the administration building, then down the stairs to a little office with prison bars. "This will be your office," he told me, "while you work with us." It had been the jail when Fort Ontario was filled with soldiers. It was a tiny room with a desk and a chair. Light came through prison bars at the top of the wall. I chuckled—one more jail to add to my list in my imaginary book, *Jails and Outhouses I Have Known.* Later when the administration building became a museum, architects discovered a secret door that led to the street and a secret window. Some jail.

The refugees were under a one-month quarantine when a phone call came from Helen Rogers Reid's secretary, Kay. "Mrs. Reid would like to know if you can come to dinner on Sunday evening. She thinks some of the guests may be helpful to you with the refugees."

How typical of her, I thought. Always thinking of ways to help.

Helen greeted me at the door of her house dressed in a long silk gown. As each guest entered, she introduced me to them. Wendell Wilkie, whom she and Dorothy Thompson had supported for president in 1942, came with his close friend Irita Van Doren, the editor of the *Herald Tribune* book review section. Several correspondents and politicians were there, as well as John Cowles and his wife, Betty. Cowles was the owner of the *Des Moines Register,* the *Minneapolis Tribune,* and *Look* magazine.

Led by Helen at the head of the table, talk at dinner centered on the war. My thoughts were on how these influential, moderate Republican leaders could help create a climate of sympathy for the refugees.

Demitasse was served in the living room, where Helen asked me to describe my journey on the ship with the refugees. I was talking about taking the train to Oswego, when Betty Cowles shouted, "Oswego! That's where I was born. My mother, Florence Bates, is the queen of Oswego. She can open any door for you. I'll call her tonight, but you must go to see her as soon as you are back there."

I called Florence Bates the next day. She became an important leader in the Oswego Advisory Committee, made up of the town's leading citizens. In the community, most people were friendly and eager to help. But there were some, not many, who spread rumors that the refugees were living in luxury. After a month, the quarantine ended. The gates of the camp were flung open. Townspeople entered the barracks, and saw the truth. Their reputedly elegant furniture consisted of an army cot covered with an army blanket, a small wooden table, and two chairs. No one had a private bathroom. The toilet and showers, army fashion, were all clustered together at the end of long hallways. The mess halls were barracks with long tables and wooden chairs. The attitude of the few hostile locals changed.

On Yom Kippur, I sat in the little synagogue singing the prayers that Jews were singing all over the world. As we sang the immortal words, "It is sealed, who shall live and who shall die," many wept and I wept with them remembering the loved ones who had died. The sun set over Lake Ontario as the rabbi blew the ram's horn. The Day of Atonement ended and we were filled with joy. In the mess hall we broke our fast.

Two days after the holidays, Eleanor Roosevelt drove into the camp with her good friend Elinor Morgenthau, the wife of Henry Morgenthau Jr.

The refugees marveled. "The first lady of the world," someone pointed out, "and she comes without police guards, soldiers, or ladies in waiting. In Europe, who would believe this?"

Eleanor went from barrack to barrack, amazed at how young women had turned army quarters into colorful homes with walls covered with pictures from newspapers and magazines. She asked them how they liked America, what their lives were like in the camp, and whether their children were in school. She held their babies, stroked their children's hair, and thanked them for presents they brought her.

She entered the hospital and paused at each bed to talk to the patients. David Levy was a young refugee whose entire family had been killed in Yugoslavia. Eleanor asked, "How do you like America?"

He responded quickly, "I love America, and I love the camp. But I want to go to college."

Eleanor turned to Joe Smart, the camp director, in surprise. "I thought all the young people were in school."

Joe explained that the State Teacher's College (later called SUNY Oswego) wanted to accept some of the students, but they were stymied by rules, regulations, and financial concerns about who would pay for the buses to transport them.

Eleanor extracted a promise from Joe to have the students accepted for the spring term.

David shook her hand. "I have the feeling your coming here today was *beshert*—destiny—like the hand of God."

After lunch with the refugees, we ushered our two guests into the auditorium, where the camp musicians and actors put on a joyous performance for them. Eleanor applauded as Leo Mirkovic, the former premier baritone of the Zagreb National Opera, sang "Figaro" with a passion that shook the walls.

After the performance, Eleanor mounted the stairs to the stage and spoke to the people. "I know you are upset by the fence here," she told them. "But all army camps have such fences. My visit to the shelter," she continued, "has been one of the most wonderful days I have spent."

She looked out at the audience, most of whom understood not one word she said, but all felt her love for them. Later I would tell them she had fought for them for years, trying to overcome the restrictions that had kept millions out, condemned to death by the rigid quotas.

That night she wrote in her newspaper column, "My Day": "Somehow you feel that if there is any compensation for suffering, it must someday bring them something beautiful in return for all the horrors they have lived through."

Chapter Twenty-One

WAR COMES TO THE WALDORF ASTORIA

I n December 1944, Elsa Maxwell invited me to another of her parties at the Waldorf Astoria. The party was in honor of Russell Davenport, a journalist and politician who had broken with his Republican affiliations to work for President Roosevelt's reelection. Elsa told me she had tried to get Secretary Ickes to come, but he hated parties too much.

This party was a wild assortment of star-spangled glitter. The first Mrs. William Randolph Hearst and Mrs. Roy Howard sat talking to each other. Judy Garland attended with her husband, Vincent Minnelli, who kept his arm around her protectively. Dorothy Thompson, the *Herald Tribune*'s fiery columnist, in a short black cocktail dress, moved restlessly around the cocktail lounge where everybody looked at everybody and sipped martinis. At nine o'clock we traipsed into the hotel dining room. Elsa had seated me next to herself, with Russell Davenport at my right, then Dorothy Thompson, and Dorothy "Dolly" Thackrey, the owner and publisher of the

New York Post. Dolly was radiant in a pink-sequined jacket and a large fresh carnation at her throat. She struck me as the kind of woman who would remain young, excited, and enthusiastic about life, even as she aged.

During dinner, Mrs. Thackrey leaned across Elsa and said, "I can't tell you how thrilled I am to meet you here. Of course you know the *Post* did a profile on you about a week ago. It was I who arranged it. I heard you on Bessie Beatty's radio show. I must tell my husband you are here."

She got up, went to the next table and called her husband, Ted Thackrey, the paper's editor-in-chief, to come to our table to meet me.

He shook my hand effusively. "We think the work that you are doing with the refugees is the most valuable and thrilling humanitarian work you could do. Will you let us help you? I know there isn't much that we can do, but we would love to help."

I assured him that I would welcome their help.

"You don't know how much it would mean to me if we can help you," he repeated. "Will you call us the next time you come to New York?"

"It would be my pleasure," I said, moved by his sincerity. Here were the owners of the *New York Post,* the paper that was doing the most courageous job in the country on the refugees, offering to help. I did not know how soon it would happen.

Immediately after ice cream and coffee were served, Elsa stood up. "I am very happy to have you all here, this glittering group out of various social registers." Elsa was wearing the same long black evening dress that I had seen her wear on the rare occasions I had seen her out of bed. It had a red belt and a black-sequined jacket. She once told me that one of her secrets is to put everything she owned in one suitcase. Then she could travel. Her thin, straight black hair was combed roughly back. As usual, she wore no cosmetics. She now called on each of the guests to speak.

Her first speaker was Bennett Cerf, the founder of Random House. He was short with a weak frame and a small face. Smiling broadly he said, "Every author knows that every publisher is a crook. And every publisher knows that every writer is a moron. Since I am both a publisher and an author I can tell you both are true." He then told a dreary joke from his new book about an insane brain specialist.

The next speaker was Russell Davenport, who read from his new book, *My Country*. He chose a passage about the flag and our responsibility to America. He said it had been the favorite of FDR's political opponent, Wendell Wilkie, who had died two months earlier. When Davenport was finished reading, he sat down, bowing his head modestly as we applauded.

Elsa then turned to Dorothy Thompson. "Dorothy, come on, say a few words, won't you?"

Thompson, turning a little red, said from her seat, in a voice that had just the slightest fringe of hysteria to make it really exciting, "Elsa, we are all glad you are back. You add to the gaiety of nations."

"Oh, come on," Elsa said, "Dorothy, tell us what's going to happen to the world?"

Robert Sherwood, the playwright, and speechwriter for FDR, leaned over from his table and whispered to Dorothy, "Don't take any longer than eleven hours."

She stood up and told everyone that Bob Sherwood had just told her to limit herself to eleven hours. "But I am not going to speak about the world. I want to speak about Russell's book. I think he has done something very important. For about thirty years we were ashamed to show emotions. If you said you believed in God, people thought you were being a little silly. The people who had the right feeling didn't dare express it except in the most esoteric terms. Now we are bringing our emotions out into the open. We can be eloquent and not be ashamed."

We applauded enthusiastically, and Mrs. Roy Howard, wife of the publisher of the Scripps-Howard newspaper chain, said loudly to a friend two tables away, "She's right!"

Elsa called on Judy Garland. Judy shrank in her seat, and in a low, breathy voice said, "Elsa, I'm a singer, not a speaker."

Elsa accepted Judy's apology. "We all know how much Judy has contributed to FDR's campaign."

Elsa then introduced me as "the lady of the snows," the title she had given one of her articles. "Do say a few words on Alaska." I started to say a few words about Alaska when she interrupted me, "Oh, Ruth, won't you tell us something about the Oswego refugees?"

I talked about Mathilda Nitsch, the rosy-cheeked Roman Catholic who ran a boardinghouse in Northern Yugoslavia and turned it into an underground station with boats that took over a hundred Jews to safety in Italy, where peasants hid them.

Elsa's guests listened intently so I went on. "The police caught her and put her into an ice storage cellar to make her reveal who helped her. Ice water dripped on her for ten days. 'Ice-cold water,' she told me, 'streamed down my face and head and the ceilings and the walls. Water was in my shoes and over my feet, but I never revealed. Some of my friends were the police themselves who helped me. But I never gave their names. Finally, they sent me to a concentration camp called Ferramonte. Please tell the people of America that I give them a thousand thanks.'"

They laughed at the story of the baby born in a jeep,

bringing a whole group from Bari to our ship. "The soldiers who had helped in the delivery named him 'International Harry' and predicted he would become a brigadier general. His mother refused to let him be circumcised on our ship, and waited until we got to the camp, and all the refugees watched to see how it's done in America. When the proud mother began serving wine to us, I asked her, 'How's the general doing?' His mother, who was already Americanized, said 'What general? He's going to be a doctor.'"

Then I told them the story of the Weinstein orphans, who thought their parents had been murdered in Auschwitz, only to one day receive a message that their mother was alive in Switzerland. Elsa's guests gasped.

By that point I could see several guests blowing their noses, and several women were weeping openly.

"This is just a group of nearly one thousand," I said. "It's nothing when you consider the millions who are still in danger. But they have served an important purpose. They've made this country and other countries aware of our responsibility to refugees. They're more than anonymous people to whom we send evaporated milk; they're human beings who need shoes, underwear, food—commonplace things which are unromantic, yet terribly important."

I ended by saying that the refugees, more than any group I knew, would understand Russell's book.

The audience applauded. Mrs. Thackrey came up to me and said, "People think they have to crack jokes all the time. It is good to awaken their consciences.

"By the way," she added, "I shouldn't ask, but I'm terribly curious. Where did you meet Elsa?"

"At Helen Reid's," I answered innocently.

Upon hearing her rival newspaper woman's name, Mrs.

Thackrey put her head down on the table. "Those are fighting words!"

Dorothy Thompson strode toward me and said, "Beautiful." But the congratulations that meant the most came from a Greek man at the party, "I am a refugee, too, and you made me cry. My family is in Athens and I cannot get food to them. I cannot do anything for them while the fighting goes on. You have a big job to do. Do it well."

The refugees had brought the war to the Waldorf Astoria.

Chapter Twenty-Two
THE END OF THE WAR

One day in early 1945, my friend Louise Herz Leopold called me from her apartment in New York. I had lived with her family when I was an exchange student in Cologne, Germany, in 1931 and 1932. "By any chance, does your brother Irving's army unit serve in Holland?" She asked.

"He's there right now," I answered.

"I'm hoping my parents are alive somewhere in the country. The last time I heard from them was in April of '44. They were hiding in a safe house in Amsterdam. Do you think he could look for them? I'm so worried about them."

I wrote to Irving immediately and described the situation. "She's not hopeful, but she knows that miracles are happening every day. She asked me to tell you that if you do find them to bring them food and anything else they might need. I told her you would know exactly what to do."

Irving searched everywhere. Three months later he still had not found them. He wrote to me on March 12, "Maybe I'll soon make some better contacts."

• • •

April and May of 1945 were heady with victory in Europe yet replete with tragedy at home. On April 12, President Roosevelt died in Hot Springs, Georgia.

Washington was stunned by the news. I sat at my desk at Interior weeping. After a while, I went to the ladies room to wash my face. Two black women were weeping as I entered. We nodded at each other in silence, bonded in our grief. One of the women said slowly, "I feel as if I lost my father. I am sixty years old, and he is the greatest president I ever knew and ever will know. He thought of all the people, of all the little people. He was doing something for everybody all of the time."

A week later, while we were all still in mourning, Ickes called me into his office.

His face was ashen. "I feel very low today," he told me. "I'm in a low frame of mind, have been for several days. I haven't gotten over the shock yet. None of us believed he would die. Just as we never believe in our own death. He was an extension of each one of us. He couldn't die."

There was a long silence. I had learned by now to understand him; to sit quietly while he was tossing things over in his mind.

Finally, he said, "This is the most goddamned job."

"You've got to stay," I said, interpreting his remark to mean he'd like to quit. "You've been fighting the good fight all these years in this people's war, and you can't call it quits now. Nobody can take your place. Who could learn all about coal, and oil, and territories, and Alaska and Puerto Rico in such a short time?"

Ickes looked pensive.

"I don't know what kind of president Truman will make," he said, "I don't know what he thinks about things, who his friends are. Hannegan and Ed Pauley—big city bosses around him—that's not so good."

We talked department business for a while. On each issue we discussed, the strain on him was visible. Finally he exclaimed, "The Division of Territories and Island Possessions is a god-awful mess!" There was another long silence. "I'd like to get drunk," he said matter-of-factly. There was another long pause. He looked unseeingly at his desk, his lips moving a little, his glasses covering his eyes. "I'd like to forget this whole business for a while."

The war was beginning to wind down. Mussolini and his mistress, Clara Patacci, were discovered in the home in which they were hiding at Lake Como. They were captured and shot. On April 28, their bodies were taken to Milan, where they were hung by their heels in a filling station. Two days later on April 30, word spread that Hitler had married Eva Braun, then killed her and committed suicide in their Berlin bunker.

On May 15, 1945, a week after the war ended, my brother Harry called me. "You have to come right home," he told me. "Papa is dying."

I rushed back to Brooklyn. Papa, who had had a stroke, seemed wide awake. I bent over to kiss him.

"It's good you came," he whispered.

Four of Papa's children huddled around his bedside. He smiled at all of us, and then his head dropped. Harry rose, looked at him, and said, "Papa is dead."

Mama, strengthened by the way Eleanor Roosevelt had held herself after FDR's death a few weeks earlier, arranged the entire funeral herself. She called two elderly men who came to the house and sat at Papa's bedside all night praying. His body was brought into the little synagogue, where the rabbi chanted the prayers for the dead, and where the people who loved him stood up and spoke. Mama wept for the first time at the graveside when Papa's body was lowered into the earth and each of us put stones on his coffin.

We knew how much it would have meant to Irving to come home for Papa's funeral. But we felt his presence there. Irving, the closest to Papa in his gentleness and wisdom, wrote me, "I've been in a fog since Papa died."

Six months after Irving began his search for the Herzes, he found a new trail to follow and knocked on the door of a house in Amsterdam.

A startled young woman answered the door.

"I'm looking for Otto and Frieda Herz," Irving said.

"Who are you?" her voice trembled as she stared at the tall, handsome young officer in a captain's uniform.

"I am Ruth Gruber's brother," he replied.

"My God!" she said. "Wait here!"

She ran to the stairs and called, "Uncle Otto! Tanta Frieda! Come down quickly! You have a surprise."

Irving watched two emaciated, elderly people hurry down the wooden staircase.

"Here's Ruth's brother!" the young woman said.

Mama and Papa Herz flung their arms around Irving's neck. Tears ran down their faces. They had no words. Finally Irving said, "Wait here—I will come right back."

As head of a medical unit, he had an army truck at his disposal. He dashed to the PX, loaded it with fresh fruit and vegetables, and dashed back to the Herzes' with the first fresh food they had seen in years. He then cabled Louise to tell her he had found her parents.

After the war, Louise was able to bring Mama and Papa Herz and Louise's mother-in-law to America. It was a bittersweet ending to their ordeal—the young Dutch man who had hidden the Herzes was caught and executed, but the family survived.

Chapter Twenty-Three
PANIC SPREADS

Back at the camp in Oswego, the joy of VE Day soon gave way to depression. Hanging over the refugees' heads was the release they had signed in Naples, promising to return to their countries of origin when the war ended. How could they go back? The countries they were born in were no longer even the same countries. Poland was under Stalin's control and Eastern Europe was in disarray.

A memo came from the War Refugee Board, telling Ickes that they were turning all responsibility for the refugees over to the Interior Department. Ickes was pleased. He asked me to draft a letter to President Truman requesting that we be allowed to close the camp in thirty days, and permitting the refugees to enter the country legally, on sponsored leave. The letter reached the president, but before he could act, Congressman Samuel Dickstein of New York, head of the Subcommittee on Immigration and Naturalization planned to visit the camp, investigate the conditions, and recommend to the full House

Committee whether the refugees should be allowed to stay or leave.

Ickes immediately called me to his office. "Travel with the committee to Oswego. Find out all you can about the members, and help them in any way that you can."

Miriam Weaver-Mendell, chief clerk to the House Committee on Immigration and Naturalization, phoned me.

"Come to my house tonight. I have things to tell you."

When I arrived she told me, "Congressman Dickstein is a good and decent man. He wants you as a witness. If you see things taking a wrong turn, tell him. He will listen to you."

I traveled on the train with the committee and soon discovered that four members were friendly, and two seemed hostile. They were Lowell Stockman of Oregon and Clark Fisher of Texas.

The *New York Post* sent one of its best reporters, Naomi Jolles, to cover the hearings. She was attractive, bright-eyed, and clever. We attended the hearings together, proud of the way the refugees handled themselves. We agreed that she would become friendly with Fisher of Texas, and I should do the same with Stockman of Oregon.

That night, the refugees put on some of their best skits in a variety show for the congressmen. After the program, Stockman and Fisher asked Naomi and me to join them for a drink.

We directed the car to the Whitehorse Inn. It was open, but dark and empty as we entered. Stockman immediately went to the jukebox, dropped some nickels in, and led me onto the empty dance floor. Fisher and Naomi joined us. They were each about five foot five and danced comfortably together. But Stockman, who was over six foot three, towered more than a foot above me. I laughed as we twirled in front of a mirror that showed me barely reaching his solar plexus. It was a good thing he was telling me jokes as we danced so I could guffaw.

The hearings, held at the camp grounds, went so well that the six congressmen voted unanimously to allow the refugees to stay. But a few days later, the full House Immigration and Naturalization Committee met on the Hill. The committee voted not to accept the recommendations of Dickstein's subcommittee. I kept squeezing my hands in despair watching the shenanigans as the committee decided that the Departments of State and Justice "should determine the practicability of returning the refugees to their homeland. If that were not practicable, the attorney general should declare them illegally present, and undertake deportation proceedings."

I returned to the camp to tell the refugees the bad news. Panic spread. The door to America was shut tighter than ever.

Meanwhile, in Europe, with the war over, thousands of survivors of the death camps tried to go back to the towns they were born in, but found everyone was dead. Pogroms broke out in Poland. The survivors, in tattered clothes, left their towns and villages, and returned to Germany, the death land. They entered the American zone of Germany and were put in DP camps by the U.S. Army.

President Harry Truman sent Earl G. Harrison, dean of law at the University of Pennsylvania, to investigate conditions in the DP camps.

Harrison was so shocked by what he found that he wrote a report in which he said, "We appear to be treating Jews as the Nazis treated them, except that we do not exterminate them."

Eisenhower, too, was shocked when he visited the DP camps in Germany and discovered that General George S. Patton was running the camps inhumanely. Eisenhower removed him. That night, Patton wrote in his diary, "Ike was wrong. These people aren't human beings. They're animals."

The bureaucratic war intensified. State, Justice, and even Treasury insisted that the refugees must be sent back to Europe. Some of the refugees were so sure they would be sent back that they bought suitcases for the journey. Ickes, with friends like Eleanor Roosevelt, fought back fiercely.

Ickes sent me back to the camp in November. "See what you can do about raising their morale."

I was startled by the changes in their faces. Some had aged badly, others looked frightened, depressed. Arthur Hirt, a former lawyer in Poland, confronted me.

"You know I was a judge," he said. "Juridically, the paper we signed in Italy doesn't hold. The Poland I would have to go back to is no longer Poland. My part of it is Russia. I don't want to go to Russia. I hate Stalin, I hate the communists. Where should I go?"

The actors and singers put on a performance to cheer me up. They opened with "The Star-Spangled Banner," and then with the camp's own anthem, "Don't Fence Me In." Leo Mirkovic sang the camp's favorite aria from "Figaro." I loved his singing, but this night it only saddened me. Others sang some of my favorite songs, but I barely heard them as questions churned in my mind. "How can we fight this edict? How can we prevent the bureaucrats from sending them out of the country."

I climbed the steps to the stage. Now it was my time to cheer them up. I told them that those of us who loved them were working day and night to keep them in America. "Wherever there is a door," I said, "we will open it." I felt tears forming in my eyes.

"That day at the Statue of Liberty," I continued, "you told

me that 'air in America smells like free air.' Believe me, we want you to breathe it."

Back in Washington, my mentor Ickes taught me how to fight the bureaucracies. "We have to change the climate here. We'll do it by getting strong letters sent to the Hill and the White House. We'll make speeches. I want you to go to New York and get tough editorials from your friends like Helen Reid and Geoffrey Parsons at the *Herald Tribune,* and your friends at *The New York Times* and the *Post.* We'll work on the Washington papers here."

Ickes was a master at confronting cabinet members and bureaucrats. A few weeks later, he said, "Go to New York again. Collect a whole group of leaders, Jewish and non-Jewish, and bring them down here to lobby."

I rushed to New York, assembled the leaders, and brought them to Ickes's office. "Don't waste time with me," Ickes said. "You know where I stand. You go to see Morgenthau at Treasury and Bill O'Dwyer, head of the War Refugee Board, and the people at State and Justice."

Morgenthau, who had been magnificent at the beginning of this project, was firm in his conviction that the refugees must be sent back. "I cannot sleep with my conscience," he insisted, "if I go back on my promise to the dead president."

"I am sure, Mr. Secretary," I urged Morgenthau, "if President Roosevelt were alive today, he would rescind that order. And if he didn't, Eleanor would make him."

On December 5, 1945, State and Justice prepared a letter for Ickes to sign and send to the Senate and House INS committees recommending that the refugees had to be sent back to Europe. Ickes called me to his office and let me read the letter. I shook my head in disbelief. "Did they really expect you would sign such a letter?"

"No, I won't sign it," he told me, his chin quivering. "Instead, I want you to draft a letter to Undersecretary of State Dean Atcheson explaining why we think the refugees must be allowed to stay."

Atcheson responded by inviting the private agencies who were advocates for the refugees to send a delegation to his office at 2 P.M. on December 14. I was asked to join them.

On Friday, the delegates from New York and Philadelphia, wearing heavy winter clothes, arrived in my office. It was an impressive group that included Joseph Chamberlain of Columbia University, Judge Nathan Perlman of the American Jewish Congress, and Bruce Molar, a personal representative of Archbishop Francis Spelman. Each of us carried a briefcase stuffed with documents, letters of support, telegrams, and newspaper articles, the ammunition we hoped would win Atcheson over.

We walked from my office to the State Department and were ushered into Atcheson's huge reception room. His secretary told us that the meeting had been postponed to 5:30. We sat for three hours, trying to keep our spirits from falling.

At 5:30, Atcheson appeared. He apologized for keeping us waiting, asked us for our documentation, and said he would be seeing President Truman the next day. We never had a chance to make our presentation to him or to the president. We were all somber. The men took their trains north and I walked to my apartment, past fake Santa Clauses jingling their bells. President Truman, I thought, is our last hope.

The next evening, I sat in my apartment listening to the radio. All day there had been bulletins announcing a special address by the president that evening. Finally, President Truman's Midwestern voice came into the room. He talked of how the war had dislocated populations.

"The immensity of the problem of Displaced Persons and

refugees," he said, "is almost beyond comprehension." He went on to discuss how countries of Europe, and the United States, were trying to solve the problem, and how he wanted to facilitate the entrance into America of some of these DPs and refugees. He could do it, he said, only by following the present immigration laws. It was obvious to me that the rigid quotas for refugees from Eastern Europe and the Balkans would not be lifted.

I was beginning to lose hope when the tone of his voice suddenly changed. He was speaking of Oswego. He pointed out that surveys revealed that most of the Oswego refugees would be admissible under the present immigration laws of the United States.

Now came the words we longed to hear:

> Under the circumstances, it would be inhumane and wasteful to require these people to go all the way back to Europe, merely for the purpose of applying there for immigration visas and returning to the United States.
>
> Many of them have close relatives, including sons and daughters, who are citizens of the United States, and who have served and are serving honorably in the armed forces of our country.
>
> I am therefore directing the secretary of state and the attorney general to adjust the immigration status of the members of this group who may wish to stay here, in strict accordance with the existing laws and regulations.

In the camp, few people slept that night, hugging and kissing each other. My phone kept ringing. What a Christmas and

Hanukkah present Truman had given us! The word "Free" seemed to dance around my room.

On Monday, Ickes phoned me, "Come up," he said. I hurried to his office, where he shook my hand. "We won," he said, smiling triumphantly. "It was a tough battle, but we won."

"You better go up to the camp again," he continued, "and help the people prepare for their new lives."

Social workers arrived in Oswego with reporters and photographers. Seventy communities asked for our refugees, offering them jobs, housing, and schools for their children. The social workers helped them decide where to go.

On New Year's Eve, the refugees arranged for the greatest celebration of their lives. In the service club, all of us, including the reporters and government officials, joined hands and danced the hora. Suddenly Otto Presser, our Eddie Cantor-like comedian, shouted, "Silence!"

"Now you all know I have been looking for a girl of seventy-five to marry. I found her. She is not seventy-five, but I want you all to know that I have proposed marriage and she has accepted."

We all looked around. Who could he mean?

Presser came toward me, and led me, laughing, into the center of the room. Someone held his hand over my head and "married" us in a mock ceremony. The audience cheered and applauded. Otto Presser spun me around the hall in a Viennese waltz.

The refugees cheered more loudly. Free at last. Free at last.

January 1, 1946, dawned clear and full of hope.

Part 3

THE DP CAMPS AND ISRAEL

Top: Riley Erickson was a Swede with an Irish nickname. **Above:** These teacher homesteaders have married and started a family in Alaska; I encouraged prospective homesteaders to see Alaska as a place to renew their lives. **Right:** Funter Bay, near Juneau, where the Aleuts of the Pribilof Islands were brought before the Japanese attacked the Aleutians.

All photographs are provided courtesy of the author.

Top: A native woman at Hooper Bay with an irrepressible smile. **Above (left and right):** At Point Hope, a Danish archaeologist named Helge Larsen found a human skeleton and a dog. **Right:** I hammered down a mileage post in a village called Platinum.

Top: At a luncheon of the Women's Division of the United Jewish Appeal in the early 1950s, I stood just to the right of our special guest, Eleanor Roosevelt (middle). **Above:** Eleanor and I then listened to a speech by Helen Keller (at the podium on the left), interpreted for us by her companion. **Left:** And then we watched Helen Rogers Reid (on the right), publisher of the New York *Herald Tribune,* receive an award from Adele Rosenwald Levy.

Herald

Copyright, 1943,
New York Tribune Inc.

Mrs. William Brown Meloney, Director of 'This Week', Die

Editor and Writer Led in Many Causes, Founded Herald Tribune Forum

Special to the Herald Tribune

PAWLING, N. Y., June 23.— Mrs. William Brown Meloney, editorial director of "This Week," the Sunday magazine of the New York Herald Tribune and of other American newspapers, died at 4 p. m. today at her home on South Quaker Hill.

Mrs. Meloney, who had been in ill health for several years, left New York on May 18 to rest from the effects of a serious attack of influenza in March.

For several weeks her recovery progressed well, but on Monday complications set in. Her son, William Brown Meloney, novelist, of Washington Square North, New York, and his wife, Rose Franken, author and playwright, were present today when she died. Mrs. Meloney's husband, Colonel William Brown Meloney, died on Dec. 7, 1925.

Requiem high mass will be celebrated at 11 a. m. Friday in St. Patrick's Cathedral, Fifth Avenue and Fiftieth Street, New York.

Mrs. Meloney's Career

Marie Mattingly Meloney—a small and slender woman—poured the energy and enthusiasm of a

Mrs. William Brown Meloney

giant into a wide variety of activities during a career of more than forty years as editor, reporter, author, executive, mother and zealous supporter of good causes.

She started as a green reporter in Washington at the turn of the century when her fields—news gathering and magazine editing— were virtually in the grip of a male monopoly. In two years, at the age of eighteen, she was a successful

(Continued on page 20, column 5

Top left: On June 24, 1943, the *Herald Tribune* placed an obituary of Marie (Missy) Mattingly Meloney on their front page. Missy had founded the *Herald Tribune* Forum, and was a close friend of Helen Rogers Reid. **Top right:** The intake process at Fort Ontario in Oswego, New York, where nearly 1,000 refugees from the Holocaust were quartered, was intimidating for some, but a joy for others. Elsa Neumann, shown to her barrack overlooking Lake Ontario, cried out, "I have a villa by the sea." Note the tag around her neck; it marked the refugees as "casual baggage," a military classification that struck the newcomers as an ironic note. **Bottom right:** Mrs. Hayim Hazan, wife of one of our rabbis, smiling as the army interrogates her. **Bottom left:** Children reading books given them on the *Henry Gibbins,* the ship that brought the refugees to America.

Left: When Eleanor Roosevelt came to the camp, she was delighted that nearly all of our children were able to attend school. But when she learned that the Oswego University [then called the Oswego State Teachers' College] had still not opened its doors, she made sure that our college-age students would soon be allowed to enter. Here, she inspects a barrack with Joe Smart (on her left), director of the camp. (Photo by Branko Kaufman) **Below:** Among the refugees were operatic singers and many talented performers; they put on plays for the other refugees and for the celebrities who came to see the first group of survivors of the greatest evil the world had known.

Above: After WW II, the *New York Post* first and then the New York *Herald Tribune,* sent me to cover the two historic committees that were considering the future of Palestine. In DP camps throughout Germany and Eastern Europe, I met people who were ill and despondent, and others who fervently hoped to emigrate to the Holy Land, proclaiming their wishes with banners: "We all want Palestine as our country!!!"

Above: I saw children in orphanages in Germany whom I secretly wanted to take home with me, though I had to settle for taking their pictures. The sadness and wisdom in their faces—and of all the children I met in my journey from Alaska to Israel—are still with me today nearly fifty years later. **Bottom right:** DPs surround me determined to tell me how they survived and how they would do anything to reach the land of Israel.

Top: In Munich, I found broken streets and broken people. **Above (right and left):** The real hero of the Anglo-American Committee of Inquiry on Palestine was Bartley Crum, a San Francisco lawyer, who brilliantly countered every maneuver that the British delegates made to keep Holocaust survivors out of Palestine. I photographed him with U.S. Army Major Robert Straus (with military cap) who accompanied us through the DP camps in Germany.

Chapter Twenty-Four
OFF TO EUROPE

A few days later, in January 1946, the telephone rang on my desk in Washington. It was Ted Thackrey, editor-in-chief of the *New York Post.*

"President Truman and Clement Attlee in London have set up the Anglo-American Committee of Inquiry on Palestine," he began. "I'd like you to take a leave of absence and cover it for the *Post.*"

My mind began to spin. The Oswego refugees were all safely settled. What an opportunity this could be! I had read how President Truman, shocked by the stories of the deplorable conditions in the DP camps, had asked Britain's Prime Minister Clement Attlee and Foreign Secretary Ernest Bevin to open the doors of Palestine to one hundred thousand DPs.

Attlee and Bevin, who had defeated Churchill in the postwar election, dared not deny Truman's request. Britain's economy was decimated; the country was in tatters—they needed everything America could send them. Their answer was, "Mr. President, let's set up a committee."

In government, committees often do good, but too often they are an easy way to circumvent action. Truman, suspicious, still asked them to spell out what this committee would be like, and what it would do.

Bevin told him, "We can have six Americans and six British. We'll call it the Anglo-American Committee of Inquiry on Palestine." He then detailed how the committee would travel through the DP camps in Germany and Austria, get Jewish and Arab leaders to appear before them, and hold sessions in Palestine and part of the Arab world. Bevin promised Truman that if the committee voted unanimously to allow the DPs into Palestine, he would open the doors to one hundred thousand survivors.

The thought of traveling with this committee and finding a home for so many people was overwhelming.

"I have to ask the boss," I told Thackrey.

Ickes's answer was, "No. As long as I am here, I need you."

I went back to my desk and told Thackrey that I couldn't go.

A few days later, Ickes called me to his office. "It's about that committee," he began.

"You know, Mr. Secretary," I said, "that as long as you need me, I want to stay, but . . ."

"I was wrong," he interrupted. "You must go. You owe it to the Jewish people."

He handed me a letter from Thackrey.

"Dear Mr. Ickes," Thackrey wrote. "I am writing to plead with you to grant a leave of absence to or, if necessary, accept the resignation of your most able assistant, Dr. Ruth Gruber, so that she may undertake for us what seems to me to be a most important and vital mission.

"I am anxious to have Dr. Gruber leave at the earliest possible moment for London to join the Anglo-American Commission created for the purpose of recommending a solution of the problem of stateless and homeless victims of the war, as well as recommending a world policy on Palestine."

My cheeks reddened as I continued reading.

"I am certain you will agree," Thackrey argued, " that Dr. Gruber's qualifications are far superior, in fact, to those of any member of the Commission, and that it is inevitable that at least the American members of the Commission will tend to rely heavily upon her for information and orientation."

Ickes waited until I finished reading the letter. "Thackrey is right," he said. "You are the one to do this job."

I returned to my office and telephoned Helen Reid.

"I've accepted an assignment from the *New York Post,*" I told her, "but I want to be sure it will not jeopardize my relationship with you and with the *Herald Tribune*. I'll be traveling with the Anglo-American Committee of Inquiry on Palestine for the four months they plan to spend in the DP camps of Europe, Palestine, and the Arab world."

"Of course it doesn't jeopardize your relationship with us," she assured me. "This story is one for the *Post* to cover completely. They're the ones who have made the story of the refugees and the DPs their major thrust. What you're doing is a public service. When this assignment is over, you know you can always come back. You're part of our family."

Relieved, I hurried home to Brooklyn to pack and say goodbye to my family. This time Mama had no objections. Her trip to Oswego had helped her understand the work I was doing.

"It's good you're going," she said. "You'll be able to help some of those poor people after what they've gone through. I read about it all the time in the paper."

She stopped talking. Tears ran down her cheeks. I knew she was thinking of her relatives in Poland and Russia. We had not heard one word from them. Were they alive? Had they been burned in the ovens of Auschwitz? Their fate haunted me, as did the fate of the thousands we could have saved and didn't.

Mama wiped her cheek. "Maybe you'll meet Irving," she said, trying to cheer herself up.

"Of course I'll meet him, Mom," I said.

I spent the next day in Dorothy Thackrey's office, a penthouse overlooking the Hudson River in lower Manhattan. The office was furnished like a comfortable living room, with soft armchairs and a fireplace. We were joined by her husband, Ted Thackrey, and Ed Flynn, the executive editor. We discussed the pieces I could write for the *Post* during my trip.

"We'd like you to call our correspondents in London when you get there," Ted told me as he gave me their phone numbers.

A few days later, my family once again assembled to kiss me good-bye.

Traveling abroad during and immediately after the war was complicated. Civilians were not allowed to travel to Europe, and army planes were filled with military and diplomatic officials. But journalists and camera people were given special premission.

On Saturday, January 26, 1946, I left for Europe on an American Airlines plane, a comfortable small vehicle that held thirty-five people. The first leg of the journey was to Gander, Newfoundland, where we refueled, had a meal, and continued to Shannon, Ireland. There, we were told we would have to spend the night in the airport.

I found a telephone and called the *New York Post* office in London.

Sam Boal greeted me on the phone. "We're all waiting to meet you."

"I'll be in London tomorrow," I told him. "Is there anything I can bring you from here?"

"Fresh fruit!" he shouted. "We haven't seen any for months. Anything you can find."

"I'll do my best."

Carrying grocery bags filled with fresh fruit and vegetables I had bought in Shannon, I traveled on to London. Sam had said he would meet me, but he was nowhere in sight, so I taxied to the London office of the *Post*. Shouts of joy filled the room as the staff watched me unload shining red apples, juicy oranges, lush green grapes, and plump, ripe tomatoes. They divided the food up, and sank their teeth into it. Sam, who had missed me, turned up apologizing.

"The first thing I have to do," Sam said, "is drive you over to the army PX and get you outfitted in an army uniform. Correspondents have to wear them in London; you can't walk around as a civilian."

At the PX, I was soon issued an Eisenhower jacket, khaki blouse and tie, a pair of army pants, a skirt, army shoes and stockings, a winter trench coat, and an army cap. A band on my sleeve and cap with the letters "WC," standing for "War Correspondent" brought laughter when I pointed out that "WC" also meant "water closet"—bathroom.

Sam then dropped me at the Royal Empire society, where the committee was meeting. I had missed only one day of the London hearings, and I was to sit through a solid week of them, morning and afternoon. The meetings in London, according to my friends in the press, were little different from the meetings held in Washington. Jewish and Arab leaders, Zionists and anti-Zionists, made speeches discussing the problems of Palestine. Some of the Jewish speakers talked of creating a Jewish state. Through the organization called the Jewish Agency they had already established the machinery of government. Politically, socially, and economically, they described how ready they were for statehood.

The Arab leaders were adamant. They demanded that not a single immigrant be allowed to enter the Holy Land. The committee listened and cross-examined the speakers, always asking if they thought Palestine could hold one hundred thousand refugees.

Robert Nathan, who had worked with the War Production Board, and Oscar Gass, who had worked in the Treasury Department, had both been in Palestine studying and analyzing its problems. These two economists were convinced not only that Palestine could easily absorb one hundred thousand DPs, but that the Arabs who had been coming into Palestine to schools for their children and health for their families would find even better conditions with one hundred thousand Jews in residence.

But there were some questions raised about the need for this nineteenth committee to study Palestine. The most prominent among them was Albert Einstein, who was given a standing ovation. Boldly, he then denounced the committee as a British smoke screen. The British Colonial Office, he said, was using it to gain more time. In a calm voice, he pointed out that he believed the British Colonial Office wanted no solution. In fact, they even helped create discord between the Arabs and Jews. So long as the two peoples fought each other, Britain could rule them. If they stopped fighting, they might realize they could rule themselves.

There were a few great speakers, including a rabbi who cried, "Gentlemen! Do not play politics with the remnants of the Jewish people!" Jewish leaders pointed out that Jews had lived in Palestine since biblical days, made the desert bloom, educated the children, and wiped out the diseases that were still decimating thousands in Arab lands. A communist group argued they believed that the Jews should stay in Europe and help rebuild it. The Arabs said that while they were not opposed to Jews, they were opposed to political Zionists. "Palestine is ours by occupation," they argued. "We don't want western Jews with modern ideas. We don't want skyscrapers. We are happy just as we are."

I listened carefully, watching the committee members as they cross-examined the speakers. I tried to get a sense of who they were and where their sympathies lay. President Truman, with the help of the State Department, had appointed six American members hoping they would open Palestine to at least one hundred thousand DPs. Ernest Bevin, Britain's foreign secretary, had appointed six British men whom he hoped would veto such action.

In 1917, as the Great War raged, Britain wrested Palestine from Turkish control. In the Balfour Declaration, issued the same year, the British declared that they favored the creation of a Jewish National Home in Palestine. As the Allies were carving up the Middle East in 1922, the British were given a mandate by the League of Nations to create a Jewish homeland. By 1939, just as Hitler was sealing off every avenue of escape for Jews trying to leave Europe, Britain passed the infamous "White Paper," which severely restricted Jewish immigration to the territory. If the war had not intervened, the anti-Semitic White Paper might have achieved Bevin's secret and subversive goal, to turn Palestine into an Arab homeland. The White Paper was dismissed as illegal by every country except Pakistan, itself a newly created country.

The committee chairmen were Judge Joseph C. Hutcheson of the fifth circuit court in Houston, Texas, and Sir John E. Singleton, judge of the King's Bench Division of the High Court of Justice in London. It was hard to imagine two more dissimilar men. Both epitomized their respective cultural stereotypes. Hutcheson was warm, effusive, and distinctively Texan. Singleton was cold, reserved, and snobbish. Later I learned that as the committee sailed for Europe on the *Queen Elizabeth* after the Washington hearings, Singleton nicknamed Hutcheson "Texas Joe." Hutcheson in turn nicknamed Singleton "Bottle John," because of the vast quantity of liquor bottles old Singleton was emptying in his cabin. Singleton was also famous as a "hanging judge" in Ireland. I realized that he would probably be the strongest advocate of Bevin's policy. The man who carried out Singleton's orders, the secretary of the committee, was Harold Beeley. Beeley, who was Bevin's chief Arabist and who later became ambassador to Egypt, found ways to control all the daily lives of the members, from transportation to dining. He pretended to be a friend and admirer of mine, even quoting some of my articles back to me. But I knew instinctively that he was my nemesis.

Of all the Americans, the most charismatic was Bartley C. Crum, the liberal San Francisco lawyer. Bart was charming, explosive, immaculately dressed, and movie-star handsome. Though I immediately admired Bart for his freshness and passion, I was also a bit wary of him. He exhibited unusual political versatility. He was a mass of contradictions—a Catholic who leaned to the political left, a Hearst lawyer, and a labor activist.

The most intellectual member was Richard H. S. Crossman, a Labor member of Parliament. Crossman, a former fellow of New College, Oxford, had also served as the assistant editor of the *New Statesman* and the deputy director of psychological warfare in Algiers for the British military. I liked him immediately, and I sensed that of all the British committee members, he might be the strongest supporter of Truman's policy.

The next morning I set out to see what the war had done to London. England on the surface looked brighter and its women more chic than I remembered in 1936 when I had met Virginia Woolf. Piccadilly was still as crowded as ever, with prostitutes, organ grinders, and soldiers; the Lyons Coffee House was as jammed as before. London on the surface looked like London before the war. But beneath the surface, England was recovering slowly from shock, cold, hunger, and exposure to the bombing. Beneath the outer calm were all the gnarled and shattered fibers of postwar British civilization.

I had the feeling Londoners were terribly tired. I listened to conversations as I sipped ersatz coffee, and heard people complaining that America should forget the money and ships we had loaned England. Others complained that American shipments of food and supplies had slowed, and commodities such as powdered eggs, which they adored, were no longer available.

On the first day of February, Lord Morrison, a Labor member of Parliament and British member of the Anglo-American Committee, invited the entire group to lunch, and I was to join them. At this lunch, a scene occurred between the British chairman, John Singleton, and the American chairman, Joseph Hutcheson, which could have come straight from a Marx Brothers' movie. Early in the trip, Hutcheson had informed Singleton that while they were in London, he would like to have fresh milk every day. Singleton had assured him that he would arrange it. They had been in London for several days, and Hutcheson had yet to see his milk.

In a loud voice, Hutcheson announced to Lord Morrison, "Thank you for this great meal. I hope maybe you can get me the milk that Sir John promised me days ago." Everyone at the table laughed, except Sir John, who sputtered something inaudible. Lord Morrison called a waiter, and within minutes, a glass pitcher of milk appeared. The scene climaxed when Judge Hutcheson, so eager to get at his treasured milk, cut his hand on the pitcher. Later, when I interviewed Hutcheson in Jerusalem, he told me, "I knew from that minute that Singleton wasn't to be trusted."

During the week in London I had my first lunch with Bart Crum, at the Café Royal. The restaurant was dark and the food awful, but Crum was engaging. He was youthful and confiding, with definite opinions—a reporter's dream.

"The British press has practically boycotted the sessions of the committee," he said angrily. "It's almost a complete blackout of news. Some papers claim that there is no interest here in London; some argue that silence itself is an editorial policy."

"How are the British treating you?" I asked him.

He had ordered food, but let it stand. He took a long sip of his drink.

"I have the feeling they are spying on me." He leaned close and lowered his voice. "Even on the *Queen Elizabeth,* I was advised not to send anything confidential on the ship's radio. Once I got to London, Harold Beeley designated one of the British members to room with me. I keep a diary, and the last thing I want is for somebody to read it. It took three days before I got my own room. Even then, I was told to be careful what I said on the telephone."

Crum's confidence in telling me made me feel less suspicious of him. It was obvious that the British had already singled him out as a potential troublemaker.

London was freezing. My hotel room had no central heating.

I would get into bed with my hot water bottle at my ice cold feet and pile all my winter clothes on top of me. Then with the little typewriter on my lap, I would type up notes. By this time, I was getting into full swing, typing stories until two or three in the morning, often waking by 5 A.M. I was tired, but felt good. It was tangible work, and I cared deeply about the stories I was cabling, making sure they were sharp and clear to told their truth.

Chapter Twenty-Five

"WE WANT TO GO,
WE MUST GO,
WE WILL GO TO PALESTINE"

A t 7 A.M. on Monday, February 4, 1946, I boarded the channel boat to sail for France. Arriving in Paris by 6:40 that night, I checked into the Hotel Rafael. Once settled, I telephoned my colleagues at the *Post,* who came right over and took me to a delicious French dinner and on to the Pigalle nightclub, where we stayed until one in the morning.

Paris had all the adrenaline of a great city. The air was luminous, the outdoor cafés full of coffee drinkers and observers, the Champs Elysees overflowing with strollers, the Bois de Boulogne smelling sweetly of the woods. Politically, Paris was seething again. The communists held the majority and were expected to capture more of the government in the next election. Everyone was debating the new constitution, which was soon to be voted upon by the people.

I attended a political review called the "Dix Heures" at a nightclub. The experience was disturbing because I realized how little the war had changed France. It could have been France of 1938. The country was recovering materially and physically, but anti-Semitism, extreme nationalism, and minority oppression persisted. Populist movements were growing all over Europe, especially east of the Danube, but on the whole, Europe recovering from war was tired, sick, and disillusioned. As usual, the evil for which the war was fought lived after it.

On February 6, I left Paris with the committee. On the train ride I found that destruction lay everywhere along the route. London had been heavily damaged, with whole sections in rubble, but Paris had been an open city with no fighting. The only damage had been done in the last days before liberation, mostly by Frenchmen inside the city. The train plowed through the ravaged countryside on our way to Germany.

Occupied Germany was divided into four zones: American, British, French, and Russian. After London, the committee had split into subcommittees. One went to Berlin, another to Switzerland, another to the French zone, and the fourth, with which I traveled, went to the American zone in Frankfurt. Each group was to hold its own meetings and interviews, then they would all reassemble in Vienna.

Gerold Frank, of the Overseas News Agency, and I were the only reporters attached to any of the subcommittees. Ours was composed of Bartley Crum, Sir Frederick Leggett, and Richard Crossman. Crossman, however, was sick with pneumonia in England and did not join us until Vienna.

Standing at the train window, Bart confided his deep concern about the committee's British members and about the British chairman, John Singleton.

"What exactly are you worried about?" I asked him.

"Their hostility and their anti-Semitism. They're out to kill the Jewish Agency," he said. "And creating the Jewish state is entirely out of the question for them. Our own James Mac-Donald is going to fight for the state, but he's using it just as his bargaining point. He knows he won't get it, but he'll be able to get more concessions by holding out for the state."

I knew Sir Frederick, standing close by, was listening, but I couldn't make Bart speak lower.

"How do you think we should handle the press from now on?" he asked me. "We don't want a news blackout like the one in London."

"I think you should be frank," I suggested. "Tell the other committee members that it would be poor public relations to try to keep reporters away from the story. It will turn them into bloodhounds."

At Frankfurt, we were met at the railroad station by Major Robert K. Strauss, who represented the American military government in Frankfurt. He piled us into cars and took us to the huge, undamaged I. G. Farben building, headquarters for the United States Forces European Theatre (USFET).

When the army takes over, it takes over completely and we were in its hands now. Every moment was planned. The subcommittee met Federal Judge Simon H. Rifkind of New York, advisor to General McNarney, liaison general on Jewish Affairs. Judge Rifkind and Major Strauss brought us up to date on the refugee situation in Frankfurt, the center of the American zone.

By this time, Gerold Frank and I were no longer treated as press, but almost as members of the committee. In fact, we were liaisons between the committee and reporters based in each town along the way. In Frankfurt, all the reporters were housed at the Park Hotel. As soon as Gerold and I entered, the reporters gathered around, wanting stories for their papers.

"After a while I left the other reporters and went back to my room. Using the telephone, I spent six hours searching for my brother Irving, who was stationed somewhere nearby in the American zone. I had nearly given up, when I asked a bellhop for help. He located Irving immediately and I was thrilled to hear Irving's voice. He told me he was with the "mobile operating dental unit" attached to the 7th Army. "Every day I'm in a different place," he said. "Yesterday, it was the hospital; today it was an army camp. But don't worry, from now on I'll find you wherever you are."

Early the next morning, Irving knocked on my door. I saw the loneliness in his eyes begin to give way to joy as we hugged. We spent the morning walking around the city together.

"I'm going to hold on to you!" I said, grabbing his arm. "I don't want to lose you."

"You won't," he said. "I'm the head of my own medical unit. I can decide where I want to go each day."

"But you're a dentist," I said.

"Here, I'm treated like an M.D.," he replied.

Frankfurt itself was crippled. Buildings were smashed, houses were transparent and naked; I saw the sky through gaping holes that were once bedrooms where people had slept. There were almost no shops open. I couldn't figure out where people bought food or clothing. Everyone walked around with a knapsack, in which the Germans stowed whatever crumbs they found.

That evening one of the generals invited James McDonald and me to dinner. I changed from my army uniform to a velvet suit—I had discovered velvet did not crease, or if it did, a little steam straightened it out—and wore one of the hats I had managed to put in my baggage. During dinner one of the army officers with us boasted, "There is not a single American who was in combat who is still here in Germany tonight."

At that moment Irving entered the dining room.

"You're wrong," I said. "Meet my brother, Captain Gruber. He was in the Battle of the Bulge, he fought with Patton, a Nazi bomb fell on one of the barracks he was sleeping in and killed the officer beside him. He's still here, and my hope is that you will send him home to his bride."

"Come join us," the officer said, making no promise. It would be months before Irving was finally allowed to go home.

The next day, I joined Crum and Leggett on a visit to the Zeilsheim Displaced Persons Camp. As we drove into the German countryside, the terrible destruction tore at me. I gasped at each hole and my throat caught and tightened with horror. But soon, after hearing stories of Nazi atrocities, I began to look upon the blasted buildings and say, "That's good. That's fine. It's just what they deserved."

Europe was on its knees, and Jews were trying to escape from it like a burning movie set. Poland was a human corridor through which hundreds of thousands poured into the American zone.

In Zeilsheim, we saw a banner that read:

"We Want to Go! We Have to Go! We Will Go to Palestine!"

Another read, *"We Jewish children will no more stay on this bloody ground where our parents were destroyed! We will go home to Palestine!"*

Three thousand men, women, and children stood outside the administration building in a driving rain, singing *Hatikvah*—the song of hope. Their voices rang high as they sang, "We will not let then kill us anymore on this bloody ground. We will go to the Land of Israel!"

The demonstrations were peaceful and orderly, but absolutely purposeful. The people knew just what they wanted.

One of the more passionate ones came up to me and said, "We ought to have a demonstration against this committee, against these spies of British imperialism. Why must they still come here at this late date? Don't they know what we want? We are tired of living on this bloody soil. Let us go to Palestine."

At Zeilsheim, three thousand people were living in 215 little buildings, which had been built by I. G. Farben to house Russian slave laborers. Every room was used for sleeping, including the kitchens. Much of the time, there were four to five people in one room, sometimes as many as eight or nine. People were always shifting around, trying to find better quarters.

I walked around the camp, talking to the children and taking photos of them. Some of the twelve- and thirteen-year-old children acted as parents for the younger ones. Some looked terrified, while others clung to me. A few held their arms out; I embraced them. I wished I could have taken some home with me, especially those whose eyes still spoke of the murders they had seen.

While communists and socialists and Catholic centrists were battling for political power in the capitols of Europe, Zionism was the philosophy, the passion, and the goal, unanimous by acclimation, of almost all the Jews in the camps.

Carefully I studied a poll taken in Zeilsheim that asked two questions: (1) If there were unlimited immigration all over the world, where would you want to go? and (2) Under the present situation, where would you want to go? It then listed other countries in the world, ending with Palestine. The poll showed that 85 percent of the people answered both questions "Palestine." Of 18,311 DPs, 17,712 wanted to go to Palestine. Most of them refused to name any country as second choice; in one camp of 1,000, about 500 named as their second choice the crematorium. In Austria, the DPs' second choice was the Danube. The United Nations Rescue and Rehabilitation Agency (UNRRA) director, Sylvan Nathan, whom I met later in New York living two blocks from my apartment, summed up the poll: "In my opinion, this entire camp wants to go to Palestine."*

At one point, Bart began talking to a little man wearing a red sweater. "Why do you want a Jewish state?" he asked.

The little man glared at Bart. "What kind of question is that?" he said angrily. "We are Jews. The Americans have America. The English have England. The French have France. We want a Jewish state. Palestine is the only state in which we can order our own existence. If you tell me that we are not Jews, but Germans or Poles or Austrians, I will give you the testimony of six million dead."

---

* Since Palestine was the name used in the 1940s for the land now called Israel, I have continued to call it Palestine throughout this book.

Chapter Twenty-Six
COLLECTING STORIES FROM DPS

From Zeilsheim, our subcommittee drove to nearby Stuttgart, a city to which many German Jewish Holocaust victims had returned. Unlike the DPs in Zeilsheim, they were not waiting to emigrate. Here they were trying to rebuild their lives on German soil. Stuttgart was even more depressing than Zeilsheim. The people were scratching around the rubble, searching for their past. In the DP camps, the Zionists had courage and hope; they were fighting for a goal. But these people had nothing. That evening we interviewed members of the community at a local hotel.

Bart observed that these people were still stunned. "They can't believe that this thing happened to them in a country where they were so assimilated. It's how my little daughter, Patti, would react if I suddenly slapped her in the face."

Each day a new realization of terror took hold of me; I tried to grasp one terrible fact at a time. First there was the shock of learning about the gas chambers. We were among the first to see them. Then there was the shock of finding that so many children had died. Women and children had been the first exterminated in the Nazis' careful plan. Even though living in Washington I had known a little more about the Holocaust than many Americans, I was still shocked by the extent of the horror.

The next day we visited Leipheim, a DP camp between Stuttgart and Munich. Irving joined us as we entered the former Luftwaffe barracks, which had been badly blasted by air raids. There had been a hunger strike the Sunday before we arrived; the people had presented the United Nations Rescue and Relief Agency with thirteen conditions. UNRRA had accepted all the conditions. Then, according to my informants in the camp, the agency proceeded to ignore all but one: They dismissed Germans from the kitchen.

Inside the camp, the administration seemed stiff and scared. During the hearings, a young man testified.

"Everyone has talked of political things," he began. "I want to say something about myself.

"I concluded my course at the university and was not allowed to work," he explained. "I am twenty-eight and have never eaten bread earned with my own hands. This shirt I wear is from the Red Cross. The sweater is from a sister in Palestine. After the war I returned to my village in Poland. Of seven thousand persons, only two small children have survived. My entire family was slaughtered. I have only two sisters left— both are in Palestine."

After talking to the director and the community representatives, we walked through the barracks. We saw little children from Hungarian orphanages who were now living a clean, simple, communal life, preparing for kibbutz life in Palestine. Bart picked up a little girl who was totally deaf and dumb from the shock of seeing her parents murdered by the Nazis. Another little girl was deaf because her father had hidden her in an ice cold river when the Nazis came, and kept her there until they left.

Just as we were about to go, our hearts heavy with the tragedy of these little children now clustered around us, a thirteen-year-old boy spoke up passionately. "After six years of all this war, it's hard to sit and wait when you know there's one piece of land where you can work and you won't be called all these names they call you in Europe."

Bart tried to console him, "You must remember the significance of the Jewish religion is faith. We are trying our best for you. You must have faith in us and be patient."

"We're tired of patience," the boy's voice rang with fervent conviction. "It's impossible for us to be patient. We've come through these six years and lived through what we have lived through, and now we don't have the right to live freely and live out the years that we have."

"The last part of the journey," Crum still tried to comfort him, "is always the longest."

"How is it possible that we are still here?" the boy continued. "We've seen so many children burned in the crematoriums. For all people the war has ended. But not for us, because we are still living on somebody else's bread. We can earn our own bread."

Crum had no answer.

A tiny girl who looked about seven but who, I later learned, was twelve cried out, "Every people has a land. We have no land. They've promised us ever since I was old enough to understand that we can have a land. I hope you not only promise us, but you will fulfill the promise."

Sir Frederick Leggett feared that the persuasiveness of the testimony might lead him to betray Bevin. "We have to be careful ourselves, or we'll all become Zionists."

We left Leipheim in the late afternoon and drove on to Munich. It was full of blasted buildings; the old landmarks were still there, but their backs were broken. The city was as crippled as its demobilized men.

Munich was our headquarters. From there, we visited Funk Caserne, a transient camp and center for refugees from Poland and the Balkans. It was a former German artillery barracks, overcrowded and uncomfortable, but the spirit of these DPs was a bit more hopeful.

A young woman who had just entered the camp was interviewed as other young people sat around her. She was pretty with shrewd brown eyes and a determined face.

"I am twenty-two," she said. "I was born in Poland. My father died at the hands of the Germans. He died in the Ukraine. I was told he was tortured."

"How did you come here from Poland?" Bart asked her.

"I traveled a very difficult journey. I came through Czechoslovakia. There were people who guided us along the way. They were Zionists."

"Were you alone?" we asked.

"No. There were twelve young men and women. We assembled on the route. There was one girl who was the leader. I was looking for people who were preparing to go to Palestine, because I wanted to go home. I mean, I wanted to go to Palestine, and I understood that through Germany we could get to Palestine."

She took a deep breath. "Everyone is leaving Poland. There is not one man in Poland who wants to remain. So many have fallen victim to the Polish Jew-haters."

"What did you bring to Germany?" she was asked.

"I stand before you with all that I have."

Her arms were empty and she carried no luggage.

"We have heard," one interviewer said, "that Polish people are coming with gold, silver, and large fortunes."

The young people exploded into laughter. The girl held up her bare hands. "Look at our rings," she said ironically. "What's the use of pursuing wealth? Another Hitler will come and take it away. The important thing was not to let anyone take our honor and our dignity."

Later at dinner, I realized how much Palestine was getting into our blood when Sir Frederick Leggett began to mumble over his glass of wine, *"Wir gehen nach Palestina"*—"We're going to Palestine."

Two leaders in the Central Committee of Liberated Jews in Munich left indelible impressions upon me. One was a young man in his twenties: Leon Retter was a dynamo who let no obstacles get in his way when it came to caring for the DPs pouring into Munich. If it were necessary, he would take on the whole American army. When he discovered that most of the children entering the camps had no shoes, he confiscated a truckload of shoes, enough to fit all the children.

The other leader was a thirty-four-year-old intense physician, Dr. Zalman Grinberg. He mesmerized the committee with the story of how he had saved his baby in the ghetto of Kovno, Lithuania. Learning that the Nazis were planning to snatch up all the children and ship them to the ovens in Auschwitz, he had injected a drug into his baby that made him sleep, and hid him in a barrel. He then smuggled him out of the ghetto and handed him over to an old friend who was not Jewish.

Dr. Grinberg was in a cattle car being transferred from Dachau to Auschwitz when U.S. planes bombed the train. In the turmoil, with Nazi soldiers shooting at them, he led his fellow prisoners to a village, where he found his way to the office of the mayor.

"I am the medical representative of the International Red Cross," he said boldly, drawing himself up in his tattered rags. "I have people with me who need medicine, food, clothing, and shelter. I request you to turn over to me all necessary facilities at once."

"Sorry," the mayor shrugged. "I have no facilities."

Thinking fast, he threatened, "The Americans are twenty-four hours behind me. I assure you that if you do not give me what I demand, you will be hanging by the neck five minutes after they arrive."

Suddenly through the window came the roar of a motorcyclist, who yelled, "The Americans are coming! The Americans are coming!"

The mayor bowed to Dr. Grinberg. "Please sit down," he said and fled.

Dr. Grinberg took over the few medical facilities in the village. Later, he founded a hospital in Munich. His wife and baby son both survived and were now with him.

He spent the next hour describing the state of mind of the DPs.

"In the concentration camps we had ample time to think. Thinking was the one privilege the Nazis could not rob from us. What could we have done to avoid falling under the Nazi steamroller before the war? Each one of us regretted that he had not gone to Palestine. We imagined the entire world would join to help us, to comfort us, to console us, and to help us reach our goal."

I had to stop writing to wipe tears from my face. No one interrupted him.

"Now," he continued in a steady voice, "months after liberation, we have come to realize, with such agony of spirit and soul as I cannot describe to you, that the world has built an even higher barbed wire fence around Palestine. They do not want to let us enter into that land."

"Why is it," he asked, "that after we have been dying for six years as Jews, the world doesn't want to let us live as Jews? To me personally, fate was kind in saving the life of my four-and-a half-year-old son. Now I must consider in what language and in what way I shall bring up my son. I am thinking about the language in which my father, grandfather, and my ancestors prayed. We had a national religion, but we had no home of our own, and that is the basis of our tragedy. My eyes, they have seen children and old people murdered, gassed, strangled. My eyes, when they look upon my child alive today, force me to a higher resolution that this child must grow up in the country to which my ancestors desired to go and speak the language in which they prayed."

Sir Frederick's eyes were red. He could take no more. He stood up ready to leave. "I am emotionally exhausted. I beg you, Dr. Grinberg and gentlemen, to believe in the good intentions of our governments. We do not intend to delay, we do not intend to retard the justice which you deserve. We shall give you that to which you are entitled as soon as certain preliminary steps are taken."

Another day we visited a farm that had been owned and run by Julius Streicher, publisher of the vitriolic anti-Semitic newspaper, *Der Stürmer*. Twenty-four teenagers in blue shorts and shirts were now working the farm. A British UNRRA worker was training them for kibbutz life in Palestine. The teenagers took us through the main house, where they showed us photos of Dr. Chaim Weizmann, who would later become Israel's first president, and Theodor Herzl, the father of Zionism, who had dreamed of a Jewish homeland. Herzl's motto was, "If you will it, it is no dream."

One of the teenagers explained that they had taken down Hitler's photograph and hung these two in its place.

"As these photographs have changed," he said, "So we are changing, and becoming new human beings."

We were waving good-bye when the young people suddenly joined hands and began dancing the hora and singing "*Artza Alainu*"—"We are going up to the Land!"

Two girls hurried toward Sir Frederick and pulled him into the ring.

"I say," he protested. "Look here!"

But the girls were strong, and soon he was dancing as vigorously as they were.

In the army car on the way back to the hotel, energized by his dancing, he made a startling announcement.

"The problem with the Germans," he explained, "are their feather quilts. No nation that struggles all night trying to keep that thing on their bodies, and keep their feet warm, couldn't be anything but mad all the next day."

Trying to control my laughter, I told him it was an astonishing discovery.

"A more astonishing discovery," he continued with a twinkle in his voice, "is that the German women are just like their feather quilts—not satisfactory."

Chapter Twenty-Seven

NUREMBERG. TRIAL OF THE CENTURY

To sit in the same courtroom with Hermann Goering.

To look at the face of Heinrich Himmler and wonder how many victims he had murdered.

To watch Julius Streicher smirk at the justices in their black robes, knowing he was the editor of the polemical Nazi rag *Der Stürmer.*

Freezing cold, I wrapped my army winter coat tightly around me. I clutched Irving's hand. We shook our heads in disbelief. Bart and Sir Frederick leaned forward, completely absorbed.

We were in Nuremberg, the once beautiful medieval city. The city Hitler had made the center of the Nazi party. Here his pet cinematographer, Leni Riefenstahl, made his Nazi rallies immortal. Here he kept his right arm rigid in the air, as thousands of brown uniformed Nazi soldiers carrying blood-red flags with black swastikas shouted "Heil Hitler."

Nuremberg. How fitting that Hitler's chief lieutenants should be on trial here. It was in 1935, just two years after he came to power, that Hitler had promulgated the "Nuremberg Laws." Jews were deprived of their citizenship, their professions, their jobs. "Marriages between Jews and Germans (or) cognate blood are forbidden," the laws proclaimed. Soon Jews could no longer attend the universities; children could no longer go to school.

We had left Munich on Monday, February 10, 1946, and driven through the snow-covered countryside to Nuremberg. If I had thought the devastation in Frankfurt and Munich, with their charred rubble and broken buildings, were the worst I would ever see, I was wrong. Nuremberg was demolished. Everything that I remembered from my days as an exchange student—the *Glockenspiel,* the town clock with its moving figures and chimes, the churches and steeples, the old stone walls—were all gone. It was as if our bombers had known it was Hitler's favorite city.

Bart Crum, Sir Frederick Leggett, Judge Simon Rifkind, Gerold Frank, Irving, and I arrived at the courthouse before the session opened. I looked around the crowded courtroom. It was small and brightly lit. Photographers were everywhere. Interpreters sat in little booths, with headsets, preparing to translate the testimony simultaneously from German into English, French, and Russian. Every word spoken in this historic trial was to be recorded. Nations were to be held accountable for their war crimes. Legally, the world was facing a new order.

Promptly at ten the marshall of the court shouted, *"Achtung!"*—"Attention!" I felt my body tense as if the curtain were going up at the premier of a play for which the whole world would be the audience. The International Military Tribunal was about to begin. Soldiers led the once powerful men of the Third Reich into the dock. We saw them being marched through a roped corridor. Several wore their military uniforms, and even in this short corridor, their high boots goose-stepped insolently just as they had once goose-stepped through the concentration camps we had toured.

Hermann Goering, head of the Luftwaffe, strode in pompously, as if *he* had won the war. Deprived of all his medals, he was still dressed in his blue Luftwaffe uniform. He was the first in line, as if whoever arranged the order in the dock wanted to emphasize that he had been the closest to Hitler.

Second in line, though he had been third in the hierarchy of Hitler's aides, was Rudolf Hess. Toward the end of the war, he had flown to Scotland without informing Hitler. When Churchill heard of this overture, he was disbelieving, and then astonished. Stalin suspected that it was a plot. It was only at the trial that the truth was revealed: Hess had hoped to negotiate peace with Britain. His face was drawn; a thousand-yard stare into an abyss.

Joachim von Ribbentrop, the former ambassador to Britain and then the Nazi foreign minister, once elegant, haughty, and powerful, slid into his chair, a broken man.

Field Marshall Wilhelm Keitel looked no more like an army general than one of the peasants we had passed on the road.

Alfred Rosenberg, who, like Goering, had plundered art treasures across Europe from museums and Jewish homes, had written books as the philosopher of the Nazi party. He tried to walk upright but in the end slumped into his chair.

Probably the most hated of all the twenty-one defendants was Julius Streicher. It was at Streicher's farm where Sir Frederick had danced the hora. Older than most of the others, looking like a seedy Bowery flophouse bum, Streicher sat brazenly trying to stare down the judges who held his fate in their hands.

Fritz Sauckel, who had commanded slave labor, kept edging away from Streicher as if he gave off a foul odor.

Dr. Hjalmar H. G. Schacht, Hitler's chief economic advisor, who had helped him become chancellor—and whose factories had continued working throughout the war with Jewish slave labor—had a constant look of outrage on his face, as if he were demanding to know why he was in the dock with these criminals.

Franz von Papen, who had become vice chancellor and premier of Prussia, seemed to be confident that no court could find him guilty.

Among the others were Albert Speer, Hitler's chief architect and later armament minister. Just months before, Speer had turned on the Führer. Armed with poison gas, he attempted to kill Hitler and several other prominent Third Reich leaders by injecting the gas into a bunker in Berlin. When his plans were foiled, he confessed his guilt to Hitler, and expected to be executed, but Hitler, already preparing for his own death with his bride, oddly forgave him.

Some were missing from the dock: Heinrich Himmler, the head of the SS and the man—other than Hitler—most responsible for murdering innocent people, had tried to escape justice by disguising himself in the uniform of an army private and a patch over one eye. He was caught, and when he realized he would be executed he swallowed the potassium cyanide he carried with him in his flight. Dr. Robert Ley, chief of the *Arbeit's Front* (Worker's Front), also cheated the executioners. He hanged himself before the trial could begin.

Sitting together in the dock, these men who had always seemed too big, too threatening in the newsreels, now sat picking their noses and ears and scratching their chins. Goering, well fed with ruddy cheeks, didn't seem particularly interested in the proceedings. He kept yawning like one of the lions he kept as pets. Hess, in a natty gray suit, sat self-consciously immobile. Keitel dozed. Streicher chewed gum ceaselessly.

Field Marshall Friedrich Paulus—who in June 1941 had led Operation Barbarossa, the campaign against Russia, and was defeated at Stalingrad—was on the stand as a witness for the prosecution.

Bart shifted toward me in his chair. "Imagine Paulus turning against Hitler," he whispered. As Paulus was being cross-examined by the defense counsel, Bart whispered again. "The defense attorneys are over cross-examining the witness. They're ruining their case."

At eleven, a messenger approached Bart. "We're showing a film of the concentration camps," the young man explained. "We think you'd like to see it."

Bart nodded. Our group followed the messenger into a small room. The lights were turned off; the picture began. Of the eighty thousand feet of film shot by Allied troops, one thousand had been selected for the trial. We saw the unbelievable horrors for the first time: cattle trains unloading hundreds of emaciated, terrified people. Some were sent instantly to be gassed and burned, and others to barracks to become slave laborers. They would be burned after they had worked themselves nearly to death. I clapped my hand over my mouth when I saw the faces of the women and children.

After seeing human bodies being pushed by tractors and naked skeletons heaped upon each other in rows, we went back to the courtroom. The trial had now changed for me. I saw the men in the dock as beasts, and I could have killed each one myself. I whispered to Irving, "I wish we were closer and I had a gun."

We were invited to lunch with some of the judges and were then taken on a tour of the jail. We found Goering, Hess, Streicher, and the others resting in sparkling clean cells and eating a hearty lunch provided under the Geneva Convention. Their laundry was done for them, and their suits, even the faded ones, were pressed every day. They had at their disposal a library of eight hundred books. The deluxe way these murderers were living, compared with the deplorable conditions in the DP camps, struck me with sickening force.

The trial lasted for months. On October 16, 1946, having been found guilty, ten of the defendants were hanged in the Nuremberg prison. Among them were Rosenberg, Keitel, Ribbentrop, and Streicher. Goering, sentenced to hang, took potassium cyanide two hours before soldiers came to take him to the execution chamber. The three top leaders, Hitler, Himmler, and Goering, had each committed suicide.

Von Papen and Schacht were later given prison sentences by the German de-Nazification courts, but they were set free almost immediately. Albert Speer was given only twenty years in prison. He later told his story in a best-selling book.

While we were in Nuremberg, Bart told me of documents he had read about the ex-Grand Mufti of Jerusalem. They showed how the Mufti had conspired with Hitler in pushing for the annihilation of the Jews. The agreement with the Nazis gave the Mufti an expense account of fifty thousand reichsmarks per month for his activities in fighting common enemies—the Allies and the Jews. In total, the Mufti received 1,800,000 reichsmarks from Nazi leaders.

"I read," Bart told me, "how the Mufti insisted to the Nazi leaders that no matter what deals might be paid to ransom some of the Jews, no Jews would be permitted into Palestine."

We left the trial of the century bound for Prague.

Top: I was photographed with George Polk of CBS, alongside two Arab guards at the Allenby Bridge at the border with Jordan. A year later Polk was found murdered in Greece, only hours after the State of Israel was born. **Above:** Cyprus: The refugees froze in winter and roasted in the Mediterranean summer. In three years, fifty-two thousand Holocaust survivors were imprisoned in these aluminum huts and tents.

All photographs are provided courtesy of the author.

Top: The refugees have painted the hated swastika over the British Union Jack. They were defying the British Empire; they were defying the whole world. *Life* magazine made this image their Photo of the Week. The picture, to the best of my knowledge, has never been published in Britain.
Above: Port de Bouc, France: I find 1500 refugees from the *Exodus 1947* aboard the prison ship *Runnymede Park*. When I went below deck, I was blinded by the near-darkness and unsure if my camera could capture their courage and their agony. The desperate people pleaded with me to tell their story to the world.

Top (left and right): A jubilant parade of Israeli fighters after the victorious War of Independence in 1948 when Israel defeated five Arab states. **Above:** Golda Meir's oratory was powerful and possessed of inexorable logic; she marshaled her words like soldiers on parade. (Photo by Philip Michaels)

Top: Young pioneers developing the Negev Desert. **Above:** Eilat was barely a development town when I went there in 1949; it has become a gleaming city on the Red Sea.

As soon as the War of Independence ended, rivers of Jews poured into Israel from North Africa, Yemen, Iraq, and Romania. I covered each of these migrations. **Top:** At dawn I interviewed a Romanian Jew carrying his child as they arrived at Ben-Gurion Airport. **Middle Left:** Romanian families descend to the airport. **Middle Right:** Yemenite Jews, helped by a nurse, prepare to fly to Israel in an American plane. **Bottom (left and right):** Others remain in Aden a few days resting from their dangerous journey fleeing Yemen.

Top: President Harry S. Truman directs the scene in his office, chuckles, and suggests he hold an earlier autographed photo he had given me and tells me to hold my book, *Israel Today: Land of Many Nations,* which had just been published. **Above:** Eleanor Roosevelt also chuckles as we both hold my next book, *Puerto Rico: Island of Promise.*

Above: I met Philip Michaels in Puerto Rico while covering the inauguration of the territory's first elected governor, Luis Muñoz Marin. The governor introduced the two of us during a picnic on the sands of Luquillo Beach.

Above: Phil, a social activist, devoted his life to helping people in need. We married in 1951.

Chapter Twenty-Eight
ARRESTED BY CZECH POLICE

At the palatial American Embassy in Prague, Ambassador Laurence Steinhardt shook my hand. "Glad to meet you," he said. "You resigned today."

I was stunned. "How would you know that here in Prague?"

"The news came over the air. Ickes announced to President Truman that he was resigning and was accepting your letter of resignation."

I was surprised at how relieved I felt. Working for Ickes was exciting, but now I was free to go back to my first love, journalism. The five years I had worked for the Secretary had taught me the uses of power in government, now I was ready to return to words and images as instruments of power.

Bart seemed to understand what I was thinking. "I guess you're really a free woman now."

Bart, Sir Frederick, and Judge Rifkind began asking Steinhardt about anti-Semitism. Steinhardt explained that Prague, under President Eduard Benes, was a cosmopolitan city with very little anti-Semitism. It was Slovakia that was notorious for its hatred of Jews.

After two days, the subcommittee left with a huge military convoy, flying the American flag. We were on our way to Vienna. Fortunately, our cars were heated against the winter cold. I sat next to Judge Rifkind, who wanted me to tell him of my work in Alaska.

About noon, as we approached the Czech-Austrian border town of Halanky, we were abruptly halted by the Czech police.

"Give us all your papers!" a policeman demanded.

"What is this about?" Bart asked defiantly.

They gave us no answer, but ordered us out of the cars. We stood for a while, defenseless against the frigid weather.

Czech soldiers approached, pointing their rifles at us as if we were criminals. They finally opened the door of a small one-room building and ordered us in. It was obviously a border guard house, another jail in my roster of jails with nothing in it but hard straight chairs and a potbellied stove. No water, no sink, no bathroom. The soldiers followed us with their rifles still menacing us. There, we were told we were under arrest.

Bart and Judge Rifkind were outraged.

"What right do you have to arrest us," Rifkind demanded.

"We have orders," the Czech officer said. "We had a message from Prague to arrest your convoy."

"That's ridiculous," Bart argued. "Call the American ambassador. Call President Benes. We've just been with all your top leaders."

He repeated, "We were told to stop and arrest a military convoy traveling with one woman."

I felt everyone's eyes looking at me.

"This is all highly illegal," Judge Rifkind insisted. "Where is your telephone?"

The officer seemed impressed. "We have a field telephone, but it only reaches across the field."

"Get me to a telephone that works," Bart said, incensed. "I want to call Prague."

"Yes, lead us to a telephone!" Sir Frederick chorused, excitedly opening the door and stepping out. Bart joined him. Through the small jail window I could see the officer telling them to wait, that he would search for a phone. I watched them shivering and rubbing their hands together impatiently. Finally, the officer returned and the three men disappeared.

Inside the jail, a Czech policeman began plying me with strong hot tea. After an hour or so Bart, Sir Frederick, and the Czech head policeman returned.

"I tried to reach Ambassador Steinhardt, but I couldn't get him," Bart said with frustration. "I tried the Czech minister for foreign affairs, the minister of war, and the minister of the interior. I couldn't get any of them, but everyone I talked to, I told how we had been unlawfully arrested."

After six hours during which they kept bringing me hot tea, the head policeman returned.

"I've finally gotten a message," he said. "We made a mistake. Yours was the wrong convoy. People in another convoy tried to steal some documents for the Nuremberg trials."

With our word of honor to the police that we had removed no documents from Czechoslovakia, the police finally let us back into our cars and waved our military convoy through the border.

The delay made it necessary for us to drive in the darkness through the Soviet zone of occupation, the most dangerous of the four military zones. Deserters, former Nazis, and armed White Russians roamed the area, attacking travelers and stripping them of their possessions. Just a few days before, a busload of people being repatriated to Vienna had been held up. The people were forced onto the road, and all their property, together with their bus, was stolen.

In the car I tried to take notes as we sped through the night. I had learned how to write in the dark in Siberian gold mines, holding my left thumb in place on the page to guide my right hand.

Unfortunately, the countless cups of hot tea I had imbibed began to assert themselves. I knew that if I didn't attend to the problem, disaster was impending.

Embarrassed, I finally explained my predicament to my friends. We were in the lead car when Bart told all the cars of the convoy behind us to halt. Bart sent a soldier to find a tree in the snow-covered terrain. Slowly, the soldier then took my hand and led me through the darkness across a field to a tree, where I finally found relief.

The convoy moved on to Vienna.

Still in the Soviet zone, one of the cars in our cavalcade broke down. Again we all stopped while several of the GI drivers used their strong bodies to push the car until it started again.

We arrived in Vienna long after midnight. Several of us checked into the Weisser Hahn (White Rooster), where all the other foreign correspondents were housed. Several greeted us: "Where were you? We've been waiting for you for hours."

Chapter Twenty-Nine
A PRESS BLACKOUT IN VIENNA

Vienna was to be the meeting place for the four sub-committees of the Anglo-American Committee of Inquiry on Palestine. Since we were the first to arrive, and the only subcommittee who had visited the DP camps in the American zone of Germany, Bart suggested that Gerold Frank and I hold a press conference.

We invited all the foreign correspondents to meet us in a Jewish community hall. Bart immediately began speaking: "Unless the camps of Europe are cleaned out and the Jews are allowed to reestablish their lives, there will be mass suicides or the Jews will fight their way to Palestine." He proposed his own answer to the problem. "Clean out the camps and settlements and let the people go where they want to go and reestablish their lives." Bart repeated, "Unless they're able to go, there will be mass suicides."

The words "mass suicide" hit the correspondents like a bombshell. The two words were splashed across the front of nearly every newspaper. The *New York Post* headlined my story quoting Crum, "Fears Suicide of Camp Jews in Europe." Bart's words struck chords around the world. It was becoming clear how desperate the survivors of the Holocaust were to end their homelessness.

Sir Frederick took no part in the press conference, but as reporters crowded around him later, he agreed with Crum and emphasized that nearly every DP we spoke with wanted to go to Palestine.

The press conference made Crum the best-known member of the committee. I wrote in my journal, "Crum has become internationally famous."

A few hours later, the nine other members of the committee arrived in Vienna. Pandemonium. The two chairmen, Sir John Singleton and Judge Joseph Hutcheson, were seething when they learned of Crum's successful press briefing. They decided to call their own press conference. It was packed with reporters. We kept asking each other what these two angry chairmen might do to Crum. We learned immediately.

Sir John opened the press conference with a written document announcing that from this moment on, only the two chairmen were to talk to journalists. Henceforth, all journalists would be barred from attending any hearings given not only by Mr. Crum or any other member of the committee, but by representatives of UNRRA, the U.S. Army, the Austrian government, the American Jewish Joint Distribution Committee, and the Red Cross. Until this conference, we had been free to question any official we wanted. Now we were being punished with a total blackout of our news-gathering efforts.

Reporters rarely take censorship lightly. As soon as Singleton asked for questions, a reporter raised his hand and shouted, "Mr. Crum—how many Jews in Czechoslovakia want to go to Palestine?"

Sir John reached out, grabbed Crum's arm, pushed him down and prevented him from speaking. "I don't think," Sir John said coldly, "it's going to help anyone if you have an *individual* member of the committee giving their views."

After the conference, the reporters returned to the Weisser Hahn, milling around angrily. However, the restrictive policy quickly boomeranged. Nearly every one of us wrote a piece condemning Singleton's brazen efforts to silence Crum. The next day, the hearings were open again, and Crum, as usual, spoke his mind.

Each day, the tension between Bart and Sir John Singleton grew stronger. Bart kept arguing for an interim report that would immediately open Palestine to thirty thousand DPs. Singleton, who I learned had not visited a single DP camp while he traveled with his subcommittee to Berlin, was adamantly against an interim report. He was determined that the doors of Palestine should remain shut until the committee wrote its final report.

Life in the press camp was a world of intrigue and romance. At times it seemed as if every American correspondent had a Hungarian mistress. Every morning they would sneak their girlfriends into the hotel to give them breakfast. For some it was the only good meal of the day. Our hotel, the Weisser Hahn, was reputed to have the only powdered eggs in Vienna. The reporters and their mistresses gobbled the eggs as if the world's best chefs had prepared them. To me the powdered eggs tasted like sawdust. Sometimes the reporters showed me the lacy lingerie they were buying on the black market for their mistresses.

"What is it about these Hungarian women?" I queried one correspondent. Certainly the women were beautiful. Some were even reputed to have been mistresses of Goering and other Nazi henchmen.

Vienna before the war had been a city of operas and symphonies, of beer-drinking bacchanalias and mouth-watering pastries, of afternoon teas and lilting Strauss waltzes. It was now a kaleidoscope of postwar poverty, hunger, and hopelessness. Only the black market thrived. Men and women walked furtively on rubble-strewn streets at dusk and dawn, searching for unavailable items, especially food. Old women hovered in doorways, or looked through their apartment peepholes for police while black market deals transpired in their houses. The price for cigarettes at the army PX was $20.00 a carton in Austrian shillings.

We spent a week in Vienna interviewing both DPs and Jewish and Arab leaders. One thing was clear: Anti-Semitism was alive and well throughout Europe. Amid the anti-Semitic propaganda then flourishing was one persistent rumor that America was sending over former German Jews to govern Germany and Austria in a military government.

"These people are taking revenge on us," a local Viennese man told me one day in a tearoom. "We want Christian Americans." Another slogan spreading through Germany and Austria was, "We should have burned all the Jews." If anything, I found the Austrians I interviewed more anti-Semitic than the Germans.

I realized in Vienna that the weeks I had spent in Germany and Austria were strengthening a process that had begun in Oswego. Before this journey I always knew I was a Jew. As a child I had an Orthodox background and strong faith. But at thirteen, rebellious against everything, I became an agnostic.

My experience with the Oswego refugees reignited my faith. Here, most of the DPs were Jews, and hearing their stories, I felt my identity as a Jew reasserting itself with more urgency and direction than ever. Like many assimilated American Jews,

I was riddled with guilt and haunted by the thought of what we might have done to have prevented some of the slaughter.

I spent the next three days in the Vienna airport waiting for a plane to Cairo, and the nights in a transient hotel that had been built by the Luftwaffe. In the days of waiting, I tried to live calmly inside of time by typing up my feelings and by recording what the committee had accomplished thus far. Bart had lost his battle for an interim report, but he was winning the media battle. He was doing a magnificent and heroic job and had the entire American press behind him. But the fight within the committee, led by Singleton, was gaining intensity. I felt as if I were in the middle of a pulp magazine cliffhanger. The real story of intrigue would start when the committee, now leaving Europe, arrived in the Middle East.

Chapter Thirty

FROM CAIRO TO JERUSALEM

It was evening when I arrived in Cairo and stretched out on a large, comfortable bed in the Continental Hotel.

With no hearings scheduled for the next day, I visited the pyramids and the sphinx in the March heat. I was excited to see these legendary monuments, and even sat on a camel for a quick, humpty-dumpty ride. I then explored the city, which I found depressing and disappointing. The rich lived in modern, white stucco villas, but the majority of the people were still in the Middle Ages. Cairo's poor lived in extreme poverty in mud huts, forced to beg constantly, and plagued with disease. I walked along the long, wide, and clean Nile, while its banks were filled with barefoot people in rags.

The heat, the dirt, and the endless armies of ragged children pleading for money began to affect me. I felt emotionally tense, with a nagging sensation that something was about to go wrong.

That evening, a wealthy pasha invited the committee to

dinner at his home. We drove through a huge courtyard filled with prancing white horses, and then entered the palace. Arab waiters escorted us to long tables overflowing with exotic foods. I have a delicate stomach, and the sight of the glassy-eyed sheep's heads made me queasy. I pretended to nibble, while watching belly dancers wiggle and gyrate around us.

After dinner we moved into a handsomely decorated ballroom. As an orchestra struck up some familiar American tunes, a young Arab man in western clothing asked me to dance. He ushered me onto the ballroom floor and as we spun around, he talked politics.

"You know, Arabs aren't really anti-Semitic," he assured me.

"That's nice to hear," I said politely.

"We're cousins," he insisted. "We're Semites together."

I danced with several other young men before collapsing into a chair against the wall. One of the young men pulled a chair up next to mine. We began talking and eventually got on the subject of women and education in Egypt.

"We have many women in our university here," he informed me. "In fact, Ibn Saud, the leader of Saudi Arabia, visited Cairo recently and insisted on seeing the university. Before he arrived, he sent word demanding that no women be present for his visit. It irritated a lot of us. One of my professors was so mad that he stood up at a faculty meeting and said, 'This is terrible. We have permitted girls to attend the university. Why should we bar them now because Ibn Saud is coming?'"

The next day, the committee opened its hearings at the Mena House Hotel, next to the Pyramids. Bart was furious when he learned that no Egyptian Jews were to testify. Determined to find out why, he learned that the chief rabbi in Cairo had warned Jewish leaders not to appear. The rabbi had been advised by King Farouk that it would be in the best interests of the Jews not to testify, not even to be seen in the committee room.

At the entrance to the Mena House, I was stopped by soldiers in red fezes who looked menacing when they ordered me to show my press card. I had obtained one earlier that morning. They looked a little friendlier once I drew it from my purse, and they allowed me to enter.

Several Arab speakers gave testimony. Azzam Pasha, the secretary general of the Arab League, declared from the start that all Arabs were passionately opposed to westernization. "The Jew who returns to Palestine," he said, "has returned without the intention to be an Easterner. Our old cousin is coming back with imperialistic ideas—with revolutionary ideas of all sorts."

Dr. Mohammed Fadel Jamali, the director general for the Iraqi Ministry of Foreign Affairs, argued that Palestine was actually part of Iraq.

Hassan el Banna, a leader of the ultraconservative Muslim Brotherhood, demanded that the committee invite the ex-Mufti of Jerusalem to appear before them. The Muslim Brotherhood was dedicated to fight for Islam against the infidel West. Bart later described el Banna's interview in his book, *Behind the Silken Curtain:* "A dark bearded, heavy-set figure with glowing eyes, speaking Arabic. . . . el Banna insisted that the Koran mentioned Christians and Muslims favorably, but had nothing good to say about Jews."

The message of each of the Arab speakers was clear: Any Jewish immigration into Palestine would be seen as an act of war.

The hearings ended. Our next stop would be Jerusalem.

I joined several of the committee on the *Orient Express.* Within a few minutes, we were in the desert. Bedouin women, wrapped in black gowns, their faces hidden, sat on the sand. Some were cooking over open fires; some were nursing their babies; others sat, unsmiling, watching the train pass by. The men sat idly in clusters, smoking *narghiles,* their colorful pipes. Children were romping in the sand. It seemed to me I could have seen this picture four thousand years earlier.

I felt my heart beating as we crossed the border into the Holy Land. Everything in it seemed hallowed—the hills of Judea, the camels and goats, the melancholy Arab music that drifted into the train.

We descended from the train in Lod. While the committee members were whisked away, I was greeted by Richard Mowrer, the Jerusalem correspondent of the *New York Post.* He piled me into his car and soon we were speeding along a quiet, empty road.

"The atmosphere in Jerusalem is pretty tense right now," Mowrer told me.

"It was also pretty tense in Cairo when we left," I told him. "We were warned that the committee might run into trouble on its trip by train. We were told to take a plane, but we refused."

"What were you supposed to be afraid of?" Mowrer asked.

"Of being blown up," I explained.

"By whom?"

"Of course the British say by Jews," I said, "but the Arab leaders are the ones who keep threatening to go to war."

Mowrer laughed. "According to *Kol Israel*"—the clandestine radio of the Jewish resistance movement—"the committee has nothing to fear from them. I heard the announcer say last night, 'It's not the intention of any Jewish organization to injure members of the committee.'"

We sat in silence for a few minutes. "What's Jerusalem like?" I asked, breaking the silence.

"Well," Mowrer said thoughtfully, "you'll find a lot of barbed wire fences, entanglements, and dragon's teeth, those orange pilings they line the roads with to bar people from passing. Soldiers are everywhere. You see a lot of them around the King David Hotel, where the committee is staying. With the curfew, we're forced to stay indoors so much that the song you hear most often in Jerusalem just now is 'Don't Fence Me In.'"

I chuckled. This had also been the anthem of the Oswego refugees, which they had sung for Eleanor Roosevelt, and for me each time I came to the camp.

We were driving up to Jerusalem. *Jerusalem.* I murmured the Hebrew name to myself : *Yeru-shalayim.* Shalom. Peace. I could see myself back in Brooklyn at the Passover seder—Papa, looking like a prophet in his white caftan, at the head of the table, with all of us around him. We were all smiling as he ended the most joyous festival of the year with the words, "Next year in Jerusalem."

The ancient city stretched before us, small houses of yellow stone, perched on narrow streets. Signs hung everywhere in three languages—English, Hebrew, and Arabic. Jerusalem was a patchwork of British, Arab, and Jewish human beings.

Mowrer drove me to the Jasmine Pension, an inn where several foreign correspondents were staying. Most of the twelve committee members were at the famous King David Hotel.

The next day, Cecil Holme, the British public information officer, called me. "The army has asked me to tell you that correspondents are not allowed to wear their war uniforms and are liable to be picked up and put in jail." Was this protocol or was he blind? Had he not seen that I was wearing a white summer dress? Anyway, in Cairo I had already packed my war correspondent's uniform in my suitcase.

I spent the evening with Bart and Dick Crossman in the

Regence Restaurant of the King David Hotel. Crossman, who had been ill in London, was now a full-fledged member of Bart's subcommittee.

Bart was disturbed. "We're under constant protective custody," he said bitterly. "We're not allowed to go anywhere without armed guards. The CID—the Counter Intelligence Division—are with us constantly. They're guarding us, but I'm pretty sure at the same time they're trying to find out just what we're doing every minute of the day."

"Can you evade them?" I asked him.

"Whenever I can," he said. "I've already met with some Arabs—" He stopped and looked up. I followed his gaze. Two Arab glamour girls, dressed in black velvet gowns that could have come from a Paris boutique, approached Crossman. They leaned seductively over his shoulder.

"May we join you?" they asked.

Without waiting for an answer, they pulled up chairs on either side of him. Bart whispered to me, "The Arab League has set this up."

I whispered back. "I recognize one of them. She was on the train with us from Cairo. But look," I teased him, "they have eyes only for Crossman. I guess they've written you off."

Bart shrugged his shoulders. "I guess I'm not their type."

"I think they gave up on you as an American. Their leaders probably think they can make headway with an Englishman."

The two women were still at the table when I stood up. "It's been quite a day. I'm going back to my hotel."

It was long past the 6 P.M. curfew, and soldiers and police kept asking for my ID card at every block.

The next morning British tanks, police, and soldiers guarded the streets around the YMCA, where the committee hearings were about to begin. All of us had to show our ID cards. The men were frisked; the women were told to open their purses.

The members of the committee sat at a semicircular table with the witnesses sitting in rows of chairs in front of them. Photographers, newsreel cameramen, foreign correspondents, and British and American diplomats filled the hall. No visitors were permitted into the hearings. The citizens of Jerusalem turned their radios on every hour on the hour to hear what was happening.

The meetings opened at 9 A.M., with the first speaker, Dr. Chaim Weizmann. He was over seventy and frail, with a small beard and piercing eyes. Born in 1874, he had been raised in a shtetl called Motol, near Minsk. "Motol," he wrote later in his autobiography, *Trial and Error,* "was situated in one of the darkest and most forlorn corners of the Pale of Settlement, that prison house created by Czarist Russia." But Dr. Weizmann was no shtetl Jew. His was a well-to-do family with acres of land, chickens, two cows, a vegetable garden, a few fruit trees, and a house with seven rooms and a kitchen. It was in Minsk that he attended school, grew from boyhood into manhood, became a chemist, and a Zionist dreaming of a homeland in Palestine. With wit and wisdom, with elegance and a mastery of science and diplomacy, he became a leader who developed friendships with the statesmen of the world.

He had notes before him, but he spoke extemporaneously. "We are listening," I jotted in my notebook, "to a man whose place in history is guaranteed." His eloquence found its stride and even some of the Arabs seemed to have tears in their eyes.

"We warned you gentlemen," he spoke sorrowfully. "We warned you. We told you the first flames that licked at the synagogues of Berlin would set fire, in time, to all the world."

Asked about the Arabs, he said, "I stand ready at any time,

any day, any moment, to meet with them and discuss the future of the country."

The shadow of anti-Semitism fell across the YMCA, as it had throughout our journey. Judge Hutcheson asked him, "Dr. Weizman, can you explain to me how the establishment of a Jewish state would eliminate anti-Semitism?"

"Sir," he answered, "we appear to the gentiles to be a peculiar people, suspended between heaven and earth. We must explain ourselves, and every person who does that is condemned in advance."

Wilfred P. Crick, a British member of the committee, who was economic advisor to the Midland Bank, asked the aging witness, "You said Palestine was a ghetto sealed off by the British. Wouldn't you say that was a rather picturesque overstatement?"

"I wouldn't say it was picturesque," Weizmann replied coolly. "I would say it's tragic." He described his resentment at being unable to walk freely in Jerusalem. "What would you say if you couldn't move about the land freely?" Weizmann then noted that Jerusalem had become a prison, a walled-in city like the Warsaw ghetto.

Crick persisted, "Some of us have been to the Warsaw ghetto and we are shocked to hear you compare Palestine with the Warsaw ghetto."

"That shouldn't shock you," Weizmann countered. "What should shock you is the fact that under the British flag, there is discrimination against those people to whom a solemn promise was given under the mandate for a national home."

Dr. Weizmann finished his testimony and stood up. Obviously weary, but always the courtly gentleman, he bowed to each member of the committee.

The chief spokesman for the Arab position was Jamal Effendi

Husseini, who had been in Iraq, plotting against the British during the war who later arrested him. He represented the Arab Higher Committee, a self-appointed role. He even questioned the right of the committee to exist, let alone decide a future "relating to the Arabs' natural rights in their own country."

I was shocked when I heard him bring in the name of the ex-Mufti of Jerusalem, Hitler's Arab partner. "We find ourselves in this inquiry deprived of the presence of our first leader, the Grand Mufti, for whom we can accept no substitute."

With a flourish of his hands, he defined who the Arabs are. "One nation. One people who speak one language and have a historic background. One future. One aspiration. One aim in the world—such are the Arabs."

Husseini ended his presentation demanding that the British mandate be abrogated, that all Jewish immigration be stopped, and that no more land be sold to Jews. I realized he was defining an ephemeral Arab state in Palestine.

The day ended. The doors of the YMCA, which had been tightly shut, were flung open. I hurried out to find the terrace filled with people eager to catch a glimpse of the committee that held the future in their hands.

Some of the reporters rushed to the post office to cable their stories. Local newspapers were completely censored before they went to press. We foreign correspondents were told by the British that there was no censorship of us, but we knew that every word we cabled to our papers was carefully scrutinized. We also knew that our telephone lines were tapped.

A few days later, David Ben-Gurion opened the afternoon session. While the West honored Dr. Weizmann as the representative of the Jewish community, the Jews of Palestine regarded David Ben-Gurion as their true leader, the George Washington and Moses of the future state.

Short, square, and dynamic with keen blue eyes and a halo of white hair encircling his head, Ben-Gurion was the symbol of the new spirit of Palestine. He was a man with a plough in one hand and a gun in the other. Born in Plonsk, Poland, in 1886, at twenty he had sailed to Palestine where he began his new life as a farmer. He soon made his mark as a tough labor leader and a passionate visionary. He appeared before the committee as the chairman of the Executive of the Jewish Agency, the shadow government the Jews had created under the nose of the British Mandatory Government.

"What do you mean," the committee asked him, "when you speak of a Jewish state?"

"By a Jewish state we mean independence," he spoke in the voice of a leader whose fists were always clamped, ready for action. "We mean Jewish safety and security. Complete independence as for any other free people."

The next speaker, Golda Meir, appeared before the committee in her usual dark skirt and white blouse, with a cigarette between the fingers of her right hand. Her face, devoid of makeup, was strong, her lips tight with tension. Still, she had a warm motherly look, with long dark hair laced with silver and pulled into a bun at the nape of her neck.

Her story as an American woman who became a leader in the male-dominated society of the Middle East intrigued me. She was born in Kiev in 1898, escaped from pogroms when she was five, landed in Milwaukee, and became a schoolteacher. Rebelling against her mother's strict control, she ran to Denver to live with her sister, Shayna, who inspired her to become a socialist and a Zionist. In Denver, she fell in love with Morris Meyerson and agreed to marry him on the condition that he join her and go to Palestine. They arrived in 1921, settled in a *moshav,* a colony of farmers, where Golda worked washing other people's clothes. But her idealism and her passion for the land caught the attention of leading politicians, who molded her, Pygmalion fashion, into an articulate leader. It was she, not the tough labor activists around her, who was chosen to speak, representing the Histadrut—the powerful General Federation of Labor in Palestine. I watched the Arabs shift uncomfortably in their chairs as she spoke.

"I am authorized," she said, "on behalf of the close to one hundred and sixty thousand members of the Histadrut to state here, in the clearest terms, that there is nothing that Jewish labor is not prepared to do in this country in order to receive large masses of Jewish immigrants, with no limitation and no conditions whatsoever."

That evening, George Polk of CBS, whom I knew as a neighbor in Washington, shared a cab with me to attend a party at the home of Gershon Agronsky, the American editor of the *Palestine Post*. After the long day of jotting notes and sending a cable off to the paper, I relaxed in the car, breathing in the clean fresh air of Jerusalem.

"George," I said, "look at this night sky. And look at the stars. They're so close I can almost touch them."

"I see them," George said, when he was suddenly stopped by a blinding light flashing in our faces.

A soldier opened the car door. "Your identity cards," he demanded.

He turned his searchlight on our ID cards first, and then on our driver's card, checking our photos to make sure they matched our faces. "Move on," he said.

The driver's hands were shaking. "You never know what to expect from these guys at night They can just pull you out of your car, lock you up, no charges, no trial, and you're in jail for a couple of months, or a couple of years."

Gershon Agronsky greeted us at the door. Behind him the party was in full swing. "How often were you stopped?" he asked.

"Once. But it was a bit scary," George told him

"Now you know," Gershon said with typical chutzpah, "what our life is like in Jerusalem."

Chapter Thirty-One
"IF I FORGET THEE, O JERUSALEM"

Early one morning I cornered Judge Joseph Hutcheson in the lobby of the King David Hotel.

"Judge Hutcheson," I began, "I would like to write a profile of you for my paper."

"Let me think it over," he said.

"I'll be waiting right here," I pointed to a comfortable-looking armchair.

It was no hardship to sit in this lobby. This was where you saw nearly everybody who made front page news—Jewish and Arab leaders, foreign diplomats, army officers, and sometimes even the British high commissioner for Palestine, Lt. Gen. Sir Alan Gordon Cunningham, whose mission was to execute orders given him by the Colonial Office and Foreign Office in London.

I was jotting down questions to ask the judge when Clifton Daniels of the *New York Times,* dapper, elegant, and competitive, stopped in front or me.

"I just did you a favor," he smiled broadly.

'That's a comradely thing to do."

"I just left Judge Hutcheson. He told me, 'There's a lady from the *New York Post* who wants to do a profile on me. What do you think?'"

"And what did you tell him? That you thought he should give you his time instead?"

Cliff laughed. "I told him, 'You'd better let her do it. If you don't, she'll do one anyway and do a terrible job on you.'"

Late that afternoon Judge Hutcheson invited me to his hotel room. "We can speak up here without interruptions," he explained. Twilight was settling over the Old City, giving a warm glow to the room where the judge talked in rich, biblical phrases.

Raised in the strictest Presbyterian tradition, Judge Hutcheson was a perfect fusion of a deeply religious Southerner, who now found himself in the Land of the Bible. He was a small-town Oliver Wendell Holmes, who had become a judge and the mayor of Houston. He knew the Bible as well as a preacher, and quoted it constantly. "At night when I pray," he told me, "I say: 'Dear God, please don't put me in a place where my weakness won't let me act the man.'"

In the accents of Virginia and Texas he continued, "If I could state my philosophy of life to you according to all the things I have done, I would say that in me there's an absolutely stout feeling that justice is right and injustice is wrong. St. Paul's dictum, 'Quench not the spirit, despise not prophesying, prove all things, hold fast that which is good,' is good enough for me or any man who calls himself a liberal."

He stopped talking and looked through the door of his terrace at the Old City below. He was a slender man with blue eyes framed in light tortoise-shell glasses. His white hair was soft and cut short, his lips were firmly set, as befit a judge.

He told me he was born on October 19, 1879, in Houston, and he adored his father, a captain in the Confederate army. His mother died when he was a baby, and he was raised by two maiden aunts who instilled him with virtue, fear of the devil, and love of the Bible. His father scolded him for being so good; he preferred a rough-riding, two-fisted son, not a sissy. "You've made me unhappier than any of my children," his father told him. "You've given me more worry than any of the others."

"Why is that, Father?" he asked.

"Because you're always so good," came the reply. "I want to know that you can take care of yourself."

Around the committee he was known as "Texas Joe," the name Sir John had fastened on him. He told me that he loved children and that he had a son, a daughter, and one grandchild. I once caught him window shopping in Jerusalem; he was watching some children who were looking longingly into a window filled with candy. He asked the children if he could buy some candy for them. They nodded their heads, so he gave them each half a dollar.

Throughout the interview he kept saying, "Please don't make me out to be a sissy. My wife keeps strict watch over me, and I'm afraid of what she's going to say to all of this."

"I wouldn't worry," I assured him.

The next day, Hutcheson searched for me in the lobby of the King David Hotel and gave me a typewritten sheet with an evaluation of his work that he himself had written. It was too good to be true—I couldn't resist. I wrote the profile dead-pan, using his own evaluation whole, saying it was written by a man who had known him all of his life.

Shortly after the profile appeared in a two-page spread, I received a letter from Mrs. Hutcheson in Houston thanking me for describing her husband so sympathetically. She ended her letter with the words, "Tell him to be very good to the children you meet." I could picture her giving him orders, though that one didn't seem necessary.

In Jerusalem Bart asked me to accompany him and Crossman to the Hadassah Hospital on Mount Scopus. Many of the doctors and nurses were Americans who had introduced Western medicine and techniques that had wiped out the diseases endemic to the entire Middle East. The wards were filled with Jewish and Arab patients, but the three of us were especially intrigued in the maternity ward to see young Arab and Jewish mothers nursing their infants.

From the hospital we walked to the Hadassah-Henrietta Szold School of Nursing, where young student nurses were being trained. The school had been created by the Baltimore-born Henrietta Szold, who had founded Hadassah in 1911 and had built this nursing school according to American standards.

Still on Mount Scopus, we visited the Hebrew University. Judah L. Magnes greeted us at the door. He had left his position as rabbi of Temple Emanu-El in New York City and emigrated to Palestine during the First World War. He no longer used the title *rabbi,* and as Doctor Magnes had founded this university. He had been one of the last witnesses at the hearings and so impressed Judge Hutcheson that the American chairman praised him, "You are not denominated a Christian, Dr. Magnes, but you talk as I should like Christians to talk. I recognize moral power when I see it."

When the hearings ended we packed our bags and traveled in a cavalcade of shiny black Studebakers to Beirut, Lebanon. Once again we were entertained in villas with belly dancers, and dined at tables laden with Middle Eastern food. Some of the committee went back to Jerusalem, others visited Arab lands. Sir John Singleton, Frank W. Buxton, Major Reginald

Manningham-Buller, and Harold Beeley were going to Baghdad in Iraq and Riyadh in Saudi Arabia; I decided to join them.

We flew first to Baghdad, where our hosts took us on a tour of the Iraqi Museum. I walked alongside Frank Buxton, the Pulitzer Prize–winning editor of the *Boston Herald,* who told me how pleased he was that I had come with them.

"The world must know," he said, "how these two Arab countries, Iraq and Saudi Arabia, both rich in oil, feel about immigration to Palestine."

"I can't wait to get to Saudi Arabia," I told him. Beeley who was trailing us, overheard.

"I think you had better ask Sir John for permission," Beeley advised. "I'll take you to him right now."

We found Sir John sitting on a museum bench. I made no effort to sit beside him, and he did not offer me a seat.

Beeley leaned over Sir John. When Beeley was excited, his eyes blinked rapidly and he stuttered.

"S-s-sir John," he blurted, quickly finishing the sentence. "Miss Gruber is hoping to fly with us to Saudi Arabia."

Singleton jumped up. "I will not permit you on the plane," he shouted. People in the museum turned to stare at this tall, thin man shaking with anger. "You are not coming with us."

"But Sir John," I kept my voice low, "I've been traveling with the committee for three months and no one has ever stopped me."

Still shouting, Sir John replied, "Well, I am stopping you now."

I was not going to let Sir John keep me off the only plane I could take to Saudi Arabia. The next day, I called on the Saudi consul. In the consulate, a charming young officer welcomed me, offering me a chair.

I told him that I was planning to accompany the sub-committee to Saudi Arabia.

"We welcome you to our country," he smiled, as I handed him my passport. He opened it, stamped it with a visa, and returned it to me.

"Thank you," I carefully placed my passport back in my purse. "Can you recommend a hotel in Riyadh?"

"There are no hotels," he shook his head. "You will probably be staying in the women's quarter of the king's household."

"His harem?" I exclaimed. "That will be a new experience."

The consul was amused. "I suggest you obtain an *aba*—that's what we call the long black wrap that our women wear. And also get a black face veil. We call that a *yashmak*."

Confident that Sir John could not stop me now, I spent the next few days interviewing officials. I had been barred, along with all other journalists, from the Baghdad hearings, held in secret in the Amanah Municipal Hall. I learned that all the witnesses were selected by the government and told what to say. Only two Jews, both anti-Zionists, were allowed to testify. One was Chief Rabbi Sassoon Khadouri.

I planned to interview the rabbi when I was diverted by a Kurd who joined me at my hotel for lunch. The young man, fair-haired with blue eyes, speaking fluent English, told me that because of the way his people were treated we were on the threshold of World War III. The Kurds, an ancient mountain people who lived in the northern tier of Iraq, were rebelling against the Iraqi government.

"Every promise this government has made to the Kurds has been broken. We are a proud people, and since the beginning of history, we have always been fearless and independent. Now in many ways we are like the Jews, a minority without a state, treated like second-class citizens. Our children cannot learn our own language in schools; our literature is not taught. We are in other countries, too. In Iran alone we represent about seven hundred fifty thousand Kurds, and altogether we are about four million.

"We live in the richest area for Iraq's oil, yet we get nothing from the land we inhabit, from the wealth of our own country. We just pay taxes. We are victims of the 'oil curse.' Everyone, even foreign countries, benefits from our wealth except us."

More than half a century later, the Kurds are still suffering.

I cabled his story to New York and then kept my promise to myself to interview Rabbi Sassoon.

I found my way to his office in the Jewish Community building. Two soldiers stopped me at the entrance, demanded identification papers, and then allowed me to enter the court-yard. I climbed a flight of rickety stairs to the balcony, where the rabbi sat waiting for me.

His head was wreathed in a paisley turban. His heavy body was covered in a long dressing gown of soft gray cloth; a wide paisley sash encircled his ample stomach. His twenty-four-year-old son, Dr. Meir Sassoon, sat next to him, interpreting for me in British-accented English. Two other rabbis joined us. One was the head of the religious court; the other, the head of the Council of Rabbis.

"Tell me all your questions," Rabbi Sassoon asked.

Quickly, I pulled three or four questions out of my brain.

"I have met many foreigners," he stroked his chin, "but none has asked me better questions than you."

He then avoided answering a single one.

"The meeting is over. My son here will show you around the city."

As I stood up to leave, the rabbi blessed me. Young Dr. Sassoon took my arm and led me outside the courtyard. On the street Dr. Sassoon whispered, "We'll be followed. Watch what you say very carefully; don't say anything provocative." He looked over his shoulder and continued to whisper, "The Jews are not safe here. My sister is already in Jerusalem, and I hope to get there myself very soon. My father is opposed to Jews entering Palestine. He will stay here, but the rest of us are making plans."

At the entrance to the synagogue, beggars stretched out their hands. I gave some money to an old, blind man, and was immediately surrounded by a dozen old men and women chattering fiercely in Arabic. I gave them each some money.

Inside the synagogue, men sat up front on wooden benches over which Persian rugs were thrown. Women sat above in dark galleries. I was surprised to find Jewish women wearing rayon *abas*. Dr. Sassoon later explained, "It's poor women who wear the *abas* because they are cheap and last for years. The rest of our women dress like they do in Paris and New York."

In the center of the synagogue was a high platform squarely enclosed with tables, where the richest Jews worshipped. The holy scrolls were kept in elaborate, rounded cases of gold and silver. On the walls were a series of framed and glassed lettering all bearing the name of Jehovah. Dr. Sassoon told me that wealthier members of the community donated the Torahs when someone in their family died. The *abas* of the poor women and the Torahs of gold donated by the rich were symbols of the difference between the hungry poor and the wealthy elite.

We left the synagogue and walked through the narrow, winding streets of the bazaar. Poverty and filth pervaded the air. I felt the same depression I had felt in Cairo: of life not being worth living under such poverty. The tiny booths were run by Arab, Christian, and Jewish merchants, who sold fruits, vegetables, meat, and fish for the local people, while foreigners entered in fancy booths buying expensive English cloth and Persian rugs. Merchants kept calling to us to buy their wares. People were haggling over prices. Everywhere there were blind and starved-looking beggars with hands condemningly outstretched. Everywhere there were children, their eyes already clouded with trachoma. This land was once the cradle of civilization; now much of it was a graveyard.

Dr. Sassoon, still speaking in a whisper, said, "An Arab newspaper in Baghdad, the *Saut-el-ahali,* estimates that at least two million people—more than fifty percent of the population—are infected with malaria, and there is a high incidence of tuberculosis. Ninety percent of the people are still illiterate."

We stopped at a booth where Arab gowns hung near the entrance. I selected a black silk *aba* and a *yashmak* that covered my face. After the ritual game of bargaining, my purchase came to eighty U.S. dollars.

Sassoon kept turning his head to see if we were being followed.

Back at my hotel I telephoned Beeley, asking him to meet me in the lobby.

"I've just gotten my visa to join the committee in Saudi Arabia," I said exultantly

Beeley blinked nervously.

"You-you-you got a vi-vi-visa!"

"Yes," I said, "Is anything wrong?"

"I- I- I mu-must t-t-talk to Sir John."

He turned on his heels, rushed to the elevator and disappeared. I waited in the lobby, and within a few minutes Sir John appeared with Beeley at his heels.

Sir John's normally cold face was icy. "Don't you know that women are not allowed in Saudi Arabia?"

I opened my passport and showed him my visa. "I've been invited," I said. "Here's proof."

The anger seemed to rise up in his throat, "I am in charge here, not you, and I have said you will not go. I simply will not allow you on board our plane."

"By whose authority?" I demanded.

"By mine," he said, and walked back to the elevator.

I was furious, but I knew I had lost the battle. I could never win with Singleton. Having watched him closely interrogate the refugees in the DP camps, I realized now that I was everything he disliked—an American, a Jew, and especially, a woman.

Months later Frank Buxton wrote me a letter, "I will never forgive myself for not having fought Sir John and gotten you on our plane, a twenty-passenger plane with fifteen empty seats. I was especially furious when I learned that we were paying for it; it was an American plane."

The next day I donated my *aba* and *yashmak* to the synagogue and left Baghdad to return to Jerusalem.

Chapter Thirty-Two
WE VISIT THE KING

King Abdullah of Trans-Jordan made an official announcement: He was planning to rename his country the Hashemite Kingdom of Jordan. Word reached us in Jerusalem. I suggested to three of my friends that we scoop the press camp and interview the king.

George Polk, with Columbia Broadcasting, John Palmer of the Associated Press, Gerold Frank, and I hired a car to take us across the Jordan River to Trans-Jordan for the historic day. The Arab guards on the border, learning we were journalists, begged us to take their photographs. Then we took photographs of each other with the friendly police, who congratulated us on being the first journalists to enter their newly named nation.

We drove across desert land to Amman, reached the palace, and told one of the guards that we wanted to interview the king. He nodded and disappeared. In a few minutes, young Prince Hussein, the grandson of King Abdullah, entered the room. He invited us into the palace.

Hussein was handsome and spoke English flawlessly in a deep, rhythmic voice. He explained that he could not answer any political questions.

"These days are so critical," he said, "and there is so much at stake, that I hope you will understand."

We knew better than to press him, and after a short tour of the palace, we returned to the Press Information Office (PIO) in Jerusalem.

Though the press corps was largely male, I experienced very little gender discrimination. On the contrary, most of the men recognized that I was as serious about my work as they were. Many were eager to share information and often asked to read the carbons of the stories I was cabling to New York. Instead of scooping each other, we often covered stories together. The men I worked with, and the people I interviewed, trusted me to report the truth.

Still, there were occasional disadvantages in being a woman journalist. A few of the men were jealous of the friendships I was making with leaders. One day in Jerusalem, Moshe Sharett, who would become Israel's first foreign minister, came to the PIO and took me aside.

"My wife would like you to join us at dinner tonight if you're free," he offered.

When he left, the correspondent for Agence-France confronted me. "What scoop did he give you?" he demanded.

"He invited me to meet his wife and children at dinner," I said.

"That's what you say; I don't believe it."

I shrugged my shoulders.

Fortunately, such incidents were rare.

The committee spent the next days traveling through Palestine, visiting farms, factories, kibbutzim, Arab villages, biblical sites, and the cities—Tel Aviv, Haifa, Nazareth, and Bethlehem. It struck me that the three major cities, Jerusalem, Tel Aviv, and Haifa, were like the hours of the day.

Haifa, with its workers hurrying at dawn to the factories and oil refineries, was the morning city.

Tel Aviv was High Noon. It was as busy and hectic as Times Square on matinee day. The city shrieked, honked its horns, jammed on its brakes, and beat its Persian carpets on its terraces.

Jerusalem was the evening city, where the sun set, not on the golden stones, but within them.

One day I made a special trip to visit my mother's cousin in Kibbutz Tel-Josef in the northern Emek Valley. It was an extremely well-run kibbutz, with white cottages, green fields planted in straight lines, and a huge communal dining room.

"Your father saved my life," my cousin flung her arms around me. "I loved him. He gave me the money for the *Schifffskarte* [the steamship ticket] that brought me here. My family sat shiva, mourning me when I left our shtetl in Poland. They were sure that Arabs would take huge knives and cut my head off. My brother, Yankel, and I are the only survivors."

Yankel soon joined us. He told me the story of how everyone in my mother's shtetl, Beremlya, in the Wolyn province of Poland, was murdered.

"The SS man came in and yelled, 'everybody out.' It didn't matter what they were doing—eating, sleeping, nursing their babies. Everyone had to get out of their houses and run toward the river. Those who didn't run fast enough were beaten by Nazi soldiers and Ukrainian and Polish police. When everyone reached the river, the SS officer, who now was on a white horse, shouted, 'Everybody undress.'"

I shuddered, picturing orthodox women forced to stand

naked in front of men. Humiliating. But that was the Nazis' technique—Jews were not people, they were animals or roaches that you stepped on and crushed.

Yankel continued: "Then the SS officer shouted, 'Shoot.' The soldiers and police shot everybody. The ones who didn't fall into the river, they shoveled into the river."

"Where were you?" I asked Yankel.

"I was hiding behind some trees. I didn't move until midnight. Then I ran."

Hearing how my relatives had died gave new meaning to the work of the committee. If only my aunts and uncles and cousins had left for Palestine before Hitler sealed Europe's borders in the late 1930s and before Britain tried to shut the doors of Palestine in 1939.

I rejoined the committee in Jerusalem, determined to work harder than ever, I wanted my words and pictures to shake my readers, to shout to them:

> *Wake up. We must get the people out of those God awful DP camps. They survived the worst torture of the Nazis because they had a vision. The vision of coming to the Holy Land. The vision of coming home.*

Chapter Thirty-Three

ALL'S WELL THAT ENDS WELL?

The hearings ended in Jerusalem, and by April 5, the committee members settled at the hotel Beau Rivage on Lake Leman in Lausanne, Switzerland, to spend a month writing their report. Gerold Frank and I were once again the only correspondents attached to the committee. We were talking to the concierge when Bart Crum caught sight of us.

"I will ask you both a big favor," he said confidentially. "Please don't stay at this hotel. We want to feel as though we can have our discussions without the press."

"I think you're wise," I told him. "I'll even cable my paper that I won't be sending stories about the hearings until a decision is reached. Anything I write would look like a leak and could throw suspicion on you."

The concierge regained my attention: "By the way Miss Gruber, a cable arrived for you, and Mr. Beeley forwarded it to the American Council in Bern."

"Mr. Beeley did what?" I was incredulous.

"He's out on the verandah," Bart offered. "Why don't you go ask him?"

I hurried out to find him seated in a wicker rocking chair.

"Where's my cable?" I demanded.

"What cable?"

"They told me at the desk that a cable had come for me and you had forwarded it."

"Oh, yes—that cable," he replied innocently. "I thought it was a cable from you to the committee so I opened it."

"You what? You opened a cable addressed to me? And what was in it, Mr. Beeley?"

"I don't know," he shrugged, trying to look bored.

"But you opened it," I repeated.

"Yes," he admitted, "but as soon as I saw it was not for me, I didn't read it."

I realized I would get nowhere with this man. I approached Bart to vent my frustration.

"It's just as I told you in Jerusalem. He and the CID are spying on all of us," Bart told me. "We know that he has already paid off the concierge to watch us and report our every move."

Crum invited me to join the committee for dinner. During the meal, in the presence of most of the committee, I waited for a lull in the conversation.

"I must telephone the American council in Bern," I announced loudly, "I need to find out whether money came for me from my paper. I'm expecting some, and a cable that came for me from New York earlier today was opened."

"How do you know it was opened?" Buxton asked. "Who opened it?

I was silent.

Beeley, feeling the finger of suspicion, said, "I did. It came addressed to the Anglo-American Committee."

When the cable was finally returned to me, I confirmed that it was addressed, not to the committee, but specifically to me. I was relieved to see there was nothing in the cable that I didn't want Beeley to see. But in the days that followed, tensions in the committee rose to the level of a spy novel. Everyone suspected everyone else with Beeley serving as the arch villain.

I found a small hotel in nearby Montreux. Gerold and I were soon joined by four Jewish leaders: Moshe Sharett; Nahum Goldman, head of the World Jewish Congress; David Horowitz, the country's chief economist; and his wife, Reba.

We spent nearly every lunch and dinner together and began calling ourselves "Kibbutz Montreux." Sharett and Goldman, both master storytellers, convulsed us in laughter, vying with each other to tell hilarious anecdotes of their colorful careers. The other guests in the hotel couldn't decide if we were a group of international spies, dignitaries, or crooks. Telephone calls for them came every few minutes from Rome, London, Jerusalem, Washington, Cleveland, Paris, and New York. There was a musical comedy air in the dining room, utterly different from the brawling, name-calling suspicion mounting at the Hotel Beau Rivage.

After I had been barred from traveling to Saudi Arabia by Singleton, I sent an article describing my experience to the *Post*. The Colonial Office flew a copy to Beeley, who showed it to the British committee members. Manningham-Buller, white-faced with rage, confronted me.

"You posed as a secretary of the British committee to get that visa," he yelled. "That was an illegal trick."

"Me? A British secretary?" I shot back. "But I have an American passport, so who would believe that? You and Beeley had better concoct a better fiction than that one."

Beeley, standing bravely behind Manningham-Buller, stuttered, "You're a w-w-wicked woman."

"And you," I exclaimed, my frustration finally exploding, "you are a mean S.O.B."

"This does nothing for Anglo-American relations, you know," Manningham-Buller said forbodingly.

"Neither does defaming my character with such a ridiculous lie," I shot back.

Meanwhile, infighting in the committee was reaching fever pitch. Judge Hutcheson had become the true leader for the American side, strongly advocating the opening of Palestine to refugees. After a story about the committee's wrangling appeared in the *Palestine Post,* a great rift developed. Crossman became a firm ally of the American side, and Sir Frederick seemed to be following his lead. Meanwhile, two American members, Frank Aydelotte, the director of the Institute for Advanced Studies at Princeton, and William Phillips, the undersecretary of state, appeared to be joining ranks with Singleton.

Bart warned me that the debates were growing fiercer by the day. At one point, talks broke down completely. Hutcheson flew secretly to Washington to see President Truman, and Singleton took most of the British committee members to London to see Foreign Secretary Ernest Bevin.

The night before the committee was to make its final vote, Beeley tried to appease me. In celebration of our four-month journey, he gave a formal dinner party at the Beau Rivage and invited me to join them. He had the menu printed with each course named for someone connected with the hearings. The main course was beef steak au Truman. He went down the list, with courses including potage Hutcheson and champignons Singleton. The dessert was Zabaglione à la Gruber.

I flew to London and remained in contact with the committee by phone. The spy story reached its climax the morning of the vote. The *New York Times* had sent its London correspondent, Flora Lewis, to cover the final report. She had breakfast with Beeley, who told her that the committee was in chaos; they had agreed on nothing and there would be not a single recommendation to open the doors of Palestine.

At the same time I was on the phone with Bart.

"Ruthie," he shouted. "We won."

"How did it happen?" I could hardly breathe.

"It was Hutcheson," he said. I heard the wonder in his voice. "The change in him in the last several weeks is one of the minor miracles in Jewish history. He was absolutely fearless. First, he whipped Aydelotte and Phillips into line. Then, he called each of the British into his room separately, demanding to know where they stood on the immigration of one hundred thousand, asking, "Is you is, or is you ain't?"'"

I burst into laughter. Only Texas Joe, the courtroom judge, fond of down-home expressions, would demand of each member that he reveal honestly where he stood on immigration.

"But what happened with Singleton?" I asked. "Did he answer?"

"Hutcheson and Singleton, who you know hate each other, had a final knock-down, drag-out fight. Texas Joe kept threatening Sir John, saying, 'My ancestors helped behead Charles the First, and I will do the same thing to you if you don't come to your senses.'"

They had argued until early in the morning, and finally Singleton said yes.

Elated, I wrote a letter to Ickes, explaining what had happened. I told him, "I have found my first breathing space to write you. For your own information, and completely off the record, the report is infinitely better than any of us dared hope a few weeks ago . . . The most important recommendation is that the one hundred thousand Jews in the DP camps will be allowed to go to Palestine or other countries by the end of this year. That means the camps will be cleaned out. The mandate was reaffirmed and the White Paper of 1939 repealed. The suggestion was made that a Jordan Valley Authority be created, but with the cooperation of the neighboring Arab states."

President Truman was delighted. Bevin had promised him that if the committee voted unanimously to open the gates, he would agree.

When word spread around the world that this historic committee had indeed voted unanimously to allow Holocaust survivors to go home, people danced and sang in the streets. In Jerusalem, families hugged and kissed and wept and told each other that soon they would be seeing relatives they had not seen since the beginning of the war.

In London I was asked to escort a group of Jewish orphans of the Holocaust aboard the SS *Uruguay* bound for New York. I was happy to play surrogate mother to these delightful youngsters, who would be living with new mothers and fathers in America. The purser became so involved that he gave me the bridal suite so I could entertain the children in style.

New York harbor on the sixth of May was packed with photographers taking pictures of the newest orphans to arrive on American soil. Soon they were gathered up by representatives of the Hebrew Immigrant Aid Society (HIAS), who assured me the children would be united immediately with their new parents.

I hugged them good-bye, then ran down the gangplank, first into Mama's arms, then Irving's, who had finally been allowed to leave Germany, and kissed my sister-in-law, Fannie, radiant with joy as she clung to Irving.

Chapter Thirty-Four

"1947: THE FATEFUL YEAR"

Our joy in the Anglo-American Committee's unanimous report lasted exactly three days.

Bevin announced that Great Britain would not accept the report. Of all the recommendations the committee had finally agreed upon, the British government would accept only one—that music should be banned from the shores of the Sea of Galilee.

Angry and heartsick, I exchanged condolence calls with Hutcheson, Crum, and Buxton. How could we not have foreseen that Bevin would betray his promise to Truman? He had assured the president that if the committee voted unanimously to open the gates of Palestine, he would accept it. How stupid I was to have believed him. Bevin's crude slap in Truman's face tested my ability to go on working and living inside of time. We had traveled so many thousands of miles, and built up the hopes of the DPs as well as our own. Now, it was difficult not to give up in the face of Britain's restrictive foreign policy.

Dick Crossman, in a May 1946 article in London's *New Statesman,* vented his anger with his government by stating coldly that "British pro-Arabism is not so much love for the Arabs as concealed anti-Semitism." He warned his British readers that the next stage in the Arab game of blackmail would be a demand for the return of the ex-Grand Mufti to Jerusalem.

I consoled myself—we hadn't yet lost the war, just one more battle. I had to go on using words and photos to tell the truth about what was happening in Palestine. In New York I began to write articles I could not have cabled from Jerusalem without endangering my sources. Many of my friends, I was sure, would have been put in jail. But now the gloves came off.

The first story in a series of four articles was banner-headlined on the front page of the *New York Post* and pasted across the side of every bus in New York.

PALESTINE TODAY IS IRELAND OF 1921
AS "BLACK AND TAN" TERROR RULES

Writing in white heat, I tried to capture what life was like in the Palestine of 1946. "The fierce hatred of the British, the concentration camp atmosphere, the destruction of civil liberties, the growth of a people's army—the same social and political explosives which made Ireland the tinderbox of the last postwar period, make Palestine the time bomb of this one."

Midway through the article, I explained that I wasn't against the British people; I opposed British foreign policy. "The Foreign Office is being run by men who have never broken with the old British imperialists, men who think back through their grandfathers, men who, knowing that the days of grabbing and expansion are over and only the days of clutching and hoarding are left, are now imperialists by despair."

"Keep going," Ed Flynn, the tough Irish American editor of the *Post* phoned me. "You're breaking new ground."

Next day the banner headline read:

> HOW BRITAIN RECRUITED PRO-NAZIS AND
> SPENT $20,000,000 ON JAILS

"Palestine is a police state," I wrote. "At the outbreak of the war with Nazi Germany, the British recruited fascists from the Mosley gang. These men, who loathed the idea of fighting their friends, the Nazis, embraced with passion the idea of fighting Jews. These fascists walked the streets of Jerusalem and Tel Aviv, a city built by Jews, singing the Nazi song *Horst Wessel*. They would march into crowded market places giving the Heil Hitler salute. They drove in British police trucks with swastikas chalked on the side. Underneath the swastikas was the familiar slogan—"Kill the Jews."

It was clear that anti-Semitism was at the heart of British colonial policy in Palestine. In an article titled JEWS AND ARABS GET ALONG WELL—UNTIL BRITAIN RAISES FALSE ISSUES, I wrote, "Divide and Rule are familiar tactics with the British. They used the same tactics in Ireland. There were grave and historic differences between the Catholic south and the Protestant north, but without British intervention, the Irish might have worked out their domestic differences. To this day, almost every Irishman blames the British for aggravating the differences between the north and south."

The series took on a life of its own. The *Post* continued to plaster signs on New York City buses reading "PALESTINE—THE IRELAND OF 1921." A New York congressman had the series reprinted in full in the *Congressional Record*. Letters and cables piled up on my desk congratulating me on at last lifting the curtain on Britain's role in the Arab-Jewish conflict. I felt good that I had reached so many people, but it was the *Post* itself that gave me the greatest pleasure when Ed Flynn called me into his office and said: "The reporters themselves are excited about the series."

A few days later, David Ben-Gurion arrived in New York. By rare good luck, he had been in Paris on "Black Saturday," June 29, 1946, escaping a massive dragnet by the British police. Early on the Sabbath morning, British police and soldiers had broken into homes, rounded up every Jewish leader they could find, and locked them all up in the Latrun Fortress jail. They then arrested thousands of others, including scientists, economists, and educators. Only Golda Meir was free to keep the shadow government functioning, and Ben-Gurion, who happened to be abroad was safe.

I suggested to Ed Flynn that the true leader of the Jews in Palestine, who was still not well known in America, was Ben-Gurion. I told Ed I wanted to do a "*Post* Close-up" on him. Ed agreed.

Ben-Gurion was staying at the unofficial Jewish embassy— a suite at Hotel 14 on Sixtieth Street, next door to the Copacabana nightclub. I phoned, telling him I wanted an interview.

"Come right now," he said.

It was a hot June day. I was dressed in the coolest outfit I owned, a sleeveless black-cotton sheath.

Ben-Gurion greeted me, "Why are you wearing black?" he demanded. "Who died?"

Surprised that he even noticed what I was wearing, I said, "Nobody died. Black is fashionable this summer."

"You shouldn't wear black," he laughed. "Now what do you want to ask me?"

I read him a list of eight questions, which he jotted down. I was not surprised when he refused to answer any of them. In a low voice underlined with sorrow and foreboding, he explained why he could not dwell on such "piquant" subjects as Bevin and Attlee defying President Truman.

I knew the weight he was carrying. I also knew how complex he was, warm-hearted and sincere, but when need be he was uncompromisingly tough. He was intense in everything he did, from the way he moved his thin lips to the way he squeezed his eyes shut when he was thinking. "I should be home," he said. "I'm very restless."

"I can imagine how much the people must miss you," I told him.

He was silent. Then he looked my way as if he were waiting for me to go on.

I spoke slowly. "I think that if Abraham Lincoln had been forced to leave my country in the middle of the civil war, we would have missed him the way the people of Palestine must miss you today."

Ben-Gurion jumped up from the sofa, his high voice rising, I thought, to the ceiling as he shouted, " Lincoln! When I think of a great man in history, I think of Lincoln. And who am I? A little Jew."

There was a knock on the door. Tony, the *Post*'s best photographer, whom I knew only as Tony, came in to take Ben-Gurion's picture. Tony wanted a photo of him smiling, but Ben-Gurion, who laughed easily in conversation, froze each time the camera was focused.

Finally, in despair, I said, "B. G., you're worse than a child."

He grinned, "And what's wrong with a child?"

Tony caught the grin, shot a few more photos and left.

"Now you can help me," Ben-Gurion said. "Take me to a

couple of bookstores. I want to buy every book they have on Lincoln."

Still despondent at the failure of Britain to open the doors of Palestine, I left the *Post* and decided to write a novel about a young couple who meet in the DP camp of Bergen-Belsen in the British zone of Germany. My work on the novel was continually being interrupted by requests for speeches at universities and by organizations whose members were eager to learn more about the DPs and the British betrayal of the Anglo-American Committee of Inquiry.

Meanwhile, in Palestine itself, the British continued to bar Holocaust survivors from entering. Defying the British, the people left Eastern Europe, crossed mountains, trekked across frontiers, and squeezed themselves into a motley fleet of ships sailing from ports in southern France and Italy bound for the Holy Land. Some broke through the British blockade and landed secretly; others were caught and imprisoned.

In 1947, Bevin threw in the towel. He told the United Nations, in effect, that he couldn't handle these "ornery Jews any longer." The mandate was over. Many suspected that he was sure the UN would get down on its knees and plead with him to reconsider. I thought so myself. I could almost envision the UN saying, "Please, Mr. Bevin, you're the only one who knows how to handle them. Please don't give up."

But the UN fooled us all. They decided to create their own committee—the United Nations Special Committee on Palestine (UNSCOP). It was made up of the representatives of eleven countries This was the first of the twenty committees that had studied Palestine that did not have a single British representative.

Helen Rogers Reid invited me to dinner. Since Ogden's

death from alcoholism and cancer on January 3, 1947, Helen had become legally what she had been unofficially for several years: the owner and publisher of the New York *Herald Tribune*. She told me that she and editors George Cornish and Joe Barnes had agreed that I should cover UNSCOP for the New York *Herald Tribune*. I told her I was honored but I needed time to think it over.

The next day I was interviewing the German-Jewish novelist Lion Feuchtwanger at the Waldorf Astoria. His story fascinated me. He had been living in Sanary in southern France when he and his wife, Marta, were arrested by the Vichy French as "enemy aliens." They were placed in separate prisons. Marta managed to escape and learned that Lion was so bruised and exhausted that he was near death. With the help of Varian Fry, the American who was saving Jewish artists and writers in southern France, and the American Consul, Hiram Bingham Jr., she rescued him.

"I have a problem," I told Feuchtwanger. "I'm in the middle of writing a novel and my former newspaper, the New York *Herald Tribune,* wants me to travel with UNSCOP."

He spoke with fire: "Drop the novel. You can always go back to writing it. But to travel with this UN committee—the most important committee yet—and do something to help the people in those terrible camps is the chance of a lifetime. How many young women—or young men—get such an opportunity to be on the forefront of history?"

I took his advice. I called Helen Reid and told her I would go.

Chapter Thirty-Five
THE LAST COMMITTEE

A t the *Herald Tribune,* I went first to Helen Reid's office.

"Our man in Jerusalem, Homer Bigart, can be a help to you and you can be of help to him," Helen told me. He'll be covering the political events while you cover UNSCOP." She walked around her desk and hugged me, "We're so happy you're going for us."

Armed with my New York *Herald Tribune* credentials, my typewriter, my cameras, and a fresh batch of empty notebooks, I departed New York at 2:30 A.M. on Saturday, June 28. My TWA flight, which was delayed for three days, now acted like the local subway train from Brooklyn to Manhattan. We made stops in Newfoundland, Ireland, Paris, Geneva, Rome, Athens, and Cairo. Finally, on Monday at 1:40 A.M., two full days later, we finally arrived in Lydda Airport (later renamed Ben-Gurion Airport). It was 7:40 P.M. in New York. I taxied to Jerusalem and found a room in the Jasmine Pension at 4:30

A.M., but was too excited to sleep. As the sun came up, I walked through the streets. The state of war was omnipresent. Tanks, with their guns ominously extended, blocked the road. Soldiers and police carried machine guns ostentatiously. Every few blocks, buildings that had been bombed looked like a stage set, with three walls surrounding beds, tables, and chairs.

At 8 A.M., apologizing for the early call, I phoned Homer Bigart.

I knew his reputation as the dean of foreign correspondents, so admired and so envied that other correspondents often trailed him trying to find his sources.

One of the many legends I heard about him in New York was about one night when Homer went to a movie. The other correspondents shook with disbelief, "Homer is at a movie! He must be meeting with one of his contacts." Several correspondents trailed him into the movie house. They returned to the press office dispirited and frustrated. "Homer just sat in the movie; he didn't meet anybody."

On the phone Homer invited me to lunch in the garden of the Eden Hotel. I had expected a giant, but Homer was a small, modest man who stuttered. He spent most of the lunch interviewing me, asking questions about the Anglo-American Committee of Inquiry on Palestine. I became aware of the thoroughness with which he worked. He often repeated sharp, probing questions the way a good prosecuting attorney would, shaping each new inquiry with a slight twist.

Lunch over, Homer showed me to the British Public Information Office to be photographed and fingerprinted for my press card. I spent the rest of the day visiting my friends at the *Palestine Post,* Gershon Agronsky and Ted Lourie. While we were talking, George Polk, my old friend from Washington dropped in. He told us he had just been involved in an altercation with an Arab cab driver. He had been riding with a girl from the Public Information Office. At one point, he had put his coat around her shoulders. The Arab driver looked back.

"He stopped the car," George explained, "and shouted that we were immoral. I demanded that he take me to his manager."

The argument dissolved into a fist fight when the cab driver spat at George, who then smacked the driver. The Arab press picked up the story, screaming about American imperialists coming into the Middle East and trying to run everything.[*]

My next stop was at the office of Teddy Kollek, who was Ben-Gurion's chief aid. He told me that the members of UNSCOP were planning to sail across the sea of Galilee and land in Kibbutz Ein Gev, which he had helped establish in 1937. "I have to go up there myself, so I'll take you there by bus tomorrow morning," he told me.

In the bus traveling north I instantly came to admire the man who would later become the beloved mayor of Jerusalem. Teddy, a dynamic thirty-six-year-old Viennese Jew, had escaped to Palestine in 1934, a year after Hitler came to power in Germany.

We arrived at Ein Gev just as the United Nations committee stepped off their ship. The entire kibbutz of four hundred settlers stood on the beach to greet the eleven committee members, their eleven alternates, members of the UN secretariat, and two hundred reporters. The hardest-working member of the UN secretariat was the brilliant African American diplomat Ralph Bunche. We became friends after he had asked me to do him a favor: Would I introduce him to members of

---

[*] The next year, on May 16, 1948, George Polk was in Greece covering the guerilla war there. He was shot and his lifeless body was left on the shore of Solonika Bay, one day after the founding of Israel.

the Irgun underground? He wanted to understand their motives and their philosophies. I was glad that I could fulfill his request.

We greeted each other warmly now in the kibbutz. The committee, tired from its long journey, looked refreshed at the sight of simple white-stucco houses surrounded by flowers, palm trees, green lawns, and flaming jacarandas nestled on the shore. Behind the house, soft mountains spread up like velvet, dotted with a few trees. Syria was just the other side of those mountains.

All of us, the committee men, their alternates, and the eager press were offered chairs on the lawn. With dates and banana trees hanging over our heads, we watched smiling young girls in blue kibbutz shorts and white T-shirts as they served us homemade ice cream, luscious grapes, and ice-cold lemonade.

The American committee press officer, George Symeonides, with a perpetual worried look on his furrowed brow told the press they could ask questions, and Mr. Hood, the Australian delegate, would answer.

Questions came fast. "How does it feel to be watched in the world's goldfish bowl?"

"Not too bad."

"Does the presence of two hundred correspondents from all over the world help or hinder the proceedings?"

"It helps sometimes and it hinders others."

"How do most of the members feel about the terrific world interest in their work?"

"How do you feel about the Arabs boycotting the hearings?"

Hood answered most of the questions with a simple "yes" or "no." But the question about the Arabs he turned over to the UN delegate from Uruguay, Professor Enrique Rodriguez Fabregat.

"We have been all over the soil of this land," he spoke in Spanish-accented English. "We have gathered a good impression of the work in Palestine." He looked at the settlers, who were following his words intently. "I speak from the heart. We want to listen to everybody who has something to say to us in order to put it before the UN assembly when we get home. We are sad that the Arabs are boycotting the hearings. We can meet them individually outside and hear their stories, but it would be better if we heard them in a full session."

Fabregat grew emotional, speaking of children and the Holocaust. "I know as everyone knows that hundreds of thousands of children have been sacrificed under the persecution in Europe." Trying to control his voice, he went on. "I have gathered in my heart very strongly the life you make for your children, the way you bring them up."

While he spoke, I had a chance to study the members of the committee. Eleven men with different mentalities, different tempers, different countries, and different interests held in their hands the fate of Jews and Arabs.

The Australian Hood held himself crisp and erect. The Canadian representative, a judge, was tall, aloof and austere, in sharp contrast to the two effusive South Americans, Dr. Fabregat of Uruguay and Jorge Garcia Granados of Guatemala. English was the official language of the committee. Most of the delegates spoke English, but several spoke their own languages, which were translated.

With the conference over, the committee members, their alternates, and the press returned to their cars, twenty-six shiny Studebakers, five of which were designated for press. Many local reporters drove in their own cars. I climbed into one of the press vehicles. We drove briefly around the kibbutz, and then headed back to Jerusalem.

The barriers all over the city made it difficult to meet my deadlines. To get a story from the YMCA, where the committee was holding its hearings, cabled to my editors required me to run a gauntlet of blockades and checkpoints. Symeonides eventually arranged to have messengers pick up our stories at the YMCA and deliver them to the cable office. But the difficulties increased again when UNSCOP decided to close its meetings to the entire press. After each committee session, Symeonides would read a communique to us.

"One of our worst problems," Symeonides confided at one press conference, "is when we have to travel through Arab neighborhoods. The Arabs have told us that Jewish correspondents— foreign as well as local—will not be permitted."

"Don't quote me," he insisted. "I asked one of the Arabs: 'What's the idea of excluding a journalist just because their grandmother was Jewish?'"

Arabs continued to boycott the committee hearings, wasting their opportunity to present their case. UNSCOP, hoping to change their minds, kept the chairs for Arab members open during the hearings. The chairs remained eloquently empty.

On July third, the committee held a meeting at the Seiff Institute, later called the Weizmann Institute of sciences. Though the press was barred from the meeting, I soon learned from my sources that Dr. Chaim Weizmann was planning to recommend that Palestine be partitioned into a Jewish state and an Arab state. Comparing Palestine with Switzerland, he spoke at the Y. "Switzerland has no natural resources, yet has light and heavy industries. Switzerland is landlocked and Palestine is not. The best resources of Switzerland are the brains and discipline of her people. Our people also have brains and discipline."

Dr. Weizmann then told the UN delegates: "We can't afford a single failure in Palestine. We can only live or die. The dif-

ference between countries like America and us is like the difference between swimming in an ocean and swimming in a
bathtub. We have learned to swim in a bathtub."

One delegate asked if it was true the Jews were buying up
the best land in Palestine. Dr. Weizmann answered: "They say
we take away their best lands, but we took nothing but sand
and stone. Over twenty years ago we bought land in the Jezreel
Valley from an absentee owner when it was a marsh. The
neighboring Arab villages disappeared because the people died
from malaria. Years later I met the former owner who said to
me, ' I'm sorry I sold you the land then. If I had waited until
now I could have gotten much more from you.' I replied, 'The
land is improved because we sunk into it twenty-five times its
price apart from the work we put into it. If you had not sold it,
it would not be what it is today.'"

I waited outside the institute until the committee left, and
then entered to talk to Dr. Weizmann.

"I'm so glad you came," he said. "I would have called you
myself."

"I had a feeling you would," I answered.

He offered me a cup of tea. Knowing how strong he drank
tea, I brought my own tea bag with me.

"Look at you," he teased. "You take that rag, pull it once
through the cup, and call that tea." Sipping his own heavily
brewed, nearly black tea, he asked, "Who is on the committee?
Tell me, where do they stand?"

"The Australians are not very friendly," I said, "nor the
Canadians, nor the Peruvians or the Dutchmen."

"So most of them are against us," he said.

"Yes," I answered, "and the Swede, a judge, will always
carry on his conscience that because the Arabs boycotted the
meeting, he didn't hear the Arab case."

"But the Arab case is on the record," Dr. Weizmann argued. "He can read." He was silent for a minute. "Do we have any friends on the committee?"

"Oh, yes," I said enthusiastically. "The Czech delegate is good. So is the Yugoslav, Vladimir Simich. And we have two genuine friends."

He looked startled. "Who are they?"

"Dr. Granados, the ambassador from Guatemala, and Dr. Fabregat, the ambassador from Uruguay. These two men don't have an ounce of anti-Semitism in their bodies."

Dr. Weizmann put his hand on my shoulder. "My child, every non-Jew carries anti-Semitism with him in a haversack on his back."

I was adamant: "Dr. Weizmann, I disagree. The two most important people I've worked for—Harold Ickes, the secretary of the Interior, and Helen Rogers Reid, who owns the paper I write for—are not prejudiced. They, too, don't have an ounce of anti-Semitism in their hearts."

"How can you prove it?"

"You get to know people when you work for them. Ickes worked harder during the war than any member of the cabinet to open America's doors to refugees. And Mrs. Ogden Reid has sent me here to cover this story knowing exactly where I stand."

Years later, a book about the *Herald Tribune* called *The Paper* was published. Its author, Richard Kluger, accused Helen Reid of being hostile to Jews. Those who knew Helen best were outraged. I certainly was. George Cornish, who spent thirty-five years with the paper, wrote to Helen's son Whitelaw, denouncing Kluger's charges: "I told Kluger that I had seen your mother, your father, and you daily over long periods of time, and had never heard one of you make an anti-Semitic statement. Certainly no one was refused a job for religious reasons during the period I knew what was happening in the editorial department." Despite her accomplishments, Helen was a modest, private person who rarely talked about herself. Because she didn't reveal her own history, her detractors were able to create demeaning myths about her life and work.

Several months later, in the fall of 1947, Helen Reid invited Dr. Weizmann to appear at the *Herald Tribune* Forum. In her letter thanking him for his contribution, she wrote, "I have wanted you to know how proud I was of having you on the program. You made a great speech and it gave me personally a new understanding of the Jewish faith. In fact, I had never heard it defined so movingly before, and there were many people to whom you gave the same experience. I feel sure your effort must have proved of lasting value for the cause of Palestine."

What anti-Semite, I thought, would write such a letter?

A few days after my conversation with Dr. Weizmann about anti-Semitism, I saw him again. He was one of the two recipients to receive the first honorary doctorates at Hebrew University in Jerusalem. The other recipient was Dr. Judah L. Magnes, president of the Hebrew University. The two men had founded the university twenty years earlier. Both men, now in their seventies, differed in their politics and their scientific interests. Dr. Weizmann believed in partitioning Palestine into two states, one Arab, one Jewish. Dr. Magnes believed in one binational state where Arabs and Jews would rule the country together.

Hundreds of people listened to a Bach aria played by a string quartet, as Dr. Weizmann, wearing a crimson doctorate gown and black cap, and Dr. Magnes, attired in a blue business suit, marched down the aisle in the Institute of Jewish Studies building.

In the audience, refugee professors, who had seen such ceremonies in now-destroyed universities, moved their hands to wipe their eyes. Visiting scholars famous in the universities of Europe and America watched the solemn ceremonies with American leaders from Hadassah, sitting with doctors and nurses from the Hadassah Hospital.

Native coeds wearing skirts and blouses, and young men in open-necked shirts and khaki pants crowded in the doorways and in the gallery. American youths, studying in Israel under the G.I. Bill of Rights, struck an interesting contrast with their bow ties, bright collegiate shirts and tailored gray slacks. I was happy to see several Englishmen, including the director of Barclays Bank and the head of the British Council in Palestine.

As an anticlimax to the dignified ceremony, a road check near the university was conducted by British personnel in armored cars. Scholars, poets, and community leaders were ordered by the British to get out of their automobiles. They were frisked by soldiers and their cars and briefcases searched thoroughly. No bombs were found.

The leader whose absence everyone noted at the ceremonies was David Ben-Gurion. He was testifying at the hearings in the YMCA, undergoing hours of questioning on whether Israel could protect itself if the British left. I hurried back to the Y, now open to the press, to hear the Czech delegate asking B. G., "If the UN gives the Jews a Jewish state, will the Jews be able to stop the violence?"

"The first thing we would do," Ben-Gurion explained, "is go to the Arabs, and say, 'We want to sit down with you and settle the questions amicably.' If their answer is 'no,' and they will use force against us, we will take care of the problem ourselves."

The next day, July eighth, Dr. Weizmann appeared in open testimony. He still looked tired and frail, but his voice was strong and his words decisive. He wore a blue suit and heavy tortoise-shell glasses. The galleries were filled with press.

The committee members kept asking him, "Why don't the Jews go to Germany and rebuild it?"

"Why should they build up Germany," he said, "only to be destroyed by the Germans again? Gentlemen, I am an old man. Last year I took it on myself to advise the Anglo-American Committee that time is of the essence. I am old enough to repeat the warning. For us, the question is of survival, and it brooks no delay."

The word "survival" reverberated through the walls of the YMCA.

Chapter Thirty-Six

STORMING ACRE PRISON

While UNSCOP was closeted in secret again at the YMCA, I was free to cover other stories. The British were planning to hang Jacob Weiss, a young Czech man, whom they'd condemned for his part in the storming of Acre Prison by the Irgun Zvai Leumi. The operation had freed many political prisoners who had been condemned to death. The prison was an old Turkish fortress that even Napoleon had found impregnable. Edith Weiss, Jacob's sister, had come to Palestine from Czechoslovakia, trying to save her brother's life. She told me that their parents had been burned in the crematoria of Auschwitz. Edith, two years older than her brother, was taken to Auschwitz in 1944. She showed me a picture of herself as a young woman of twenty-two—big, strong, with ruddy cheeks, and black shiny hair. The Germans made use of her strength, sending her to Allendorf to manufacture bombs and grenades.

In 1945, liberated by Americans troops, she returned to Czechoslovakia, looking for anyone from her past who was still alive, but everyone was dead. Her house had been bombed, the contents looted. The only possession she found was a green signet ring that her mother had given Jacob for his Bar Mitzvah. He had left it with a Christian neighbor, who gave it to her upon her return home.

Jacob had spent the war years in the underground, smuggling Jews out of ghettos and death camps. After the war, he piled survivors into ships than ran the British blockade into Palestine. To the Jews whose lives he saved, Jacob was a great hero. To the British, he was a criminal they were determined to hang.

"Will you come to the prison with me to see my brother?" she urged me. "I'm really too nervous to go alone."

"I'll have to make some changes in my schedule," I explained. "Come to the government press office with me—I'll have to see if I have any messages."

Homer Bigart was hunched over his typewriter, working on a story. I introduced him to Edith.

"She is Jacob Weiss's sister," I told him.

His eyes focused on her face, which was riddled with anxiety.

"Homer, she wants me to come to Acre with her," I said. "Would I be stepping on your turf?"

"Not at all, Ruth. I've got enough keeping me busy here in Jerusalem."

Edith and I spent the evening dining in Jerusalem, where she seemed optimistic. "I have great hopes everything will be all right. He and I will be able to live together when he's released."

At dawn, we took an overcrowded bus to Haifa. Edith's mood had changed. She had not slept all night.

When we reached Acre, we were led into a courtyard. Saturday was visiting day for the Jews, Friday for the Muslims, and Sunday for the Christians. Now, with some twenty other members of prisoners' families milling around, Edith was beginning to tremble. We kept walking back and forth while the sun beat down on the weathered, yellow bricks of the fortress.

The police kept us waiting for two hours in the hot sun. At 11:30, a sergeant called, "Weiss!" She rushed to the gate, and walked up the concrete road of the fortress toward the cell block. Still in the blistering sun, she waited until Jacob came from solitary confinement to the door, which was completely covered in grillwork, so tightly latticed that at a distance we could hardly see through it. At last, she could see him coming to the door through a narrow corridor, stopping behind the grill, wearing the blood-red pants given to all condemned prisoners.

Jacob found a tiny hole torn in the grillwork and put two fingers through it. Edith grasped his fingers. It was their first touch since the beginning of the war. Jacob was silent a moment and then began to laugh. I realized he was trying to cheer up his sister. "You have nothing to worry about," he told her. "Everything's going to work out all right."

They talked for fifteen minutes, when the guard told Edith, "Time to go."

She asked the guard, "May I give my brother his Bar Mitzvah ring?"

"No."

Jacob was led away.

Edith walked blindly back to where I was waiting.

"I have such a terrible feeling," she told me.

I took her arm and we both sobbed walking back to the bus.

Shortly after our visit, Jacob Weiss was hanged.

I thought, *I'm living in a culture of good and evil. The good comes from people who have survived the worst atrocities in history, and who are now trying to make a new home. The evil comes from those who perpetuate the atrocity by persecuting, imprisoning, and executing those who are trying to go home.*

Chapter Thirty-Seven

EXODUS 1947

I was in the YMCA covering more speeches, when one of the messengers who carried my cables to the post office entered the hall.

"We just heard," he told me breathlessly, "there's a battle at sea. The British are attacking a ship named *Exodus 1947,* with forty-five hundred refugees aboard."

I dashed off a brief cable to my editor, Joe Barnes, at the *Herald Tribune*. "The British are battling another refugee ship. I'm going to leave UNSCOP and cover the ship."

Without waiting for an answer, I found a friend who was willing to drive me from Jerusalem to Haifa.

Jerusalem was paralyzed. Factories were shutting down; offices closing; shopkeepers boarding up their windows and doors. Two British tanks attempted to drive through the chaotic streets, but were stopped, at least briefly, by three men who jumped in front of the heavy vehicles flailing their arms. I watched a soldier standing up in the turret of his tank, white-faced and shaking, as he called on his walkie-talkie for help.

On the road, we listened to the radio station *Kol Israel*—The Voice of Israel. We heard the voice of John Stanley Grauel, an American student-preacher who was on the ship describing the battle. Grauel spoke urgently: "This is the refugee ship *Exodus 1947*. Before dawn today we were attacked by five British destroyers and one cruiser at a distance of seventeen miles from the shores of Palestine, in international waters. The assailants immediately opened fire, threw gas bombs, and rammed our ship from three directions. On our deck there are one dead, five dying, and one hundred and twenty wounded. The resistance continued for more than three hours. Owing to the losses and the condition of the ship, which is in danger of sinking, we were compelled to sail in the direction of Haifa, in order to save the forty-five hundred refugees from drowning."

Our car was stopped by soldiers outside the Haifa docks. I walked to the waterfront. The harbor was a war zone with coils of rusted barbed wire, British Army tanks and trucks, and some five hundred troops of the 6th Airborne Division. The air was charged with the anticipation of soldiers waiting for the enemy.

The *Exodus* was still not in sight. The British officer commanding the dock was Major Cardozo, a diminutive martinet carrying a stick. He never walked, he danced. Dancing after him, I said, "Major, those three ships sitting out there—the *Runnymede Park, Empire Rival,* and *Ocean Vigour*—what are they doing there?"

"They're hospital ships," he answered. "We're going to put all the people into them and take them overnight to Cyprus."

"I'd like to go aboard one."

"Oh, no, no. But I can tell you they're a hell of a lot better than that tub they're on now. We've got beds for them, sheets and blankets and food."

I was to remember those words later.

British soldiers kept dropping depth charges to make sure the waters stayed clear of sabotage. At last the battered ship came into the harbor. It looked like a matchbox splintered by a nutcracker. One whole deck had been blasted open. I could see plumbing, broken staircases, and children running, their faces tormented with fear. Thousands of people crowded on the uppermost deck. The blue-and-white flag of Zion flew fore and aft. A sign on the ship read:

> HAGANNAH SHIP
> EXODUS 1947

The voices of people singing came to us on the quay. They were singing, "*Hatikvah*"—the song they sang at every crisis.

The people began coming down the gangway. Some of the British troops carried children; others dragged refugees who fought against disembarking. Some walked wearily, looking up at Haifa's Mount Carmel. Others, helped by their fellow passengers, had bandages on their heads, their legs, their arms, even their faces.

Nearly everyone carried a green bottle filled with water. It was the mark of the immigrant; water on the ship was scarce. Water meant survival, and it was the first thing the soldiers grabbed, smashing the bottles on the dock.

Next, their tattered bags and bundles were taken away. When the people clung to their few precious possessions, they were told: "You'll get everything back in Cyprus." Soldiers confiscated scissors, knives, razors—anything that might be a weapon. The British pulled off all the bandages to make sure refugees bound for the waiting ambulances were really wounded.

Men were separated from women. Some began screaming.

In the concentration camps, separation meant death. Here, they were forced into search pens, lean-tos made of strips of wood and potato sacks. I entered the women's pen and watched as four Arab women with holes in their black stockings frisked the women, and even the babies. Then the refugees were sprayed from head to toe with DDT.

The British had tried to prevent members of UNSCOP from coming to Haifa to see this latest tragedy. But they failed as two members of the committee appeared, escorted by the brilliant, young diplomat Abba Eban. They were Justice Emil Sandstrom of Sweden, UNSCOP chairman, in his immaculate white suit, and Vladimir Simich of Yugoslavia. As ambassadors to the United Nations they shrugged off British attempts to control their movements. Sandstrom was so moved by what he saw that he pronounced, "Britain must no longer have the mandate over Palestine."

The British arrested the first mate, Bernie Marks, the best American seaman on the ship, and Cy Weinstein, a tall, handsome seaman who limped from polio. Others, including the captain, smuggled themselves off the ship.

Emotionally exhausted, I left the harbor and joined some of the American members of the crew who had also smuggled themselves off. They took me to a small hotel in Haifa, where we joined American sailors who had come off earlier ships. From them, I learned during the battle, Yossi Harel, the political commander, and Ike Aronowitz, the short, young captain had ordered the crew and passengers: "We will not shoot. We will not fire any guns. We will fight back with fruit, potatoes, and cans of kosher beef."

The British, armed with stanchions and pistols, tossed firecrackers and tear-gas bombs onto the ship. In the black smoke and confusion, eighteen sailors managed to board.

In the end there were three deaths and one hundred fifty wounded. One of the victims was Bill Bernstein, the beloved second mate from San Francisco, who had been clubbed to death protecting the wheelhouse. The other two were sixteen-year-old orphans. One of them armed with an orange tossed it at a British soldier, who then shot him in the face.

Several months later in San Francisco, Bill Bernstein's brother gave me a letter Bill had written to his mother explaining why he was returning to Europe after a brilliant career as a lieutenant in the U.S. Navy during the war.

"You ask me to settle down, go to school," he wrote. "That's all very fine, Mom, but one doesn't find happiness by continually telling himself he's happy. Don't you think I would like a nice wife and kids and a good job? Of course I would, but I can't do that now. I say this knowing that your thoughts and heart are with me wherever I am and whatever I'm doing. If I lose that, I lose the only things that I own."

At midnight, I returned to the harbor in Haifa. There was an eerie silence. The refugees of the *Exodus 1947* were now all aboard the three ships I had seen in the harbor, bound, I had been led to believe, for Cyprus.

Chapter Thirty-Eight
CYPRUS AND PORT DE BOUC

Cyprus, the British crown colony, was being used as a prison island for Jewish refugees who were caught trying to enter Palestine. I had flown there, following Major Cardozo's assurance that this would be the destination of the *Exodus* refugees. I waited, but the three so-called hospital ships never came. They had disappeared, and no one was sure where they were.

The prison camps on Cyprus were a hellhole of desert sand and wind. The architecture was straight out of Auschwitz, with two rows of metal fences topped with barbed wire. There was no water, no privacy, no sanitation. Cyprus had to be smelled to be believed. Married couples hung army blankets in their tents to lend privacy to their lovemaking.

I had thought the DP camps in Germany and Austria were a disaster, but they began to look better when I saw Cyprus. At least in Europe, there were buildings and walls to protect the people from the weather. On Cyprus there was no protection from the elements at all. The DPs froze in winter and blistered in summer. I sent cables and photos to the *Herald Tribune* each day describing what 52,000 DPs transiting through Cyprus for two years were being forced to endure. Each month, the British allowed 750 to leave and enter Palestine legally. The order was "first in, first out"—those who had been there the longest would be the first to leave.

Golda Meir visited the camp one day with a message. She was still acting as the head of the political department of the Jewish Agency. She had convinced Sir Godfrey Collins, the commanding officer in charge of the Cyprus camps, to let parents with babies under one year old leave immediately. The doctors were afraid that a typhus epidemic would reach the most vulnerable in the camp—the babies.

Collins agreed to let parents and infants go, but only if those already slated to leave for Palestine offered up their spots. Golda had to persuade them to give up their places.

She climbed on top of several crates on a makeshift platform and addressed the crowd of refugees.

"There is typhus here in the camps," she said. "We cannot allow Jewish babies to die. We owe them life. I am asking you to make a sacrifice."

A man in the crowd shouted, "Hitler did enough to me in Europe. Now I've been in this hell for six months—I want to get out!"

"Friends, hear me out," Golda urged. "They are talking about us right now at the United Nations. I am sure you will not have to remain on Cyprus much longer. Eventually, all of you will be released, and you will be free to come home to us. If we delay getting the children right out, they may be dead. We want them to live. We want you to live. We want all of you to come home."

"She's right!" a woman cried, tears running down her cheeks. "I've waited so long, so many years. I can wait another month. Golda, take my certificate. I have no babies anymore to be saved. My babies are dead."

The people agreed. The "baby transport" sailed out of Cyprus to Haifa. But Golda's promise that the others would soon follow proved premature.

After more than a week of futility I left Cyprus and rejoined UNSCOP, traveling with them first to Lebanon and Syria, and then to Germany, where we visited more DP camps, beginning in Bergen-Belsen and ending in Vienna. While the committee left for Geneva to write its report, I flew to Port de Bouc in southern France. I had finally learned that the three ships, each carrying fifteen hundred Holocaust survivors, were docked at this small harbor town.

Late in the afternoon, I went out in a small motor launch to circle the three ships. They were anchored just inside the three-mile limit on the ocean side of a bleak gray stone lighthouse. Huge wire cages with coils and rusted barbed wire fenced in the tiny area on each ship where a handful of refugees, most of them women and children, were allowed on deck. They waved frantically, beckoning us closer.

A French longshoreman whom I had befriended turned to me in disgust. "The French people are ashamed of this," he shook his head. "Many of us have been in German prison camps during the war. I was in one for five years. I know who the enemy is. The people on those ships are not the enemy."

Now on August eighteenth, exactly a month after the refugees had been dragged off the ship in Haifa and transferred on these three ships, telegrams smuggled off the ship announced that the people were going on a twenty-four-hour hunger strike. Pregnant women, children, and sick people were asked by the leaders not to participate. They would not agree, and joined the strike against what they considered the apathy of a world that had conveniently forgotten them. The strike began in the morning. I watched as the launch carrying food rations for two days returned to shore without unloading. After the food had been turned away by the refugees, signs were strung up in English and French:

> OPEN THE DOORS OF PALESTINE—
> OUR ONLY HOPE!

A message from the *Ocean Vigour* to the press read, "How can you allow the English to treat us in such an inhuman way on this Nazi ship?"

The captain of the *Empire Rival* ordered that all books in Hebrew and Yiddish brought on deck burned. Among the books were prayer books and the Bible. The DPs sat grimly for hours, mourning the Book.

A letter of condolence and hope from Haganah men was smuggled aboard the *Ocean Vigour*. It began by greeting the refugees with the news that the press was finally waking up to their condition. I was startled to read in the letter: "The New York *Herald Tribune* sent one of its top journalists, Ruth Gruber, who was the first journalist sent by that paper to cover the UNSCOP inquiry into Eretz Israel. She also covered the Anglo-American Commission of Inquiry a year ago. She understands us well and her articles have special importance. Last night she tried to obtain permission to board the ships from the consul of 'rats', and he refused. She did manage to get to the vicinity of the ships and take photographs. Maybe she will get permission yet to board."

Three days later, on August 21, the British government delivered an ultimatum to the refugees ordering them to disembark before 6 P.M. the next day, or they would be transported to Hamburg, Germany. Soldiers distributed leaflets explaining that the people had two choices: leave the ship in France or be taken to Germany. The leaflets were translated into German, Yiddish, and Polish to make certain they were understood by everyone.

One of the refugee leaders made a speech denouncing the policy of the British in sending survivors of the death camps on Germany's blood-stained soil. When he finished, the refugees burst into applause. No one disembarked.

The world press was filled with outrage. Dozens of reporters descended on the little port city, demanding to be taken aboard the ships. The British consul, Edward Ashcroft, called us together on the wharf. "I cannot take you all aboard," he explained. He selected three journalists, one for the British press, one for the world press, and then chose me to represent all the American journalists.

Ashcroft sat next to me on the British launch as we rode out on a rough sea to the *Runnymede Park*. I was greeted by a young captain who led me to the fore section of the bridge. Hundreds of half-naked people were squeezed together in an open cage.

"It's good up here!" they shouted with bitter irony. "There's air here!"

"Air!" I thought. Inside the cage there was a green wooden toilet with six holes for fifteen hundred people. At the far end of the cage, half-naked young men and strong-looking women unfurled a huge flag. They had painted the swastika onto the British Union Jack. They were defying the British Empire; they were defying the whole world. I took several rolls of film of this flag of defiance. I felt I was not shooting a flag. I was photographing history.

The bolted wire gate was suddenly unlocked. The people

shouted to me, "Don't stand up here—go below. Go see our floating Auschwitz!"

The so-called "hospital ship" was in truth a prison. It was a former American Lend-Lease vessel that President Roosevelt had sent the British when their backs were against the wall. Ironically, they had even given the ship the noble name, *Runnymede Park*, the site where the Magna Carta was signed in 1215. Now, instead of returning it to the United States under the Lend Lease agreement, the British had converted it into a prison ship.

I descended a flight of slippery steps into the hold of the ship. The scene was a black-and-white image out of Dante's *Inferno*. Heads here, legs there. When the people heard that an American journalist who spoke their language had come aboard, they handed me slips of paper with telephone numbers—"Call my cousin in Chicago," "Call my mother in New York," "Call Detroit," "Call Los Angeles." I said I would make the calls as soon as I returned to New York.

Seeing that I had a camera, the people cried out, "Take pictures! Show the world how they treat us!"

I took pictures, though I wasn't sure if I could manage any decent shots. The only light came through little prison bars. I was blinded by the darkness and by their agony.

A young mother handed me her baby. I held it. "It's a beautiful baby," I told her. She looked at her child in my arms.

"Yes," she agreed, "but my life is over."

"How old are you?" I asked.

"Twenty-four."

"You musn't say that! You musn't talk that way!" I pleaded. "This will be over soon. You'll get there."

Everything I said sounded stupid. What few words I could summon seemed inadequate. But she was much wiser than I was.

"I know," she responded, "I'm going to live for this baby. I'm going to stay alive so my child won't be burned in a gas chamber. I'm going to live so my child can grow up in decency, without being afraid. There are no frontiers on Jewish hope."

Mr. Ashcroft, the consul, shouted, "We have to go now."

Back on the dock, Ashcroft held a final press briefing telling us when the ships were likely to arrive in Hamburg. Suddenly his eye fixed on my camera. He began to sputter in rage.

"I insist you give me that camera instantly, and all the film that you exposed."

I shook my head in disbelief. "Impossible. They are the property of the New York *Herald Tribune*."

"You had no permission to take pictures. You were the only American we allowed on board. You saw that we barred all photographers."

The photographers had indeed been barred, but so had all other newspaper people, all of whom were now watching this escalating scene.

"You—you," Ashcroft raged, "you smuggled that camera on board."

"Smuggled?" I repeated his word. "Smuggled! My camera kept hitting you in the thigh all the time we sat in the launch."

"Nonsense! I never saw that camera in my life."

"And where do you think I could have hidden this Rolleiflex?" I looked down at the scoop-necked cotton dress I was wearing, the only garment I could wear in the burning summer heat.

"I don't know where women hide things," he said testily. His face grew redder. "But I demand that camera and the films."

I clutched them tightly. "I'm sorry. They belong to my paper."

"You hand them over or the British government will bring charges against you and against the *Herald Tribune*. Your career is at stake. I warn you, both you and the *Herald Tribune* are in serious trouble."

"Sorry, Mr. Ashcroft," I said defiantly. "You'll have to get the British government to talk to my editor."

I turned on my heels, and as soon as I was out of sight, ran to get a cab. I told the driver to drive to Marseille as fast as he could. Back in the Hotel L'arbois, where everybody sat in the cocktail lounge, whispering about who was spying on whom for whom, I wrote my story of the final scenes in the prison hold and telephoned Paris so the story could be transmitted immediately to New York.

Then I asked the operator to connect me with Eric Hawkins. Eric was the editor of the *Paris Herald Tribune*. Eric, an Englishman, had never lost his British accent, nor his passion for justice.

He listened carefully as I told him of Ashcroft's threat. "Seems to me," Eric said, "that man is acting rather high-handed. Still," he paused. I thought we had been disconnected when he went on. "We don't know what he's up to. Where are the films now?"

"I've got them."

"Good girl. Can you catch a plane and get here first thing tomorrow morning? We'll decide how to handle the pictures and the British Empire."

The next morning I flew to Paris.

"I don't know what he may have up his sleeve," Eric said, "but we'd better see the pictures right away. Particularly since nobody else has any pictures of those prison ships."

Eric had the pictures printed. I didn't know if any of them would turn out, especially those taken in the dark hold of the ship.

"The pictures are great," Eric told me. "I never cry over pictures, but these made me weep."

"I wept taking them."

"Now listen," Eric said, "we've got a world exclusive. But we've got to figure out what the British are up to. Whom do you know at the Foreign Office? Anybody? Maybe we could get some inkling of what this consul has up his sleeve."

I knew Charles Campbell. Charlie had been in charge of the American press for the British government when I worked in Washington. Now he was a top official in the information section of the Foreign Office.

Within hours, I flew to London and telephoned Charlie.

"I'm in London for a few hours," I said. "Will you have a drink with me?" In Washington, Charlie could drink anybody under the table.

We met at a bar near the Foreign Office. We reminisced about the good old days in Washington. Then, trying to be casual, I told him I had just been in Marseille covering the *Exodus* prison ships. "The British consul accused me of smuggling my Rolleiflex aboard. Now he's threatening me and the *Herald Tribune*."

Charlie burst into laughter. "Some of those characters we have in little jobs out in the provinces love to play God and the British Empire." He downed his scotch. "It reminds me," he said, "of the time the Nazi government threatened the *Boston Globe*. It was during the late thirties. The paper had been printing some pretty grim things about Hitler, and one day the Nazi consul called up the editors of the *Globe*: 'If you don't stop printing lies about Der Führer, we won't send you any more press releases.'"

I left Charlie hurriedly, and dashed to a phone to call Eric Hawkins in Paris.

"The pictures belong to the *Herald Tribune*," Eric said, "but I think we have got to give them to the world."

He turned the pictures over to the Associated Press. Within about eight seconds, they were flashed around the world. The picture of the swatstika painted on the Union Jack became *Life* magazine's Photo of the Week, and the most famous photo I have ever taken.

After the pictures were published, I thought of the words of a young Haganah girl who had stood near me in Port de Bouc, watching the three prison ships sail for Germany. We both wept as they sailed past us.

"Now," the young girl told me, "you will see the birth of a Jewish state."

Her words were prophetic. In Germany, the people of the *Exodus* were once again forced off the ships and taken to camps near Leipzig. One by one, they escaped, found their way across Europe, boarded more "illegal ships," and set sail again for the Land of Israel.

Chapter Thirty-Nine

A LINE OF FIRE AND BLOOD

UNSCOP's report on Palestine was due September 1, 1947. In Geneva, amid fierce debate, the eleven committee members finally reached their decision. They voted to partition Palestine into a Jewish state and an Arab state. Their conclusions would have to be voted on in November by the United Nations General Assembly.

On an Indian summer day in September, Helen Reid's secretary, Kay, called. "Mrs. Reid would like you to spend the weekend at her home in Westchester."

The leaves were gold and crimson as I reached Ophir Cottage, the Reid estate in Purchase, New York. As soon as I settled in, Helen took me into the study. She stretched a huge map across the floor and beckoned to me to come kneel with her.

"Now let's just follow where you traveled, and what was happening there," she said.

Her excitement and enthusiasm energized me. Her questions about the *Exodus* and the prison camps in Cyprus were filled with compassion and anger. Here she was, through marriage, part of British royalty; her husband's sister, Jean, with whom Helen had spent many months in London, was married to John Ward, a member of British aristocracy. Yet Helen turned out to be the strongest and most powerful advocate the refugees had in both the American and international press.

Most of the weekend, from a gala dinner party to breakfast and lunch, was spent discussing UNSCOP and its conclusions. It was still unclear whether Britain would accept the UN committee's report. A split appeared to be developing in high government circles and inside the Foreign Office itself over the soundness of their Middle East strategy. Some were still clinging to the belief that Palestine was important to the empire as a military base; others were beginning to feel it was not so strategically important after all.

Though she rarely talked about herself, I began to learn more about Helen that weekend, and in the weeks that followed. This tiny woman who was a giant in the publishing world.

Helen Rogers was born in the small town of Appleton, Wisconsin, the youngest of eleven children. Her father, a much-loved leader in the community, died when she was three. The only thing she remembered of him was that he had taken her to the circus, and hen her handkerchief fell between the seats, her father bent down to pick it up. Her mother, left to cope with a huge family, dragged Helen from pillar to post, and when she was ten, left her in a boarding school run by Helen's oldest brother. I wondered if her passion for DPs came from that experience. She was a DC—a displaced child.

When she was sixteen, she left for New York to attend Barnard College. She looked back upon the Barnard years as the happiest of her life. When her money ran out during her sophomore year, she worked in the bursar's office to pay her way. At her senior prom, sitting with a boyfriend, a classmate approached her. "A Mrs. Whitelaw Reid, whose husband owns the New York Herald Tribune, is looking for a secretary. I thought you might like to apply." Helen had hoped to become a teacher of Greek, but decided to look into this job opportunity.

Mrs. Whitelaw Reid, who was even tinier than Helen, hired her immediately. She liked what she saw in the young woman from the midwest: Helen was serious, dependable, bright, and ambitious. When Mr. Reid was named ambassador to London, Helen traveled with the family and became an intimate friend of their daughter, Jean.

It was in London that Helen met the son and heir to the Reid fortune, young Ogden, home from Yale. Ogden was smitten, and soon began taking her to dinner and the theater. Their courtship was stormy, with Helen worried that the elder Reids did not consider her an eligible wife for their only son. Ogden paid little attention to his parents; he was determined to marry her. When Helen tried to end the relationship, he followed her back to Wisconsin, and they were married in Racine in 1911.

The headlines were giddy:

ENGAGEMENT OF AMBASSADOR'S SON AND MISS
ROGERS SURPRISES SOCIETY

AMBASSADOR'S SON TO WED SECRETARY OF
HIS MOTHER

ROMANCE OF POOR GIRL AND YALE ATHLETE,
NOW A REPORTER AND HEIR TO MANY MILLIONS

Helen gave birth to three children: Whitelaw, called "Whitie"; Elizabeth, called "Betty"; and Ogden, called "Brownie" as a youngster, and later "Brown." Helen told me the greatest tragedy of her life was the death of her nine-year-old daughter, Betty, from typhoid.

Tears filled her eyes. "I could have brought the greatest specialists in the world to save her. But I failed."

I wondered if this tragedy was one of the reasons Helen worked so hard helping young women become journalists.

In 1918, the *Tribune* was failing when Ogden asked her to become a salesperson in the advertising unit. She had no formal training in journalism, but she had the heart of a journalist. Soon she was a power in the editorial department. She was interested in everything—politics, economics, society, family, and especially children. She broke new trails, dividing the paper into sections so that people could turn easily to the parts that fit their lives. Other papers soon copied what she had done. The *Herald Tribune* became the morning rival to the *New York Times*.

During that first weekend together Helen urged me to write a book telling the story of *Exodus 1947* and Cyprus. I began immediately and wrote the manuscript from my heart, in six weeks. I then telephoned William Shawn, the editor of *The New Yorker* who invited me to his office at five o'clock, on Friday, November 14. Shawn was a legend in the publishing business. We talked for a while; he told me he had read my articles and knew the whole story.

"Leave the manuscript with me," he said. "I'll call you in a few days."

A week later we lunched at the famous writers' table in the Algonquin Hotel. "We're going to print it," he told me. "I've made some suggestions." He handed me the manuscript with his notes. Again, working swiftly, I made the corrections he suggested to help tighten and shape the manuscript. I called H. R. to tell her the news.

"Good. The story belongs in *The New Yorker,*" she agreed.

My excitement was short-lived. Shawn again called me to his office.

"Mr. Fleischman, the owner of *The New Yorker,* has cancelled the story."

"Why?" I murmured in shock.

"He feels it's too Jewish," Shawn explained. "But, wait a minute."

He telephoned Bruce Bliven, the editor of the *New Republic*. Sight unseen, Bliven bought the story and printed it in three editions under the title "Exodus Memoirs: The First Complete Story of a Tragic Voyage."

The *Exodus* and Cyprus continued to be front page news. *Collier's* magazine asked me to write an eyewitness account and filled it with my photos. They ran ads in the *New York Times* announcing the "exclusive story of the British prison camps on Cyprus." I prayed the stories would help open the gates to Cyprus. To no avail.

On November 29, 1947, the United Nations General Assembly debated UNSCOP's report. I sat in the press gallery on the edge of my chair. How would the fifty-eight member nations vote? The resolution needed two-thirds of the assembly to be adopted. The role call reverberated through the vast assembly hall. One by one, in alphabetical order, the delegates called out "yes," "no," or "abstain." By a vote of 33 (including the United States and the Soviet Union) to 13 (including all the Arab nations), with 10 abstentions (including Great Britain), the United Nations voted to recommend the partition of Palestine into a Jewish state and an Arab state. When the final count was announced, Saudi Arabia's delegates, Azzam Pasha and Prince Faisal marched out of the chamber, followed by a small army of robed men with checkered headdresses, their faces rigid in anger.

"Any line of partition drawn in Palestine," Azzam Pasha declared, "will be a line of fire and blood."

I watched them stalk through the hall, filled with mixed emotions: joy that the DPs would at last have a home, and fear that this home, like the birth of a child, would certainly be born in blood.

Part 4

THE BIRTH
OF ISRAEL

Chapter Forty

THE NATION IS BORN, THE WAR BEGINS

S itting at her home in Jerusalem, Golda Meir had listened to the entire debate on the radio. The stunning vote in the United Nations sent her into the streets of Tel Aviv. People were dancing and singing.

She hurried into the huge courtyard of the Jewish Agency, filled with hundreds of revelers. Even British soldiers, against orders, were joining in and dancing the hora. Some people shouted to her, "Golda, speak, speak." She stepped out onto the balcony and addressed the people, with a special message to the Arabs:

"You have fought your battle against us in the United Nations. The majority of countries in the world have had their say. The partition plan is a compromise: not what you wanted, not what we wanted. But let us now live in friendship and peace together."

Instead, fighting broke out almost immediately. Jamal Husseni, the spokesman for the Arab Higher Committee, who had earlier announced that Arabs would drench "the soil of our beloved country with the last drop of our blood," now proclaimed: "We will fight for every inch of this country." In

Egypt, leaders in the Al-Azhar University exhorted the Muslim world to proclaim a *jihad*—a holy war—against the Jews. Arab irregulars began infiltrating the borders; Arab nations were already collecting guns and munitions to strengthen their armies for the inevitable war.

The Jews had no real militia, and President Truman and the State Department banned sending arms to the Jews. Ben-Gurion was prepared to travel to America to raise money, but the Jewish Agency decided he was too valuable in Palestine. He sent Golda Meir instead. I met with her several times in her suite in New York's Hotel 14, the unofficial Jewish embassy.

In her first speech, given in Chicago for the non-Zionist General Assembly of Jewish Federations and Welfare Funds, she spoke passionately:

"My friends, we are at war. There is no Jew in Palestine who does not believe that finally we will be victorious. That is the spirit of the country. But this valiant spirit alone cannot face rifles and machine guns."

Her six-week trip in America raised over fifty million dollars. It was used immediately to buy munitions in Europe. Ben-Gurion congratulated her on her return home. "Someday," he told her, "when history will be written, it will be said that there was a Jewish woman who got the money which made the state possible." Golda told him that the people of America had given the money not to her, but to Israel.

In January 1948, one thousand Arabs attacked northern Palestine, and in the next weeks, Arab armies from neighboring countries also invaded. The British openly sided with the Arab, training the army of Jordan and providing them with arms and officer leadership. The British stayed on for six months, blocking Jewish immigration, outlawing Jewish militias, and confiscating any Jewish arms they located.

In the prison camps of Cyprus, young men of military age were barred from leaving. Even those whose turn had come were forced to remain on the island. Britain wanted to make certain they would not join the Haganah and fight the invading Arabs. Still, many made their way onto the ships, posing as crippled or frail old men. While I was on Cyprus waiting in vain for the forty-five hundred *Exodus* refugees to arrive, I became a minor Picasso, painting wrinkles on the faces of twenty-year-olds, and helping fit ugly false teeth in their mouths. Some were caught when British officers tested their biceps and sent them back to their tents. But many succeeded in fooling the officers and received certificates to leave. They promptly jumped onto one of the ships headed for Haifa, and immediately joined the secret army.

American Jewish leaders mobilized for action. Rabbi Abba Hillel Silver of Cleveland, Ohio, was granted an interview with President Truman. The rabbi, tall, dramatic, and famous for his florid oratory, pounded the president's desk in an impassioned speech. Truman was furious.

"No one pounds my desk," the president later told me. He ordered that no more Jewish leaders be permitted into the White House.

The one Jew whom Truman never barred was Eddie Jacobson. They had fought together in World War I, with Truman as a captain and Eddie as his sergeant. After the war, they opened a haberdashery shop in Kansas City, Missouri. During a recession, their shop went bankrupt, yet both men repaid every penny they owed to their creditors.

I met Eddie in the spring of 1948 on a speaking tour in Kansas City. We soon became such good friends that Eddie's wife, Bluma, invited me to leave my hotel and come stay with them and their two young daughters.

Eddie was asked by Jewish community leaders to intervene with the president and urge him to see Dr. Weizmann.

"I was sitting in the White House with my friend," Eddie told me in his living room, "and I said, 'Mr. President, you have a hero—Andrew Jackson. I have a hero—it's Dr. Chaim Weizmann. I would like you to see my hero.'"

Eddie paused and reflected. "I saw the president look out the window. I was silent. I knew what he was thinking. Then he turned to me and he said, 'I'll see him. Send him here Saturday, but have him come in the kitchen entrance. The British ambassador will be leaving though the front door.'"

Years later in Independence, Missouri, Truman described his meeting with Dr. Weizmann to me. The Jewish leader, frail and nearly blind, was ushered into Truman's office. "I was so impressed with him." The former president said, "He presented me with a Torah." Truman's hand shaped the holy scroll in the air. "It was something I had always wanted. Then we went to my globe, and he showed me the Negev Desert and why the Jews needed that desert."

The president had become cool to partition, but Dr. Weizmann won him over. However, the State Department was determined to destroy the plan. Our UN representative, Warren Austin, prepared to give a speech to the United Nations suggesting that partition be forgotten, and that a temporary trusteeship over Palestine be established.

Defense Secretary James Forrestal announced that the Pentagon, also opposed to partition, would not send any munitions to Palestine. The State Department was so hostile that General George Marshall, the secretary of state, warned Moshe Sharett, with undiplomatic furor, "Do not declare a state."

But Ben-Gurion allowed no obstacles to stop him. Helped by the funds Golda had raised, Ben-Gurion was able to purchase airplanes from Czechoslovakia. They arrived on April 1, 1948. A few days later, machine guns and rifles followed.

The Arabs, with munitions from all the neighboring states, continued their attacks. A convoy carrying seventy-five doctors and nurses of the Hadasah Medical Center was attacked by Arabs and burned alive.

On Friday, May 14, 1948, Ben-Gurion spoke at a museum in Tel Aviv and read the world's newest Declaration of Independence. The whole audience stood up and applauded when they heard him say, "The state of Israel will be open to Jewish immigration and the ingathering of the Arab people dwelling in Israel to keep the peace and to play their part in building the state." He then offered his hope for "peace and good neighborliness" with the Arab states that had already begun the war. He ended his speech with the words, "I do hereby proclaim the establishment of a Jewish state in the Land of Israel—the State of Israel."

While people danced in the streets, Ben-Gurion went home and spoke solemnly to his wife, Paula, "I feel like the mourner at the festival." He envisioned terrible bloodshed.

That afternoon, I was sitting in the press gallery at a United Nations meeting in Lake Success, New York watching Warren Austin hurry to the podium to discuss the State Department's trusteeship plan. He had not quite reached the podium when one of his staff stopped him and announced: "Ben-Gurion has just declared statehood in Tel Aviv." Austin returned to his seat and soon, dejected, left the building.

Eleven minutes after Ben-Gurion's declaration, President Truman recognized the new state, the first world leader to do so. At the UN, an American delegate went to the podium.

"This government has been informed that a Jewish state has been proclaimed in Palestine. The United States government recognizes the Provisional Government as the *de facto* authority of the State of Israel."

In the visitor's gallery, in the press section, all of us burst into applause. Our excitement continued unabated. I joined friends at a party in New York, where we sang and danced and asked each other, "Can you believe it?"

Before dawn a radio operator pounded on Ben-Gurion's door in Tel Aviv.

"You must speak to the American people, thanking President Truman."

Ben-Gurion flung a coat over his pajamas and drove to the radio station. It was 5:20 A.M. Saturday morning in Israel, 10:20 P.M. Friday in New York.

At midnight, Sir Alan Cunningham, British High Commissioner for Palestine, closed the door of Government House on the Hill of Evil Counsel in Jerusalem and departed. The mandate was over. Britain no longer controlled the Holy Land.

Tears rolled down my face. The months I had spent with the Anglo-American Committee and UNSCOP telescoped together. I had learned so much, experienced so much tragedy and hope. How worthwhile it had all been. How gratifying that the DPs would no longer suffer in the DP camps in Europe. Cyprus would be cleaned out. The Jews of the *Exodus* had come home.

Around me, my friends were still singing and dancing when someone turned on the radio.

"Listen everybody, Ben-Gurion is talking."

A hush fell across the room. I could picture him—this short, sturdy man of the people speaking with passion about the country he had done so much to create. In the middle of the speech there was a loud explosion. Then silence. Ben-Gurion said solemnly, "An Egyptian bomb has just fallen on Tel Aviv."

Chapter Forty-One
LIFE AS A WAR CORRESPONDENT

W e want you to go back to Israel and cover the war."

Helen Reid was at her desk, her jade eyes shining at me as she gave me the paper's most coveted wartime assignment.

I stood up, leaned across the desk, and took her hand. "I promise you I'll cover this war with every cell in my body."

"I know that. That's why we chose you to be part of the team."

Later I learned from Herb Kupferberg, the *Herald Tribune*'s music critic, that L. L. (Lessing Lanham) Engelking, the city editor who could be crude and nasty, and then apologetic, had confronted H. R. at a staff meeting: "How can you send Ruth? What does she know about covering a war?"

Helen looked at him and said, "I'm sending her."

Now in her office, Helen gave me another assignment. "Before you go, I want you to talk to the Federation of

Women's Clubs. They're meeting right now in New York. They represent thousands of women across the country. I want you to tell them about the *Exodus* and Cyprus. They should know those stories. I'll arrange for you to address them."

Almost from the moment I entered the Hotel Commodore, I felt their hostility. Their president, Mrs. LaFell Dickinson of Keene, New Hampshire, announced in an irritated voice, "Mrs. Ogden Reid has asked me to break into our program to listen to a speaker who has to leave tomorrow to cover the war in Israel."

My heart was thumping as I walked to the dais. How could I make these women understand these dark historic years from the end of World War II to the birth of Israel?

I never speak from notes. Here especially, I wanted to see the audience, feel whether they cared about a subject that was consuming me. How could I make them see DPs not as statistics, but as human beings, with faces and hearts and souls?

Words failed me. There was no connective tissue; even the ideas were choppy. I could almost touch the women's impatience, their restlessness, their resentment that their program was being messed up. I could tell my speech was an utter failure.

I cut it short, thanked the audience, heard some polite applause, and hurried home to pack. The next day the *Herald Tribune* carried chunks of the speech. It gave me no comfort.

Early in the evening, I sailed for Israel on a freighter called the *Meridian Victory*. All airlines had canceled their flights to the brand new country at war.

The freighter was small, but in its hold, it carried many of the gifts friends asked me to bring to their relatives in Israel. Among the gifts were a refrigerator, bags of coffee, a tub of butter, salami, and cartons of cigarettes.

The passengers were all people determined to be in the newly founded state. Pnina Zaitman, later Shallon, was hurrying back to her home in Tel Aviv, where she taught art in a high school. She later became one of Israel's most creative dress designers. Relationships develop quickly aboard a ship, and almost from the first day, Pnina and I began a close friendship. We were sitting on deck chairs one afternoon when a steward approached us, offering coffee. He asked Pnina, "Why didn't you stay in America instead of going back to all the shooting?"

Pnina answered, "When something is being built for the first time in two thousand years, you must go back. Everyone has to do his or her part. Even if I can just cook meals for the soldiers, it is something."

I remembered one of Golda's speeches in America: "We have a secret weapon," she told her audience. "It is *ein brera*—no alternative. We will stay, because we have nowhere else to go."

In twelve days we would be reaching a new democracy, where the butcher and baker, the prima donna of the Habima theater, and the leading physicist of the Weizmann Institute all drank coffee in the same cafe. My mind flashed back to Alaska. There, too, millionaires and sourdoughs ate lunches together. But while pioneers in Alaska cut down trees to develop new towns, in Israel they had planted trees to reclaim the once fertile ancient land from the desert's grip.

Another passenger determined to go home was Professor Jacques Faitlovitch, a small old man who had startled the world when he discovered there were black Jews living in Ethiopia. Each day, walking the decks, he told me how these unknown people had clung to their Jewishness through the ages. They thought they were the only Jews alive; they could not believe there were any other Jews in the world, let alone white-skinned ones. Faitlovitch was devoting his life to saving them from extinction. His words inspired me forty years later to travel to Ethiopia to help rescue them in Operation Moses, and to write a book called *Rescue: The Exodus of the Ethopian Jews.*

Now, sailing through the Mediterranean, we listened to the radio broadcasting news of the war. The fighters of the Haganah were moving rapidly against five Arab states. Egypt on the south and west, Lebanon and Syria on the north, Jordan and Iraq from the east.

We arrived in Haifa on July 10, joined immediately by immigration, quarantine, and police officials who came aboard the ship and greeted us effusively.

"Welcome. Shalom. Shalom. Shalom."

On earlier trips, British officials often had made me feel like a criminal. Now, I was in a country of Jews where I was wanted. Still, the customs official charged me one pound twenty-five piasters, about four dollars, for each carton of cigarettes.

"Israel needs money," he apologized.

Tel Aviv was my home base. The mood of the city was one of freedom. The nightly curfews I had lived under while the British were there were gone, along with the barbed wire and the air of a police state. Whatever restrictions were there now were war-imposed and self-imposed. The Hebrew word one heard most often in Tel Aviv was *shelanu,* meaning "ours." Our land. Our culture. Our language. Ours.

Despite the war, the people walked along the beautiful promenade and the beach on the Mediterranean. They sat in cafes, danced and sang, or sipped coffee and ate ice cream. They told me, "It's all ours."

Egyptian bombs kept dropping on the city six or seven times a day. Sirens shrieked and people raced into the air raid shelters below their houses or their basements. As soon at the "all clear" sounded, they came out walking tall and proud, a free people building a new state.

I was in an apartment in Tel Aviv interviewing a refugee family when a bomb dropped on the three-story building. We heard the siren and rushed into the basement. A few minutes later, another bomb fell on the building, plummeting straight down. On each floor, it killed the people directly in its path; on the top floor it killed a rabbi, on the next, it killed a mother and child. I was shaken. When the "all clear" finally sounded, those of us who had found refuge walked up the stairs to the street. The families of the victims came out weeping. Surveying the rubble, I thought about the randomness of war. *Why the rabbi? Why the mother and child? Why not me in the basement?*

One day I learned that Joe Weiner, a red-headed former officer in the Canadian army, now commander of the 7th armored regiment of the 71st Battalion, was hoping to capture Nazareth. He had sent word to his troops, "I want no reporters and no photographers. If any show up, tell them they are barred."

I jumped into a jeep with a photographer and managed to convince one of the soldiers that I was an old friend of Joe's. If Joe didn't want me, I would go back.

We reached Joe at the head of his unit.

"What in the name of—" he exploded. "What are you doing up here? Don't you know I said no reporters?"

"This is a battle I want to cover."

"I'm a Canadian. You can get me into trouble with my government."

"I promise I won't mention your name."

"Follow me," he ordered.

We fell in behind him leading the convoy up winding hills to the outskirts of Nazareth. Joe jumped out of his jeep, halting the convoy. He motioned to me to join him as he climbed to an isolated house on a high hill. He knocked on the door, shouting "Open. This is the Israeli army."

The terrified owner raised his arms in the air, "Don't shoot. Don't shoot."

"We're not going to shoot you," Joe said calmly. "Send one of your sons to bring the mayor and the Moslem and Christian leaders of Nazareth up here."

Soon the leaders climbed up the hill carrying a white flag. Joe talked with them, assuring them no one would be harmed.

At 11:30 that night Joe and the Israeli army officers sat at one side of the dining room table, while the Moslem and Christian leaders sat at the other side signing a document of peace typed in Hebrew on plain white paper. One of the conditions on which Mayor Yusef Effendi Yahum agreed to surrender was that he would remain as mayor and represent his people with the occupying Israeli forces. Joe agreed. He had captured Nazareth with the surprise tactics of a Saturday afternoon college football game. The city where Jesus had lived and preached was unscathed. Not a single bullet had been fired. With a full moon lighting up the hills, the bells of Nazareth rang out peace.

A few days later, traveling with another army unit, I heard the commanding officer tell his troops, "We are about to enter an Arab village. We will not touch a single mosque."

I cabled the paper describing the care the soldiers took protecting the mosque. Joe Barnes sent me a message: "Your story changed the vote at the United Nations. They were going to censor Israel. But when the Israeli delegate stood up and read your article to the General Assembly, the debate ended."

Chapter Forty-Two

BRUSHES WITH DEATH,
BRUSHES WITH GREATNESS

G olda Meir had just been named Envoy Extraordi-
naire and Minister Potentiary to the Soviet Union
when she invited me to her apartment in Tel Aviv.
Dressed in her usual white blouse and black skirt, she served
the two of us tea and chocolate chip cookies she had baked. In
her kitchen she was the consummate hostess, talking about her
early life, her arrival in Palestine with her husband, and her
philosophy of activism.

"The thing that mattered most in my life," she told me, "was
that if a thing has to be done, you don't waste time with theories and debates. You just do it. In America, when I realized
that Zionism was the solution to the Jewish Problem, I came
here. I realized that Israel could only be built by Jews who were
ready and willing to come."

Her voice was a little hoarse as she spoke. I remembered how
she had electrified American audiences with her inexorable
logic and the inevitability of her words. With Golda there was

no oratory, no dramatics, not a single stage trick; each word followed the other like footsteps of soldiers in a parade so that the cumulative effect was overwhelming.

"I foresee," she said, "that for a number of years we will have a government made up of a variety of parties. The effort on everyone's part will be to build a state and absorb immigrants. Immigration will remain the chief aim of our government for quite a few years."

During one of the truces that usually lasted about ten days, I was able to make the trip from Tel Aviv to Jerusalem. I traveled on the road the American West Point graduate Mickey Marcus had built to circumvent Arab snipers and bring supplies to Jerusalem under siege. It was dubbed the "Burma Road" in memory of the famous road that had helped save Burma. I was covered in dust from the long drive, heading to the home of my friend Hanna Ruppin, where I was to spend the next few days. Hanna's husband, Arthur, was one of the creators of the kibbutz movement in Israel.

"I'm going to give you a shower right away," Hanna told me, leading me to her bathroom.

"But Hanna," I protested, "there is so little water in Jerusalem—don't waste it on me."

"We use water four ways," she explained. "First for cooking, then for showering, then to sponge the floor, and last, for the toilet." Soon I was covered with soap while Hanna poured water on my head from one of her cooking pots, and saved the water.

I spent the next few days walking the streets of Jerusalem. Unlike Tel Aviv, Jerusalem looked like a city coming back from the dead. There was an unearthly stillness. Some of the people walked slowly, as though they had forgotten how to walk and were rehearsing. Jerusalem was not a conquered city, but a city that had held up under a long siege and was just beginning to breathe air again.

At a party one evening I heard Major Memi de Shalit say, "I'm taking a convoy to Tel Aviv tomorrow."

Memi, the son of one of Israel's pioneering families, was a smiling, easygoing officer who looked more like a vice president of a bank than a senior military man.

"Can I go with you?" I asked. "There are some stories I want to cover in Tel Aviv."

"Of course," he agreed, "You can even ride with me in the lead jeep."

We set out early the next morning leading what looked like a mile-long caravan of public buses, taxies, heavy trucks, motorcycles, and private cars.

Memi explained how the convoy worked. "We travel as far as the Latrun Monastery and jail. Yes, it's the famous jail where the British locked up all our leaders on Black Saturday. You know we've made several attempts and haven't been able to capture Latrun yet."

I nodded. I had covered one of those disastrous battles with the army.

"Don't worry," Memi said, squeezing the steering wheel as if it were a shotgun, "we'll succeed one of these days. Latrun is a nemesis. Meanwhile, to get back to the convoy, we drive up to the outskirts of the monastery and wait there for a United Nations escort. He takes us across the monastery grounds to the other side; there he waves us off and we're free to go on to Tel Aviv."

I leaned back in the jeep, the day was beautiful; the Jerusalem sun was shining, no bombs were falling, and no shots were exploding in the air. I felt safe knowing that Memi and the UN were protecting us.

We were approaching Latrun, when Memi said, "I have

some business with the Father Superior. If you would like to stretch your legs, you can come out and sit on the porch. No women are allowed in this monastery, and only the Father Superior and interns are allowed to speak."

I settled into a wicker chair on the terrace and watched him enter the monastery. Within minutes, an Arab wearing a black-and-white striped gown, a checkered *keffiyeh* and holding a shotgun came out from behind a bush. Creeping on all fours, he began to come toward me with his gun pointed right at my head, yelling at me in Arabic. As he crawled, his shotgun began to grow until it looked to me like a cannon.

Memi heard the shouting and came running out. Soon the Arab, screaming louder than ever, pointed the gun at him. I thought this is the last day on earth for the two of us.

I'm not sure how long he held us at gunpoint; it seemed like an hour—it was probably ten minutes. He was about six feet from us when a strapping young intern rushed out of the monastery and began screaming at him in Arabic. He motioned for the man to move back. It was to no avail. The Arab continued haranguing us, his face growing fiercer with anger and frustration.

The intern warned us, "Sit still—I'm getting us help." It was unnecessary advice. We were rigid with fear.

He flew across the field and within minutes returned on a jeep with a handsome young British officer, who drove standing up at the wheel. He looked like Robert Taylor arriving to save the day in a Hollywood war film. He shouted commands in Arabic and, with his eyes flashing, waved the gunman to move back.

Even in the face of imminent death, an odd thought flashed through my head: "I hope this character doesn't shoot the officer. He's too handsome to be shot."

Whatever the Englishman said worked. Slowly, the Arab, still crawling on all fours with his gun pointed at us, inched backwards.

"Get in my jeep fast," the Englishman commanded us, "and get down on the floor. You never know where that man might be hiding."

We crouched on the floor until he drove us back to our convoy, then led the whole caravan to safety on the other side of Latrun. From there, we traveled on to Tel Aviv.

The next day, another convoy returned to Jerusalem from Tel Aviv by the same route we had taken. They were ambushed not by one but by a whole group of Arabs before they reached Latrun. The commanding officer of the convoy shouted, "Everybody into the ditches."

An American engineer stood up in a car waving his passport. "I promised my wife I would see Jerusalem before I leave. She'll never forgive me if I don't get there."

An Arab bullet pierced his chest and he fell dead. The daughter of a Dutch banker was killed as well. Major de Shalit phoned me, "They probably thought that young woman was you."

The truce ended several days later. Both sides took advantage of the pause to bring in ammunition and more soldiers. I was in the government press office when I received a cable from Joe Barnes: "Can you get an interview with Ben-Gurion."

I telephoned Nehemiah, the aide Ben-Gurion loved even more than he loved his son, Amos. "Nehemiah," I said, "Can you set up an appointment with B. G.?"

"I'll call you back," he told me.

Within minutes, the phone rang. "Come now."

Ben-Gurion was seated at his desk when I entered. "Sit down," he said, and waited for me to speak.

"B. G.," I said, "The *Herald Tribune* wants an interview with you."

"You—you ought to know better," he responded. "You know I'm not giving interviews. Not to the *New York Times,* the *Washington Post*—not even the Israeli papers."

"B. G., I won't ask you a thing about the war," I assured him. "I know you're going to win it. I'm not going to ask you a thing about politics," I continued. "I want you to shut your eyes and dream. I want you to tell me what Israel will look like when the blood has stopped flowing and the Jews have come home."

For a few minutes, he shut his eyes. The sun was setting on his halo of white hair, turning it silver. I could almost forget that Arab armies were a few miles away and that the sound of shooting never stopped. When he spoke, his words were slow and tinged with hope.

"There will be no more desert. There will be no more sand. There will be trees on every hill."

The glow on his face showed he was beginning to enjoy his dream of an Israel at peace.

"The sky will be full of planes," he went on. "The sea will be full of ships. There will be small towns and villages, not big cities like you have in America. We are a little country. There will be white cottages and lots of children—children are our future."

His eyes were still closed. I broke the silence.

"What will be the philosophy of life be in this cottage civilization?"

His eyes were open now as he spoke, "It takes too many words in English. In Hebrew it takes only three—*Veahavta reekh'a kamoh'a*. It means 'love your neighbor as yourself.'"

Chapter Forty-Three

FALLING IN LOVE IN PUERTO RICO

With the gates of Israel now open, Jews began pouring in from Europe, North Africa, and the Middle East. They came in such large numbers that the new nation was unable to build enough homes for them. Instead they were put into camps. I entered many of the camps and was shocked to see how they were living. Women in tents during a rainstorm showed me they were in mud up to their knees. I went to see Ben-Gurion.

"Of all countries," I began, "you should not be putting newcomers into camps. I was connected with a camp in upper New York in a place called Oswego. We gave the people good food and what they wanted most, education for their children. True, they lived in barracks, but they were protected from bad weather. For most of the young people who had been running for years with no schooling, it was a good experience. But some of the older people deteriorated. A camp is a camp is a camp. We brought in psychologists and no one could help them.

What they wanted was to get out of the camp and begin a new life of freedom. Life in a camp can drive some to madness, even suicide."

Ben-Gurion said, "Write me a report."

I spent the whole night writing. "Historically," I began, "the camps in Israel are one of the world's most ironic failures. Jews are running camps for Jews, and they seem to have learned nothing from their own tragedy.

"Some of the administrators just don't like people. Medical personnel is woefully inadequate. Some of the camps are so filthy, so rat-ridden, that if an epidemic broke out, the entire state would be in danger. There is leprosy; there are hundreds of cases of trachoma; and babies are dying of dysentery."

I concluded, "Camps are never good for human beings. People deteriorate amid the abnormality of camp life. In Germany and Cyprus there was hope, Israel lay ahead. Here there is no hope—unless action is taken immediately."

As I handed Ben-Gurion the report, I told him, "Not a single member of your cabinet has been inside one of these camps."

I watched B. G. reading the report. He called Nehemiah. "I want this report translated right now and sent to every cabinet member with an order that they visit the camps immediately." He stood up, came around his desk, and shook my hand.

"You are a *behriah*," he said. "Do you know what that means?"

"Sure, my mother was a *behriah*," I replied. "It meant she was a good housekeeper."

"No," he said irritated. "That's not what it means. It means you give someone a job and they do it."

The war was winding down. I said good-bye to my friends in Israel and returned to New York to spend the high holidays with the family. My book on the *Exodus* and Cyprus had come out.

Playing with the opening letters "DP," the book was called *Destination Palestine: The Story of the Haganah Ship Exodus* 1947.*

In Atlantic City, at the convention of the United Jewish Appeal, Moshe Sharett, Israel's foreign minister, and I were the keynote speakers. On the dais he whispered to me, "Because of you I had to visit those terrible camps."

"Did you make changes?" I asked.

"Of course. We're building new development towns all over the country, and planning thirty thousand new homes."

Months later, Leon Uris, the author of *Exodus,* and I were both asked to speak about our books. Over one thousand Hadassah members in a meeting, chaired by Sylvia Miller, the Los Angeles president, listened intently as Leon spoke. "I'm going to tell a story about Ruth. When Otto Preminger bought my book, he said, 'Leon, send over the three or four books that most influenced you.' So, of course, I sent over Ruth's book on the real *Exodus 1947.*"

I sat at the edge of my chair. This was a surprise.

Leon continued, "The next morning, Preminger called me and said, 'Leon, if I had read this book, I never would have bought yours.'"

The night before the movie *Exodus* was to open in New York, the Israeli consul general threw a gala party for Preminger and several of the stars.

Preminger was at the cocktail table munching little sandwiches when I told him Leon's story. "Is it true?" I asked him.

"Yes, it is true," he answered, "and do you know what I'm going to do for you?"

I waited, wondering, *Is he going to give me credit in the film?*

*Republished in 1999 as *Exodus 1947: The Ship that Launched a Nation.*

"I'm going to give you two tickets to the movie."

In December 1948, an invitation arrived from Luis Muñoz Marin inviting me to attend his inauguration as the first elected governor in the 450-year history of Puerto Rico. We had become acquainted when I worked in the Interior Department; Puerto Rico was a territory like Alaska, under the supervision of Interior. While I was working on the problems of Alaska, Luis was working on the problems of Puerto Rico. We would often bemoan the fact that our problems were diametrically opposite: Puerto Rico had too many people and too little land; Alaska had few people in a vast and empty land.

"If only there were some way," we would say ruefully, "to solve the problems of both territories at once."

Before leaving for Puerto Rico, I called Helen Reid to say good-bye. I told her I was sailing to San Juan for this historic moment in the island's history. "It's a great story," she enthused. "While you're there, cover it for us."

I did not know this journey would be a historic moment for me, too.

On the ship from New York to San Juan, getting to know Puerto Rican families and their children, I began asking myself why the United States had taken Puerto Rico after the Spanish American War in 1898. The Puerto Ricans did not ask to become part of our country. They were a spoil of the war.

By one of those acts of irony in which history abounds, the Spaniards, barely a year before the Americans landed, gave Puerto Rico an autonomous charter. On November 25, 1897, Luis Muños Rivera succeeded in getting the prime minister of Spain to grant Puerto Rico its first constitution and to give it self-government. Spain, after four hundred years of oppression, corruption, and bureaucracy, suddenly set the clock forward.

It was not too little, but it was too late. The Spanish American War intervened. The United States, with almost no political experience in ruling colonies, promptly set the clock back. It withdrew the autonomy that the Puerto Ricans had wrested from Spain in 1897.

After thirty years of neglect and indifference, the men of the New Deal, in agonizing reappraisal, made the country aware that we were as responsible for the Puerto Ricans as a parent is for the child who never asked to be born. We had much to undo.

Soon after arriving in San Juan, I checked into a hotel and went directly to Muñoz's office. He stood up to welcome me with a warm, powerful handshake and a bear hug. Everything about him was large—his frame, his thick inch-wide mustache, his bushy eloquent eyebrows, and his soft dark eyes. He loved life, people, music, conversation, good phrases, and especially good jokes. He was a prophetic man, with poetic insight; in fact, he had been a poet in New York's Greenwich Village. He was restless, deeply concerned with ideas and words. His aphorisms were famous: "Puerto Rico," he once said, "is a land of flattering statistics and distressing realities."

He was delighted that the *Herald Tribune* would be covering his inauguration.

"We'll give you a car and chauffeur," he said, "to help you see whatever you want."

The inauguration was a heartwarming combination of Thanksgiving, a bloodless revolution, and a week-long fiesta that outdid any Polish or Greek wedding. There were huge balls every night and dinners at La Fortaleza, the castle he lived in with his strong, politically sophisticated wife, Doña Ines, and their children. There were tours of the island for invited celebrities from North and South America. San Juan looked like a fairyland at night, while the days were filled with cockfights and horse races, and picnics on beaches, with pigs revolving on huge spits and tables groaning with Puerto Rican delicacies.

On January 1, 1949, the whole island seemed to crowd into San Juan to watch the inaugural parade and show their affection for Muñoz. He was the first Puerto Rican elected by the people of Puerto Rico to govern them. He was a symbol of their triumph, a symbol of their culture and tradition, of their pride in their Spanish roots.

Sitting in the grandstand, I saw a barefooted old man walk up to Muñoz and hand him a basket of grapefruit. The old man had walked down from the mountains bearing his gift. There was a reverent look on his face, the kind of look seen on pilgrims coming to a shrine. On this first day in the new year in the hot tropical sun of a once downtrodden island, two million people looked to Muñoz to lead them.

"With or without an oath," Muñoz spole eloquently as he took the oath of office, "the forces of my conscience have fought to make my life an oath of service to my people. The great masses owe it to themselves to take this oath—that every living being better the nobility of spirit that animates it, that every hand serve better the land that it cultivates . . . thus the people of Puerto Rico may within the smallness of their territory realize the greatness of their destiny."

Sitting next to me in the grandstand was Doña Felisa Rincón de Gautier, the mayor of San Juan. Doña Felisa was unique— a woman mayor in a macho society. Soon after the inauguration, she took me to see how she was cleaning up the capital city and how she was helping her people. Every Wednesday morning she held open house at city hall. At nine o'clock, she would enter. A large vivacious woman with a cameo-like face, she wore a freshly starched linen dress and long matching jacket. Her white hair was fixed in two huge buns tied with a black ribbon. She sat at a desk facing the people, a chair at her right side. Here each petitioner sat for a minute, five minutes, or as long as needed.

Doña Felisa listened, her face filled with interest and compassion, never with censure. She nodded her head, then wrote a word or two on a pad. On many she wrote, *"Mira a ver. F"*— "Look and see. Felisa." A social worker took the petitioners to the door and told them to which government agency they should go for help. Some of the requests, of course, required a thorough investigation. But many were for shoes for children, and for these Doña Felisa wrote simply on her magic pad *1 par.*

Her people expected Doña Felisa to be everything—from legal counsel to a one-woman court of human relations. A woman, sitting hopefully at her side, said, "Doña Felisa, my husband hasn't shown up for three days. If you will come to dinner at my house, he will hear about it and he will come home."

Doña Felisa came to dinner, and the truant husband returned.

She was the mother image of San Juan, and a safety valve for pent-up emotions. She was a combination of Louis XIV, a twentieth-century Lady Bountiful, and a female La Guardia running a city of half a million people.

At a picnic lunch on the sands of Luquillo Beach, Muñoz took the hand of Philip Michaels, a lawyer he had invited to the inauguration in gratitude for all he had done for the Puerto Ricans in New York. He put Phil's hand on mine and said, "You two New Yorkers should get to know each other."

We spent the rest of the inauguration festivities together. He was five feet five with brown hair, bright penetrating eyes, and a high, intelligent forehead. He exuded a love of music and art, and a passion for helping oppressed people.

He was reluctant to talk about himself, but I still managed to learn about his life. In his forties, he was a lawyer and a confirmed bachelor who had converted part of a furniture store he managed in the South Bronx into a neighborhood settlement house. Every year before Christmas, he filled the store with busloads of school children who had never been to a theater. He began smiling as the children began shrieking with joy as they watched exciting puppet shows. He mediated fights between African American and Puerto Rican gangs and ran Saturday night dances in the store to get young people off the mean streets.

In the car Muñoz had given me, I took Philip to see the slums of San Juan. He kept shaking his head in torment as we visited dilapidated shacks in a slum called La Perla. A young woman stepped out of one of the shacks, barefoot, in a torn housedress. She held a naked baby tightly in her arms. Six more children tumbled out of the shack. She told us that the people in this neighborhood were living without a drop of water or light. "To live in these slums," Phil said, "is like living in an open sewer."

I was moved by his compassion. I realized I was falling in love.

Chapter Forty-Four

MR. BEVIN AND MRS. REID

Back home in New York, Helen Reid told me that Cyprus had become her passion. While all the DP camps in Europe were almost empty, the British still held thousands of Jewish prisoners in Cyprus. Helen was determined to get them released.

At lunch in her home in New York, she confronted her houseguest, British press giant Lord Max Beaverbrook.

"Why are you keeping the Jews in those terrible camps in Cyprus?" Helen demanded.

"What are you talking about?" Beaverbrook feigned ignorance.

"Why is your government running those camps? How can you commit people to live in such terrible conditions?"

"What terrible conditions?" he asked.

"Imprisoning them in overcrowded tents and huts," she said. "Without water, without privacy. How can you do this to people who've suffered what the Jews suffered under Hitler?"

"Cyprus isn't that bad," Beaverbrook insisted.

Helen looked at him in surprise. "Haven't you read the articles we've been running on the prison camps?"

Beaverbrook said he had not. Helen telephoned the *Tribune* office. "Send a messenger with all Ruth's articles and photos on Cyprus, and a copy of her book *Destination Palestine*.

"Take these with you," Helen told him. "Read them on the ship on your way back to London."

"I will," he promised, "and what's more, I'll talk to Bevin about this problem."

He was true to his word. A few weeks later, H. R. asked me to come to dinner. Lord Beaverbrook had sent her a letter, and she wanted to answer it immediately.

We went downstairs to Bleeck's restaurant, where the *Herald Tribune* and *New York Times* journalists often met for drinks and food. People sitting at the bar jumped off their stools when they saw Helen enter. Murmuring greetings, they cleared a path for us to go to a table toward the back. We ordered quickly.

Helen showed me Lord Beaverbrook's letter.

"I know just who wrote this," I said. "It was Harold Beeley, Bevin's assistant and chief Arabist." I told Helen how Beeley had tried to sabotage the Anglo-American committee by bribing the concierge in Switzerland, opening member's mail, including mine, and giving misinformation to first-rate journalists, like the *New York Times'* Flora Lewis.

We reviewed the letter, which described in detail Bevin's reasons for keeping Jews imprisoned. Helen refuted each of his arguments, writing in the margins. Beaverbrook's arguments were riddled with Beeley's lies. "I am informed," he wrote, "by the highest authority on the subject [obviously Mr. Beeley], "that 8,000 are held there in obedience with the United Nations Decision as being of military age."

H. R. wrote in tiny script, "No UN decision on Cyprus."

"The remaining 3,000," the letter continued, "are free to go, but elect to stay."

At this I shook my head, disbelievingly. I couldn't imagine a single refugee "electing" to stay on Cyprus.

Helen had no success with the powerful "Beaver" as he was called. But she refused to give up. She made a secret trip to Paris to confront Ernest Bevin in person. They met in the home of U.S. Ambassador Alfred Duff Cooper.

"Mr. Bevin," she said, "Why do you limit the number of Jews allowed to quit the camps in Cyprus and sail to the Holy Land? The Jews have suffered enough. They were promised a national homeland, and they ought to be allowed to go home."

Bevin was polite, but definite. "I am honored by your presence, Mrs. Reid, but I must act in accordance with the White Paper with its monthly immigration quota."

Helen continued undeterred. "But Britain created that document, and only Pakistan recognizes it. Surely you can dispense with it."

Bevin paid little attention. "I don't think Palestine can absorb all the DPs who want to enter. I have sympathy with your deep interest and concern. But I cannot commit more than the number set by the White Paper."

Helen's fight for the refugees on Cyprus failed, but it was hard fought and valiant. No anti-Semite would have fought such a battle.

The courtship with Philip was changing the course of my life. Back in New York, Phil and I saw each other several nights each week, for dinner and the theater. He was a theater buff who not only saw every musical play, but learned the lyrics in every song. The longer I knew him, the more I grew to admire him.

In the summer of 1949, I returned to Israel to cover the secret operation called "Magic Carpet." The mission was to rescue fifty thousand Jews from the degradation of their lives in the Arab kingdom of Yemen.

Phil drove me to the airport and stayed with me until the plane took off.

"I wish you didn't have to go," he said.

"I'll be back soon," I assured him. "I hate leaving you." I shrugged and kissed him unashamed.

In Israel, a few days later, I flew from Ben-Gurion Airport to the tip of the Red Sea and the British protectorate of Aden. My plane was a giant silver-winged C-54 Skymaster piloted by "Flying Tigers." They were sturdy Americans from Texas who had flown freight during World War II. Now they were flying biblical-era Jews to the land of the Bible.

In Aden, the American Jewish Joint Distribution Committee was running camps, housing the Yemenite Jews before their journey to the Holy Land. I decided I needed to see and feel in my own skin the dangerous route they trekked. I chose a transit point between Aden and Yemen, in the Sultan of Lahej's kingdom. I had heard of the ransom the sultan demanded for every Yemenite Jewish man and woman, every newborn baby, for every holy scroll, and every Bible.

The JDC people warned me, "You're mad to go. They might kill you."

I shrugged my shoulders.

The British agent in charge of the Protectorate was J. W. T. Allen, a thin Englishman who wore white shorts, high socks, and a monocle. From him I obtained a travel pass for the Lahej kingdom. I hired a car and a young Arab interpreter and drove along the overland road through the Arabian land.

With customs stopping the car along the way, always with guns aimed straight at my head, we finally reached the

kingdom of the Sultan of Lahej. We entered a huge open courtyard, where I saw more than a hundred Yemenite Jews
squeezed against each other in fright. When the people learned
that I was not an Arab, they crowded around me.

My Arab interpreter translated, "Sick, Sick! Help us!"

Children pulled at my skirt, "Water! Water! We have no
water!"

Why had I not thought to bring water and food?

"Have patience," I said to the people, unsure how I dared to
use the word. "This is the end of the journey. Tonight we will
send trucks for you. Tonight you will be in the camps. Tonight
there will be doctors and food. Tonight you will be safe."

Still filled with guilt, I drove back to Aden.

Long after midnight, the lights of the trucks, like the eyes of
jungle cats, shone as the people climbed out of the trucks, some
holding a child in one arm and a holy scroll in the other. I
helped the JDC people give them bread, water, and the food
they yearned for: milk and dates.

I stayed with them for several days, learning more about
their lives while they rested, ate, read their precious holy scrolls,
and prayed as once the children of Israel had prayed when
Moses led them out of Egypt.

These Yemenite Jews, and their ancestors, had clung to their
Jewishness for thousands of years, even while their lives in
Yemen were filled with misery. They were second-class citizens.
A Jew could not live in a house looking down on a Muslim. He
could not leave the ghettos at night, have light in the ghetto
streets, or even wear shoes. Of every one thousand children
born, eight hundred died. Every orphan became the property of
the state, and was forced to convert to Islam. Prayer books were
so scarce that youngsters, sitting in a circle studying Hebrew,
learned to read the language upside down. For years, the
Yemenite Jews had trickled out illegally to reach the Holy Land,

threatened with capital punishment if they were caught. Now they were escaping in the hundreds.

Each day in the camp they sang, "Next Year in Jerusalem," and each day, for some five hundred flying home, the prayer was coming true.

I flew back to Israel in an American Skymaster with 140 Yemenite Jews. In the plane, I asked an old man, "Have you ever seen a plane before?"

He shook his head.

"Are you frightened?"

"Frightened!" he exclaimed, "Why should I be frightened? It is all written in the Bible." He quoted the beautiful passage from Isaiah: "But they that wait upon the Lord shall renew their strength; they shall mount up with wings as eagles; they shall run and not be weary; and they shall walk, and not faint."

"For all these years," the man continued, "we waited upon the Lord and He kept renewing our strength. Now we're mounting up with wings as eagles. Only, the Bible didn't say they would be American Eagle's wings."

I returned to New York carrying the story with me. Phil was at the airport with a bouquet of roses.

The next morning I brought the story to my editor, Joe Barnes. "We can't print this," I told him, "until all the Yemenite Jews are safely home. Any publicity might shut down the whole Magic Carpet operation."

Joe agreed.

I called him the moment I learned it was safe. Fifty-thousand Jews were home and the *Herald Tribune* was the first with the story.

Chapter Forty-Five
THE WEDDING

The sun was setting over Central Park when Phil asked me to marry him. We were in the penthouse restaurant of the Essex House hotel.

I felt a warm glow encircle my body. Outside the window, the park was a blaze of crimson and gold.

"I have to think about it," I said slowly.

He lit a cigarette. "I'll wait."

Thoughts raced through my head. Ours was no frivolous teenage romance. It was mature and honest. We hid nothing from each other. He was forty-six, strong and youthful-looking; I was thirty-nine. We liked the same things: art, music, theater, books—especially history and biography—good talk, good friends, and politics. We were both New Deal Democrats who admired Franklin and Eleanor Roosevelt and loved America, even as we sought to make changes within the system, always without destroying it. Spiritually, we were both proud of the truth and the beauty of our Jewishness.

I broke the silence. "I want children." I said.

"So do I," he smiled.

I leaned across the table and took his hand. Our eyes met and held.

"Let's not wait," he said. "Can you meet me tomorrow afternoon? My cousin, Abe Sachs, owns a jewelry shop on Fifth Avenue off 57th Street."

The next day at the store, Abe brought out a tray of beautiful, glistening white diamonds. I waved it away. "I'm not a diamond girl," I told him. He then brought out another tray of wedding rings. My eyes lit on a square-cut sapphire ring. Phil put it on my finger.

"That's you," he said. "It goes with your blue eyes."

At the door, Phil kissed me good-bye and rushed back to work. I walked along Fifth Avenue glancing not at the shop windows but at the ring sparkling on my finger. Finally I took the subway back to my apartment in Brooklyn and called my mother.

"God should only help you," she said.

Then I called Helen Reid in her office. "It's great news," said. "Can you bring him for tea tomorrow?"

At five the next day, we were in the wood-paneled library of Helen's Fifth Avenue apartment.

"I can't wait to see your ring," she said as soon we sat down. She studied it on my finger. "It's the deepest blue sapphire I've ever seen."

She turned to Phil. "You know, Phil," she fixed him with her jade eyes. "At the *New York Times*, when a woman writer marries, she has to take her husband's name. We don't do that at the *Tribune*. We feel that we put so much into building up a woman's name that she ought to be able to keep it. You agree, don't you?"

"I wouldn't want it any other way," he said. He didn't need me to take his name. His own ego was sturdy.

The next weeks were a blur of parties and trying to find an apartment in Manhattan. We looked at several brownstones. I hated them—I had grown up in a four-story brownstone, where everything I wanted was usually on the floor I was not on. My heart began to beat when we entered the art deco lobby of the Eldorado on Central Park West with its marble floors, ornate paneling, and murals. Phil had found the perfect apartment for us; a huge living and dining room, one bedroom, a fair-sized kitchen, and the most exciting part of all, a broad terrace that swept around the whole apartment, and seemed to me as big as the deck of the *Queen Mary*. I knew I was home.

Phil told me, "Leave all your stuff in your apartment in Brooklyn. We're beginning a new life."

We divided the job of planning the wedding. I was to take care of planning the honeymoon trip to Europe, North Africa, and Israel. Phil, a great organizer, took command of everything else. He was so capable and so indispensable that when the leaders of the South Bronx Community Council, which he had created to fight crime and improve education, decided to surprise us with a massive bridal shower, they asked Phil to organize our surprise party.

In January 1950, we drove from Brooklyn in my brother Harry's car to the wedding. Mama, who found it hard to compliment her children for fear of the "evil eye," looked at me as if she were seeing me for the first time. "You have *kalah-chen,*" she said. It meant the charm of the bride.

Only our families and a few lifelong friends were invited to the flower-filled apartment of Phil's brother, Will Michaels, on the upper west side of Manhattan. Rabbi Charles Shulman recited the blessings of the betrothal. "May He who is supreme power, blessings, and glory bless this bridegroom and bride."

He then sanctified a glass goblet of wine and explained:

"The sanctification of all great moments in Jewish life are symbolized by the drinking of the wine." He handed the wine to Philip, who sipped it and then gave it to me.

I looked at Philip and knew that I would love him to the end of days.

Phil placed the wedding band on my finger and repeated after the rabbi, "By this ring you are consecrated to me as my wife in accordance with the law of Moses and the people of Israel."

Then I placed the wedding band on Phil's finger, and, changing only "wife" to "husband," repeated the words that had just consecrated him to me.

Once again, Rabbi Shulman handed the glass goblet to Philip to sip, then gave it to me, and with great care, placed it under Philip's foot. In this day of greatest happiness, we were not to forget the destruction of the Temple in the year A.D. 70.

Philip, his face wreathed with joy, stamped on the glass with all his power. We would never forget.

The house rang with shouts, *"Mazel Tov. Mazel Tov."* Philip kissed me. Mama kissed me. Philip's tiny mother, whom I had already learned to love, kissed me. We dined and laughed and sang and laughed some more. At midnight Phil and I left for the Plaza Hotel to begin our honeymoon.

As usual, even on my honeymoon, I was working on stories for the *Herald Tribune*. Phil wanted to help me, so I taught him how to use my Leica camera for color, while I used my beloved Rolleiflex for black-and-whites.

In Paris, our hosts were dear friends from New York, Sylvia and Lou Horwitz. Lou was the Paris director of the Joint Distribution Committee. His boss, Dr. Joseph Schwartz, had sent him orders to show us everything we wanted to see. The four of us, with an interpreter who spoke fluent Arabic, traveled to

Casablanca, where the local head of the JDC in Casablanca insisted on showing us the entire city, including the brothels. I had taught Phil to focus on the eyes when photographing people. When we returned to America, we invited our families for our usual Sunday family dinner. Phil had just brought back the Kodachrome slides, and without having seen them, decided to show them. Laughter rocked the apartment as we watched ladies of the night beckoning to Phil with exposed breasts as big as watermelons.

Phil was shocked and embarrassed. "But you told me to focus on the eyes," he explained.

Still on our honeymoon, we continued across North Africa, interviewing people everywhere we went, seeing the poverty and terror under which the Jews of Morocco, Algeria, Tunisia, and Libya were living. Lou assured the needy Jews we met that as soon as he returned to Paris, he would make certain that the JDC would send them food, clothing, doctors, nurses, and teachers. He promised that as soon as possible, Israel would rescue them with ships and planes and take them to their new home.

We were in Libya, then a kingdom, where many of the Jews were living inside of caves. We were about to enter one of the caves, when a band of Arabs nabbed us and ordered us to raise our arms up and face a wall. One of the men demanded, "What are you spies doing in our country?"

Our interpreter, who spoke fluent Arabic, translated. He then responded, "We are not spies. These people with me are Americans. They've come to help the people."

"A bunch of lies," the leader of the band insisted.

Suddenly, a voice came from one of the mosques announcing it was time to pray. With their guns still trained on us, the Arabs kneeled on the ground and began their prayers. Bells were ringing, donkeys were braying, camels walked past us. I wondered if we would survive.

What a fate, I thought ruefully, *to die on my honeymoon.*

The prayers ended. One of our Arab captors raised his gun to the sky and fired some bullets into the air. Even our interpreter looked terrified. The shots that frightened us became our instruments of survival. They brought a whole unit of the French Foreign Legion to rescue us. Dressed in sparkling blue and gold uniforms, they focused their guns on the Arabs, and one of them shouted commands. The gunmen slowly slipped out of sight.

We said good-bye to Sylvia and Lou Horwitz and flew off to Israel. I was proud to introduce Phil to my friends.

Phil proved to be more than a companion. With his political skills and his humanitarianism, he became my full partner, often thinking up questions for me to ask the people I was interviewing.

We went to interview Ben-Gurion, who as usual turned the tables and interviewed us. Before we left, B. G. said, "Jews from Iraq are being brought in from the thousands. Iraq is letting them out, so long as they do it fast and secretly. They have to leave everything they own behind. It is still dangerous; I suggest you go to the airport right away and do what you did with the Yemenite Jews. Take photos, and release the story once we've brought one hundred and twenty thousand of them home."

We said good-bye to the prime minister and taxied to the airport. Again, Phil carried the Leica, and I the Rolleiflex. I kept my notebook in my hand, and one extra roll of film. All the others, I put in Phil's pockets, grateful he could carry them.

The sight of the arriving Jews was breathtaking. Women came down from the planes in magnificent purple gowns, beautifully embroidered. With my press pass pinned to my coat, I raced around the airport taking my own shots in black-and-white. I left Phil to shoot his pictures in color. The biblical words of the ancient Jews who yearned to leave exile kept singing in my head: "If I forget thee, O Jerusalem, may my right hand lose its cunning."

I shot my last roll of film and started to search for Phil to get the film I had put in his pockets. He was nowhere to be found. *Where could he have gone to?* I wondered. I was so angry and frustrated. Here were these beautiful shots calling out to be preserved. I was ready to divorce him on the spot.

I filled more pages in my notebook, and when the last of the planes landed, went to a small restaurant hoping Phil would soon turn up. The chief of security for the whole airport, whom I knew from my earlier trips, soon joined me.

"May I sit with you?" he asked.

"Of course."

We sipped tea and reminisced about the good old days, when he had smuggled DPs into Haifa harbor under the noses of the British.

"We don't have to smuggle anyone anymore," he said. "They're so happy when they come off the ships and the planes."

One of his uniformed policemen came to the table and whispered something in his ear. He nodded, and said, "Excuse me, I have to tend to some business." Five minutes later, Phil appeared. His hair and his clothes were disheveled.

"Where were you?" I tried to keep from shouting.

He slumped into a chair beside me.

"In prison."

"You were in prison?!" I asked in disbelief. "What did they lock you up for?"

"One of the police came up to me while I was shooting," he

explained. "They asked me for my press card. I kept telling them to call Ben-Gurion, Golda, Moshe Sharett. They thought I was crazy. They said, 'Do you want us to call Napoleon, too?'"

I hit my head with my hands. "Oh, dear God!" I exclaimed. "I was so eager to cover this story that I forgot you needed a press card. I'm so sorry, Darling."

"But I spoiled your story," he said. "You missed so many wonderful pictures."

"I got enough, and I'm sure you did, too. I'm just so happy that you're all right."

The story and our pictures ran not only in the *Herald Tribune*, but as a feature story in *Look* Magazine.

We returned to New York and began our lives together.

Chapter Forty-Six
ELEANOR VISITS THE HOLY LAND

One year later, I was back in Israel on an assignment from the *Herald Tribune* to cover the unending waves of new immigrants flooding the new nation. I promised Phil that I would return as soon as possible.

"Take as long as you need," he assured me. "I'll be fine. You know how busy I am."

He was busy working late, going to meetings, mediating fights on streets riven by gangs. We had two separate careers that did not impinge on each other. I admired him for all he was doing, he admired me. We posed no threat to each other. His constant encouragement became my support system. I could travel anywhere, write, and give speeches knowing I always had a place and Phil to come home to.

Now in Israel, traveling alone, I could concentrate on immigration. The camps and tent cities that I had decried to Ben-Gurion were giving way to decent homes. New small towns were springing up from the hills of Galilee to the sands of the

Negev. History, legends, and Bible stories made the land seem gigantic. I realized you could not measure Israel with a ruler. You had to measure it in height and depth, in history and dreams. The soul of this country was big. It was the soul of a people who had known death and outwitted it.

This was the key to Israel: It was a land built on a biblical vision and on the cremated bones of six million dead. It was a creative country built by a creative people. It was a country built out of death for life, with the broadest arms in the world welcoming home every homeless Jew.

One morning, returning to my hotel room in Tel Aviv, I fell on my bed fully dressed, to rest. The sun was rising on the blue turquoise sea outside my window. My eyes were shut, but memories were churning in my brain. How much my life had changed in the ten years since that day in 1941 when I first walked into Harold Ickes's office. I was a young woman then, searching for myself.

These ten years had brought my life into focus. Alaska had taught me how to use my energy and passion efficiently by living inside of time. The years that followed taught me that even in the face of great evil, I could try to help others rebuild their lives.

The telephone broke into my reverie. It was Eleanor Roosevelt.

"I heard you were in my hotel," she said.

"I have a request," she said. "I want you to show me how Israel is absorbing these newcomers. After your experience with the Oswego refugees, I'm sure you'll know what to show me."

"When do you want to go?" I asked.

"Tomorrow," she answered. "Right after breakfast."

That night, I traveled to a development town not far from Tel Aviv. The people had come from countries in North Africa and the Middle East. I sought out some of their leaders and told them, "Tomorrow I'm bringing you the widow of the great American president Franklin Roosevelt."

The next morning, as our car with our interpreter entered, we were greeted by the new immigrants standing on both sides of the road holding huge platters of food and ululating with joy.

Eleanor's eyes were moist, as she listened to the people on the dirt road shouting, "The Queen of America has come." The warmth and love she was giving to these people came back from them to her.

Only Eleanor would do what she did next. She went to each woman who was holding a plate of food, and though some of it must have looked strange to her, she tasted it and remarked how good it was. Through the interpreter, she asked her hosts the same questions she had asked in Oswego: "How do you find your life here? Do your children go to school? Do you get medical care?" The answers made her nod and smile.

Back in the car, she suddenly looked sad.

"Is anything wrong?" I asked her.

"I wish I had done more for the Jews."

I put my hand on hers. "You did whatever you could. Government policy did not make refugees our top priority. Nearly every leader in Washington insisted, 'First, we must win the war. Then we can take care of the refugees.' They didn't realize that if they waited there might not be any refugees to take care of."

She shook her head. "I should have done more."

A week later, I returned to New York. Phil took me to dinner that night to welcome me home. Back in the penthouse of Essex House, I kissed Phil's hand.

"You have something to tell me, don't you?" he said.

I smiled. "I saw a doctor in Israel."

"Why?" he asked, concerned. "Were you ill?"

"No, I wasn't ill," I paused. "We're going to have a baby."

ACKNOWLEDGMENTS

My first note of thanks goes to Herman Graf, president of Carroll & Graf Publishers, for his whole-hearted support and his passion for the writing of history.

My next note of gratitude goes to my editor, Philip Turner, for his understanding, meticulous editing and enthusiasm. Like a football coach, his constant encouragement, "Keep going, it's moving fast," often energized me to work ten or twelve hours a day. In the end, to speed the manuscript to the printer, he did something almost unheard-of for a senior editor: he sat at my computer for hours typing in the changes we were making.

I want to thank Keith Wallman, assistant editor, who took over, with grace and care and knowledge, whenever Philip was away. And thanks and admiration go to Linda Kosarin, the creative art director, who designed the cover and screened a good number of the two thousand Kodachrome slides that were then made into black-and-white photos. Warm thanks also go to Fifi Oscard, president of the Fifi Oscard Agency.

I could not have written this book, digging into my notebooks (at least the notebooks were indexed with time and place and content), my reports to Secretary Ickes, my articles and letters, without the help of my quartet of twenty-something assistants, Laura Eldridge, Allison Hiroto, Idris (Edie) Rosenberg, and Karen Berenthal. Their fingers danced like ballerinas on the keys of my laptop, typing as fast as I dictated. Except for Allison, who went to Columbia, the others were molded by Barnard. They taught me some of the culture of their generation, and I awakened them to the fact that Reid Hall, built by Barnard in honor of Helen Rogers Reid, had been their freshman dormitory.

My deepest thanks go to my daughter, Celia; her husband,

Stephen; their children Michael and Lucy; to my son David; his wife, Gail; and their children, Joel and Lila, for the warmth and love they surrounded me with while I was writing this book; and to my stepdaughter, Barbara, who took time out to read parts of the book at night after working a full day on her own. All of them have helped me, in my ninetieth year, live inside of time.

Roster of speakers at the New York *Herald Tribune* Forum in 1943, followed by Helen Rogers Reid's introduction of Ruth Gruber and her speech on Alaska.

CONTENTS

FIRST SESSION

Tuesday, November 16, 1943, 1:45 P.M.

America's Basic Responsibilities

iii

APPENDIX

SECOND SESSION

Tuesday, November 16, 1943, 7:45 P.M.

Economic Pioneering

iv

v

THIRD SESSION

Wednesday, November 17, 1943, 1:45 P.M.

Pioneering with Science

vi

FOURTH SESSION

Wednesday, November 17, 1943, 7:45 P.M.

The World We Want

APPENDIX

Dr. Ruth Gruber

Field Representative, Department of the Interior

Alaska—The New Crossroads

MRS. REID: Our next speaker is an adventure in herself. She has the keen enquiring mind, the vivid aliveness and zest for exploration among the far-flung people and places of the earth that make the perfect reporter. Her education stems from three universities—an A.B. from New York University at the end of three years, an M.A. from Wisconsin in another year, and a Ph.D. with a magna cum laude from the University of Cologne after only one year. At the age of twenty, she became the youngest Doctor of Philosophy on record.

On returning home she was given a traveling fellowship by the New Jersey State Federation of Women's Clubs to study the situation of women under Fascism, Communism and European Democracy. With this assignment she scooped the newspaper world by getting inside the Soviet Arctic and writing a remarkable book entitled, "I Went to the Soviet Arctic."

In 1941 Secretary Ickes sent Ruth Gruber to Alaska to make a social and economic study of developments. For over nineteen months she covered that vast territory by plane, train, truck, boat and dogsled with more thoroughness than has ever been done by any single person. She lived in schools, hospitals and even a jail among the

96

Eskimos of the Arctic Coast, talking to people in every walk of life, gathering a wealth of material about this undeveloped part of our country. During a trip to the Aleutians as the only woman in an Army convoy, she lived on the base at Dutch Harbor. She ate with the soldiers and sailors and came to know all their hopes and fears. Until now Army censorship has prevented her from telling the story of this great new crossroads of the world. Tonight the veil has been slightly lifted. We are thankful that we can bring you her first report on civilian life in our Arctic outpost and her picture of its future.

I am especially proud of introducing to you an important government representative and a reporter extraordinary, Dr. Ruth Gruber.

DR. GRUBER: I am happy to be here tonight, being first an alumna of the Herald Tribune and secondly an alumna of the New Jersey Federation of Women's Clubs.

The most important fact in geography and history that we have learned from the war is the fact that Alaska is only fifty miles from Siberia. Primitive man knew that when he first came to America from Asia by way of Alaska. We have rediscovered the crossroads. We have learned again that the shortest and most logical route between America and Asia is not across the ocean but directly across Alaska. Geography is Alaska's sinew of war.

Her location on the globe will make her grow as Asia grows, as Canada grows and as America grows. Alaska is our frontier to the post-war world, our key to the future. The Soviets are pushing industries and cities east of the Urals; China is unifying itself; millions of Asiatic people, whose standards of living are rising, are going to demand American automobiles, American tractors, American refrigerators and toilet soap. Alaska is the natural gateway to those markets.

Let me try to describe Alaska to you. It sits proudly on two oceans, the North Pacific and the Arctic, with the Bering Sea to link them. Behind it lies Canada; below it, in a straight line, lies Hawaii; before it lies Siberia. It is so enormous that if you put a map of Alaska on a map of the whole United States, you will find that the body of Alaska covers the entire Middle West; southeastern Alaska would reach to Georgia, and the long tail of the Aleutians would sweep out to California.

Alaska seems to have a chunk of everything American. Are you from Iowa? The interior has flat land and fertile valleys. Are you from the forest lands of Oregon? Southeastern Alaska is an almost uncut primeval forest. Are you from Los Angeles? Alaska has plenty of mist. New Jersey? The mosquitoes in Alaska are as big as Army bombers, if you believe the soldiers who have fed them blood. Planes alone can trek through time and squeeze these distances, and when you fly over sections of the highway and coast, when you see below

97

you flowing rivers of ice, and fields of glaciers, you feel almost as though you were flying over the first day of creation.

Alaska has suffered from its own picturesqueness. Travelers have come back to us telling not of the schools, not of the university and the excellent churches, but of the wild no-man's-land of Eskimos and igloos, a land stuffed like a legendary ice cream cone with ice on top and nothing on bottom. Actually, most of our Alaskan Eskimos don't even know how to build a snowhouse. They live in wooden houses or sod huts; and they are probably tuning in right now to the Herald Tribune Forum.

The other half of the population is made of Americans of all races who came yesterday or forty years ago, who speak English with all accents, including the Scandinavian, who drive Buicks and Fords, who play pingpong and bridge, who have a delegate in Congress, elect their own Legislature, drink highballs and Coca-Colas, and wear more evening clothes in a year than most people in New York wear in a lifetime.

Alaska is no Paradise on Earth. Neither is it Hell Frozen Over. It is a big land and it is an empty land. In all that geographic vastness, in a land with summers that are hotter than Florida's and winters that are cold, there live only 80,000 civilians; just about the number who watch a single football game on Saturday.

Tomorrow, I think, the story will be different. There is a new challenge in Alaska, and throughout the nation there is a new dream. Each week we in Washington receive hundreds of letters from men and women, telling us that they have heard about Alaska, that the thought of it has gotten into their blood, that they want to go North to homestead, to farm, to teach school, to open grocery stores and bakery shops, to work in beauty parlors and on the Alaska Railroad. Those letters, written not with cynicism or fear, but with a clean and healthy optimism, are shining proof that the people, the good solid people, are looking to Alaska as one of the places where men and women of all races and creeds, coming home from a war that they have fought brilliantly, can help build a decent world.

You learn a good deal from the soldiers when you live in Alaska. Sometimes, at the request of their officers, I would talk to the men in their barracks. Those long evenings, sitting on bunks and trunks out there in the Aleutians, we really let down our hair. Some of the men hated Alaska. Their remarks were devastating: "Why don't they sink Alaska?" "Why don't they give it back to the Eskimos?" "By golly, if the Japs take Alaska, it pretty well serves them right." Of course, good healthy grousing is one of the characteristics of the American Army.

But many of the men had caught the spirit and freedom of the North. Alaska had taken strange hold; and while they fought on the

98

Aleutians, flew bombers into Fairbanks and trucked food along the road, they were making plans to raise their families in Alaska after the war. A soldier, just back from two years in Alaska, came to see me the other day. "You remember how I hated Alaska when you were there," he said. "I've been home for three weeks and I've got a different angle on it now. Alaska is my self-assurance. Knowing that country is worth more to me than a million dollars in the bank. Every boy who's been up there feels that he can thumb his nose at the whole world. Alaska has shown us that there is a place where we can be more than just cogs in a great wheel."

For a long time Alaska has been called a man's country. I should like to change that, I should like to call it a woman's country. Here is where women can prove, socially and politically, that women can be leaders, just as men can be leaders, if they are given the chance. Women who go North hardly know the meaning of loneliness. Alaska is a good place for girls whose ego needs a little boost. Any girl suffering from a not-too-advanced spinsterhood might profitably trek northward. In fact, the farther North you go the more beautiful you become. A dance in a place like Dutch Harbor makes you feel like a cross between the Duchess of Windsor and Hedy Lamarr.

The United States Employment Service in Seattle has hundreds of jobs for women in Alaska who are not married to men stationed there. Everywhere you go in the Territory you hear the cry: "Send us people. Send us workmen. Send us women." The need for women is enormous. But only the strong and the courageous ought to go.

There is a glamour in the North, but life is not easy. Many of the women who went to Alaska grew weary of the isolation, tired of chopping wood in the interior, and carrying umbrellas on the coast. Others grew sullen and bitter because they found not the human warmth and hospitality, not the greatness in emergencies of the small town, but its naked cruelty and its gossip. They left, hating Alaska violently.

A man, too, needs firm eyes and the will to withstand discouragement on the frontier. Alaska is no place for city or farm weaklings. Every farmer ought to have at least $3,000 to tide him over those first heart-breaking years when his land must be stumped and cleared, when his crops are uncertain, his roads unfinished, and his markets are unknown.

A workingman, even with a job waiting for him in Alaska, ought to have some money before he goes. Living costs are very high. Amusements are few.

For men and women of courage, however, Alaska offers the same promise that America offered to the millions who were frustrated in Europe. What you need on the frontier, besides muscle and ambition, are imagination, a pair of rubber boots and a sense of humor.

99

There was a construction worker and his wife whom I visited at a new naval air station. For years they had known only reverses. Now, though they were middle-aged and had grown children, they had become twentieth century pioneers. They had bought some land facing a bay, and, until they could finish building their home, they were living in a tent. The woman had fixed that tent so that it was almost a work of art. She had hung it with pictures from magazines and with red pots from the five and ten. She baked the bread in a tiny oven; she hauled the water; she chopped the wood; she read by the uncertain light of a gasoline lantern. But she and her family were intensely happy; they were getting down to the roots of life again; they were lowering the barriers that cities and worries had created between life and themselves.

"This tent," she said to me, "this beautiful bay outside our door! You know, it's all like something I used to dream about. When my husband comes home from the naval base we walk along the beach and pick up shells—imagine, at our age! It's really our first honeymoon. The depression had hit us hard. We were sick with worry over how to meet our bills—doctor's bills, store bills, grocery bills. We never caught up. Now, for the first time in our lives, we have money, we don't have to worry. We can go into any store and look around and say to ourselves: 'I can buy that, I can buy anything I want.'" She stopped for a moment. "But, more important than having money, we have won self-respect again. Alaska has given us back our dignity."

Not only the white people, but the Eskimos, the Indians and the Aleuts (who live along the Aleutian Islands), those three native groups whose ancestral roots are in the soil and who make up almost half of Alaska's population, are helping us win the war and build the future.

Their sons are in the Army. Lieutenant Bertrand Leask, an Alaskan Indian boy, helped bomb and sink an Axis tanker in the Mediterranean. Their women are knitting and rolling bandages for the Red Cross. All of them are buying war bonds. When the Eskimo people of St. Lawrence Island, a village in the Bering Sea, a bare twenty miles from Siberia, heard that we were giving 10 per cent of our income for war bonds they voted to give 100 per cent of their community funds.

Secretary of the Interior, Harold L. Ickes, who has jurisdiction over Alaska, has repeatedly told the natives that, unlike the minorities of Fascist Europe, the Indian need not die, he must not die, he must live. Our job, he has said, is to integrate the beautiful culture of our Alaskan peoples into the stream of our entire national life. We have little enough to teach them in stories, legends, dances, fur sewing and ivory carving. They are exquisite artists and skilled mechanics. We can give them hospitals for their tuberculous patients and education in

100

how better to use their own tools. Our policy is not to make museum pieces of them, but to help them become leaders of their own people, to help them to help themselves.

Those Eskimos in the North are among the most noble, the most happy, and the most dignified people with whom I have ever lived. All the native children attend government schools. I helped run one of those schools for a few days and I have never seen children who were more hungry for information about the rest of the world. When I asked the children what they liked best to do, about 75 per cent of them said they liked best to read *Life* magazine. They get it once a year, twelve months' issues on one ship. The other 25 per cent liked to do fractions in arithmetic. Needless to say, I let them read *Life* magazine and then asked them to write what they had read. Almost every child in that room wrote about the advertisements. One child wrote—and I can think of no writer who has told that plot with such economy of words—"This is the story of a girl. She is waiting at the church. The groom has left her. She did not learn. She has bad breath."

Alaska, you can see, has its human resources, but they are over-shadowed by the physical wealth of the land. Since 1867, when Seward bought it from the Russians for $7,200,000 after a game of whist, we have gotten over a hundred times our investment; a billion dollars' worth of fish; a hundred million dollars' worth of fur; six hundred million dollars' worth of gold; two hundred million dollars' worth of other minerals: copper, platinum, silver, iron, and now we are finding oil and tin.

In one forest, the beautifully named Tongass National Forest, there are about three million acres of salable timber. Some experts believe that the lumber industry in southeastern Alaska alone could give employment to about thirty thousand people.

You all remember the dust-bowl farmers who were sent by the government in 1935 to the Matanuska Valley. Perhaps you have been told that the experiment was a failure. It isn't true. For seven years the valley has been a laboratory demonstration in democracy. Seven years may seem long in the time of a newspaper, but they are short in a farmer's almanac. Those seven years proved the two things that the experiment set out to prove: first, that farming is feasible in Alaska (most Alaskans knew this, but the nation didn't), and, secondly, they proved that you can take good farmers who have been living on sub-marginal land, give them new soil and new opportunity, and they will become citizens proud to raise their children in these United States.

Now I have some good news to tell you about these Alaskan farmers. This last summer the valley has grown to be more than a study in democracy. It has become a magnificent success. The valley's farmers

101

earned more than a million dollars in dairy, meat and vegetables. They helped feed the local Army and civilian population at a crucial time when every ship to Alaska was needed for munitions and supplies to get the Japs out. They earned a quarter of a million dollars just in potatoes. In a national fair a few years ago, Alaskan potatoes took first prize. A homesteader this summer made $2,200 from a quarter of an acre of celery. Some of the farmers are earning $800 a month in milk and cream and butter.

Fishing is Alaska's most important industry, and it, too, can be expanded by extracting vitamins and using the by-products of fish for fertilizer. The mineral possibilities of the country haven't been scratched; the fur industry can grow; power plants can electrify and industrialize whole sections of the North.

There is room, too, for small industries, both for export and for home consumption, to help make Alaska self-sufficient. There is room for small family unit sawmills, for arts and crafts with the label "Made in Alaska," tourist industries, hotels, auto camps, and so on. Alaska can become a great and beautiful playground.

But transportation is still the first problem of Alaska. I am convinced that Alaska's future lies in solving that problem of transportation. Her greatest promise lies in the air, as a terminal for the short air routes between America and Asia. We now have civilian and military airplanes latticing the whole territory. The war has taught us how to build airfields over night. The famous Alaska Highway now links Alaska through Canada to the States. That road is no Westchester Boulevard. For the most part, it is a good, graveled, two-lane country road. It was built by white and Negro soldiers, and by construction workers who knew what they were building for. That's why they could break a 1,500-mile trail in nine months through muskeg and forests. They knew that this road would help win the war faster. They knew that it would service and fuel the short, safe, lend-lease airway to Siberia.

Slowly but surely we are solving the problem of transportation inside Alaska. In the interior of the Territory, we have not only a growing highway system being built and maintained by the Department of the Interior, but we have the 500-mile Alaska Railroad, also operated by the Department, as the great transportation artery.

We know now what explorers like Stefansson predicted and what the pilots made real: that Alaska's future lies in the trade routes of peace as well as in the strategic routes of war. In a world shrunken by air transportation, Kamchatka is virtually at New York's back door. Alaska is the crossroads of that shrunken world.

We have a great deal to learn from our neighbors across from Alaska. We need Soviet weather information to plot our weather maps. Weather is still pretty much of a military secret, but it is no secret that

102

367

most of our weather in Alaska and in the North Pacific is manufactured in Siberia, and that the Arctic and the Antarctic are the weather kitchens of the world. I am revealing no military information when I tell you that we are establishing a network of weather bureau stations in Alaska which, I trust, will continue to gather and send national and international weather reports after the war. Remember, there are no politics in the weather.

You will hear many of our philosophers of despair wailing that frontier days are over, that the frontier spirit is an anachronism, and that, since we have not opened wide our doors to political refugees from Europe, we have, ipso facto, broken the frontier pattern which made us great. I believe that they are wrong. I believe that we are still a frontier people, that we have not lost our virility, our love for fearless freedom. Alaska is our newest frontier, our newest rebirth, our newest responsibility.

But Alaska won't be populated by phrases. Good pioneers won't move northward because of slogans like "Short Cut to Tokio" and "Dagger to Japan." Alaska will have to prove that it has room for industrialists and managers, for risk capital and cautious capital, for farmers and laborers. What Alaska needs is families. It needs honest, hard-working, rugged men and the kind of pioneer women who helped to build the West. With such people, the nineteen-forty-niners can write a century of history.

They can't hope to find success the first year. It takes capital to make the industries pay. It takes labor to make them function. It takes the right kind of publicity and it takes the right kind of sound, enthusiastic public opinion. The government can pour millions into Alaska as a springboard for war and as a crossroads for peace. But that money won't induce anybody to stay unless the whole nation, unless you and I, blast our ice and snow misconceptions and realize that Alaska can be opened successfully only by management, labor and government co-operating.

If Alaska takes its rightful place in world aviation, airplanes.will be flying regularly from Chicago through Alaska to Yakutsk, Moscow and cities in Europe, the way Wendell Willkie and Ambassador Joseph E. Davies flew home. Roads will link us with our next-door neighbors in Siberia and China. Many of you will be leaving your homes in New York and California and driving all around the world, by way of Alaska. This air route and land route through Alaska will help us break through the race prejudices and the medieval fears that we have been taught about Asia and Europe, even as we have been taught them about Alaska.

I once visited a hut in Yakutsk, and one of the first songs they played for me was "Who's Afraid of the Big Bad Wolf?" I knew then that the isolation in the world had been broken by music. Now, with

103

Alaska as a depot to the world, I can see that isolation broken by the strong cords of commerce and of friendship and of understanding.

This is no day dream. Was it a day dream when the first Colonists landed on Plymouth Rock and began to build their houses of logs? Was it a day dream when the pioneers went westward and dreamed of settlements in the Great Plains and the fertile valleys? Surely there was heartbreak. When, in all the wanderings of man on the face of this globe, has there not been heartbreak? In the opening of the West, historians tell us, about 50 per cent of the people turned back. In the opening of the North, we would have to expect at least the same proportion.

But if 50 per cent of the tens of thousands who have heard of Alaska, who have seen it under fire, and who think they want to live there, turn homeward, that will still leave thousands to build homes, to utilize the wealth and give their children the right to live with decency and dignity, without hunger and without fear.

104

369

INDEX

INDEX

ABOUT THE AUTHOR

Born in Brooklyn in 1911, **Ruth Gruber** earned her Ph.D. from Cologne University at age twenty, then the youngest person ever awarded a doctorate. At twenty-three, she became the first journalist to report from the Soviet Arctic. That part of her life is recounted in *Ahead of Time: My Early Years as a Foreign Correspondent,* the prequel to *Inside of Time.* In addition she is the author of *Haven: The Dramatic Story of 1000 WW II Refugees and How they Came to America,* which was also a CBS miniseries; *Exodus 1947: The Ship that Launched a Nation;* and *Raquela: A Woman of Israel,* winner of the National Jewish Book Award. Her photographs have appeared in more than 20 exhibits and documentaries, including the Academy Award-winning film, "The Long Way Home." In 1998 she received a lifetime achievement award from the American Society of Journalists and Authors. In October 2002, she helped dedicate Safe Haven, a museum in Oswego, New York, dedicated to preserving and learning from the experience of the Holocaust survivors she brought to a camp at Fort Ontario in 1944. Gruber lives in New York City and lectures frequently at venues around the country.